INTERNATIONAL TRADE AND LABOUR MARKETS

International Trade and Labour Markets

Edited by

Jitendralal Borkakoti
Middlesex University

and

Chris Milner
CREDIT
University of Nottingham

for the International Economics Study Group

First published in Great Britain 1997 by
MACMILLAN PRESS LTD
Houndmills, Basingstoke, Hampshire RG21 6XS and London
Companies and representatives throughout the world

A catalogue record for this book is available from the British Library.

ISBN 0–333–71088–6

 First published in the United States of America 1997 by
ST. MARTIN'S PRESS, INC.,
Scholarly and Reference Division,
175 Fifth Avenue, New York, N.Y. 10010

ISBN 0–312–17733–X

Library of Congress Cataloging-in-Publication Data
International trade and labour markets / edited by Jitendralal
Borkakoti and Chris Milner.
p. cm.
Contains papers originally presented at the 20th Annual Conference
of the International Economics Study Group, held at the University
of Sussex, September, 22–24, 1995.
Includes bibliographical references and index.
ISBN 0–312–17733–X (cloth : alk. paper)
1. Foreign trade and employment—Congresses.   2. Labor market—
–Congresses.   I. Borkakoti, Jitendralal.   II. Milner, Chris.
III. International Economics Study Group. Conference (20th : 1995 :
University of Sussex)
HD5710.7.I57 1997
331.12—DC21   97–22991
                                                                                  CIP

This book is printed on paper suitable for recycling and made from fully managed and
sustained forest sources.

10   9   8   7   6   5   4   3   2   1
06   05   04   03   02   01   00   99   98   97

Printed in Great Britain by
The Ipswich Book Company Ltd
Ipswich, Suffolk

Contents

International Economics Study Group   vi

Notes on Contributors   vii

Preface   viii

1   International trade, employment and unemployment
    Jitendralal Borkakoti and Chris Milner   1

2   Trade liberalization and unemployment: Policy issues and
    evidence from Chile   8
    Alejandra Cox Edwards and Sebastian Edwards

3   Lessons for policy reform in light of the Mexican experience   44
    Anne O. Krueger

4   International trade, deindustrialization and labour demand:
    An input–output study for the UK (1979–90)   62
    Mary Gregory and Christine Greenhalgh

5   The impact of import penetration on unemployment in UK
    manufacturing   90
    Jitendralal Borkakoti

6   Trade and manufacturing employment in the
    United Kingdom   118
    Robert C. Hine and Peter Wright

7   How trade hurt unskilled workers   140
    Adrian Wood

8   Occupational employment and wage changes in the UK:
    Trade and technology effects   169
    Anthony Courakis, Keith E. Maskus and Allan Webster

9   Optimum inflation, taxation and monetary arrangements
    in the open economy   203
    Peter Sinclair

10 Tied aid, unemployment and welfare   219
    Sajal Lahiri and Pascalis Raimondos-Møller

International Economics Study Group

The International Economics Study Group (IESG) was formed in 1973 to provide a forum in which professional economists with an interest in international economics can discuss developments in their field. It is concerned with both the theoretical and applied aspects of this subject. The group has a regular seminar meeting series at the London School of Economics and runs a mini-conference and major annual conference each year.

The IESG's primary funding is from the Economics and Social Research Council but other organizations sometimes provide additional finance.

IESG Management Committee

Chairman	Professor Chris Milner, University of Nottingham
Secretary	Dr Robert Read, University of Lancaster
Members	Dr. Jitendralal Borkakoti, Middlesex University
	Professor Alasdair Smith, University of Sussex
	Professor David Vines, University of Oxford
	Professor L. Alan Winters, World Bank and University of Birmingham
	Mr Henry Scott, University of Birmingham

Notes on Contributors

Jitendralal Borkakoti, Middlesex University

Anthony Courakis, Brasenose College, Oxford

Alejandra Cox Edwards, California State University and World Bank

Sebastian Edwards, University of California and World Bank

Christine Greenhalgh, St Peter's College, Oxford

Mary Gregory, St Hilda's College, Oxford

Robert C. Hine, University of Nottingham

Anne O. Krueger, Stanford University

Sajal Lahiri, University of Essex

Keith E. Maskus, University of Colorado at Boulder

Chris Milner, University of Nottingham

Pascalis Raimondos-Møller, Copenhagen Business School

Peter Sinclair, University of Birmingham

Allan Webster, Maxwell Stamp plc

Adrian Wood, University of Sussex

Peter Wright, University of Nottingham

Preface

This volume contains the papers originally presented at the 20th Annual Conference of the International Economics Study Group, held at the Isle of Thorns Training Centre, University of Sussex, on 22–24 September 1995. The conference focused on the intricate relationship between international trade and labour markets. The papers are both theoretical and empirical, and the countries considered include the UK, Mexico and Chile.

We wish to express our gratitude to the authors who accepted our invitation to present papers. We also wish to thank the discussants whose comments and suggestions were valuable. The list of discussants includes V. Balasubramanyam (Lancaster University), John Black (University of Exeter), Alec Chrystal (City University), John Martin (OECD), Henry Scott (University of Birmingham), Jeffrey Sheen (University of Sydney), Peter Sinclair (University of Birmingham), Alasdair Smith (University of Sussex), and Allan Webster (Maxwell Stamp plc). Lastly, we thank all the participants who helped to make this conference a success.

Jitendralal Borkakoti
Principal Lecturer in Economics
CRIE, Middlesex University

and

Chris Milner
Professor of International Economics
CREDIT, University of Nottingham

20 August 1996

1 International Trade, Employment and Unemployment

Jitendralal Borkakoti and Chris Milner

INTRODUCTION

During the past few decades, a variety of changes in the international economy have resulted in the increased integration of nations, both developed and developing. Globalization, or the increased openness of countries to the influences of the world economy, has accompanied or been associated with the increased mobility of factors, in particular capital, and with the growth of international trade and the increased importance of international competition in product markets. As a result the labour market in any one country has become more intricately linked with those in other countries. Indeed with the emergence of high and persistent unemployment in many OECD countries and the growing wage dispersion between skilled and unskilled workers in some countries, there has been lively debate as to whether globalization is responsible for these labour market changes. There is some irony in the extent to which trade with developing countries, relatively well-endowed with unskilled labour, is viewed as a culprit in this debate, since policy makers in many developing countries are also concerned with the labour market adjustments to the trade liberalization they have been encouraged to implement in order to expand their exports to the industrial countries!

In this volume of papers which were originally commissioned for and presented at an IESG Annual Conference and which have subsequently been revised in the light of helpful comments from conference discussants and others, we concentrate on the trade and labour market aspects of globalization. We specifically revisit the issue of the relative importance of trade and technical progress in influencing employment and relative wages. Much of the debate so far has been hampered by the fact that the empirical work has tended to relate only to the

1

United States. Here we make some attempt to redress this balance by including a number of UK-focused studies and by including also some non-OECD focus with two papers on Latin American experiences. By its nature, a conference volume is unlikely to provide comprehensiveness on a major theme such as trade, employment and unemployment, but the papers gathered here do demonstrate the large research agenda that is arising out of the increased theoretical and empirical interest in the trade–labour market linkages and from the collaborations between trade and labour market economists.

THE ISSUES AND OUTLINE OF THE BOOK

Besides confronting some of the core issues about the long run relationships between trade and employment or between trade and relative wages of skilled and unskilled labour, and about the short run labour market adjustments to trade liberalization, the volume includes papers which tackle some specialist topics such as the effects of tied aid on donor country's employment and the optimal trade-off between inflation and unemployment in an open economy. In some cases the links between the papers are strong and self-evident, in others the links are less obvious. Nonetheless the range of issues in these papers is impressive and should make a contribution to the growing literature on the relationships between international trade and labour markets. Let us comment further on some of the main themes of the book.

Reform and employment in Latin America

Chapters 2 and 3 can be grouped together because they focus on one region of the world, namely Latin America, that has seen dramatic changes in trade strategy and performance in recent decades. Each of these two papers has a country-specific focus, on Chile and Mexico respectively, but they also have a wider relevance. Unilateral trade reforms have been initiated in many developing countries in the last two decades. Given that Chile was one of the earliest of this phase of trade liberalizers and also one of the most extensive and rapid liberalizers, an analysis of the actual effects of these trade reforms on employment is particularly instructive. Similarly, Mexico was among the front-runners in adopting policy reform programmes. It has been viewed as a particularly interesting case study because of the extent of the country's debt crisis, but is also an interesting example of the way that the 'new regionalism' (involving greater integration between industrial and industrializing countries) has increased the openness of the less advanced economy to foreign competition from imports and foreign investment.

In Chapter 2, Sebastian Edwards and Alejandra Cox Edwards seek to answer a number of related questions. What are the effects of trade reform on employment? Are the adjustment (that is, unemployment) costs of trade liberalization high? How are the adjustment costs affected by policy? The approach adopted to answer these questions is both theoretical and empirical. A Ricardo–Viner model with importables, exportables and non-tradeables sectors is used to investigate the effects of economy-wide or sector specific wage rigidities (for example, associated with administratively minimum wages) on the nature of the employment (and unemployment) consequences of import-liberalizing trade reforms. Although the outcomes, sectoral employment levels and wages are often ambiguous in this theoretical framework and depend on the coverage of wage rigidities, the modelling exercise outlined by the authors establishes the possibility that trade liberalization *can* generate nontrivial (short-run) unemployment problems. The results of the analysis of Chilean unemployment survey data for a number of years support this hypothesis to some degree. Probit models of the probability of being unemployed and of the conditional probability of remaining unemployed are estimated. After controlling for individual characteristics (sex, experience, education, and so on), the degree of trade liberalization in each sector is shown to increase the probability of unemployment and the probability of remaining unemployed. Although these disprotection effects on unemployment are significant, they are also found to be rather small and declining through time. Nonetheless, they support the view that the costliness of labour market adjustment to trade liberalization will be influenced by the coverage and degree of wage rigidities.

The issues of rigidities and distortions in one market affecting the effectiveness or sustainability of reforms in other markets are themes also taken up by Anne Krueger in her paper on Mexican reforms (Chapter 3). The paper focuses in particular on the use of a nominal anchor exchange rate policy in order to speed up the deceleration of inflation. This is a policy that has been advocated by a number of macroeconomists, especially where the control of inflation is seen as of major importance. This paper draws attention to the distortion between domestic and foreign returns on investment in the 'anchored' economy that such a policy generates; involving a redistribution from 'taxed' domestic capital owners to 'subsidized' foreign capital owners. This pattern of 'taxation' and 'subsidization' occurs when the rate of nominal exchange rate depreciation is less than the domestic inflation rate and foreigners have the option to convert into the domestic currency (to take advantage of higher nominal interest rates on domestic currency) and to reconvert into foreign currency at the pre-announced exchange rate.

The author draws attention therefore to this important problem and calls for more work on the subject. Some preliminary analysis in the paper explains why the distortion may bias the allocation of resources away from tradeables into non-tradeables or home goods production. One of the areas of further research is therefore how such biases in the incentive to produce non-tradeables as opposed to tradeables affect employment levels and patterns. As argued in Chapters 2 and 3, on Latin America, there has been only limited attention given to the empirical experience of actual employment effects of trade and trade reform. Indeed, the work of Krueger (1981) is one of the relatively rare exceptions in the case of developing countries. In her paper in this volume no attention is given to this, though empirical issues taken up in the later chapters of this volume may offer some insights into the employment volume and composition effects of investment distortions.

Labour market adjustments to trade in the UK

In Chapters 4, 5 and 6, attention shifts from developing countries to one particular developed, industrial country, namely the UK. Given the decline in employment in UK manufacturing, there continues to be considerable academic and policy interest in the role of trade in general, and in import competition from particular sources (for example, European and Asian competitors), in accounting for or explaining this decline. We include in this volume, therefore, three different, but potentially complementary, empirical studies; an input-output study by Mary Gregory and Christine Greenhalgh, and a mixture of accounting and econometric methods in the studies by Borkakoti and by Robert Hine and Peter Wright.

Input-output evidence

Using an 87 sector, input-output (IO) table for the UK economy for the years 1979, 1985 and 1990, Gregory and Greenhalgh analyse the relative contribution to gross output and employment of changes in domestic final demand, import penetration (in final and intermediate use), exports and technical change (changes in inter-industry input requirements) using the approach pioneered by Chenery *et al.* (1962). They find that increased import penetration in final goods was a substantial source of gross output and employment change, but it was on average offset (perhaps with a delay until the next boom) by the growth in exports. The direct effects of increased productivity were also much more important throughout the economy than any loss of markets in accounting for reduced labour demand. But increased productivity is a feature of an economy experiencing structural change in the face of increasing international competition. The total demand for labour in the UK was lower in 1990 than 1979 and there was a shift in the pattern of labour demand away from manufactures towards financial services (directly through change in product composition and indirectly through change in business organization as firms 'contracted out' certain services) and in general away from lower to higher value-added sectors.

Accounting evidence

Accounting methods are often criticized for being arbitrary, but nonetheless they have been and remain a common starting point for trying to separate the relative contributions of demand, labour productivity and import change to changes in employment. Borkakoti applies the methodology to changes in UK manufacturing sectors in each of the periods 1979–80 to 1984–5 and 1984–5 to 1989–90 and concludes that growing (net) import penetration is a fairly significant influence in 'accounting' for job losses in a substantial number (albeit declining between the periods) of manufacturing sectors. This is rather surprising since the conventional wisdom is that the trade effect of employment is relatively small, with export expansion tending to offset the effects of import expansion. Indeed, in the next chapter, by Robert Hine and Peter Wright, further accounting analysis of UK manufacturing supports the traditional view. They conclude that the large loss of manufacturing jobs in the UK since 1979 is largely the outcome of large labour productivity growth combined with slow growth in domestic demand. The difference in the results of these two studies may be explained by the greater disaggregation of sectors and greater breakdown of the time periods in the latter study. But herein lies the limitations of the accounting approach, namely its sensitivity to the aggregation of activities and of time periods and the related difficulty of isolating trade from non-trade effects. Trade-induced productivity improvements may induce job cuts in the short term, but make them more secure and affect trade performance in the longer term.

Econometric evidence

Econometric work is relatively rare in this area. The papers by Borkakoti and by Hine and Wright serve to redress this deficiency. The former uses a two-stage approach; employment by manufacturing sector being regressed in cross section against predicted values of the sector trade balance, with these predicted values being derived from an estimated neo-factor proportion model. The conclusion is that the estimated trade balance had a small but significant negative impact on employment in 1985 and 1990 (but not in 1980). This time it is Hine and Wright that identify a stronger trade effect on UK employment, using a panel data set to estimate conventional labour demand functions with an additional and separate, disciplinary effect of trade on productivity captured.

Clearly, there is more work of this type required to reduce the dependence on 'accounting' evidence and to test the robustness of the econometric methodology, but both of these studies are very useful pioneering studies. Interestingly, Hine and Wright find that the impact of trade on labour demand is not invariant with the direction of trade. The need to strengthen our understanding of the link between the labour- and trade-theoretic approaches is clearly demonstrated.

Trade, technology and labour skills

We have seen already how the idea that the overall employment effects of trade are small is increasingly coming under some critical challenge. When it comes to the employment and wage effects of trade on specific types of labour, then there is also a controversy. The majority or conventional view is that the deteriorating situation of unskilled workers (in terms of relative wage and employment opportunities) is mainly caused by changes in technology. The counterview, propounded most strongly recently by Adrian Wood, is that increased trade with developing countries has hurt unskilled workers in developed countries. We reproduce here (Chapter 7) Adrian Wood's paper, originally published in the *Journal of Economic Perspectives* (1995). We do so because it sets out the debate, not in an agnostic manner, but nonetheless fairly comprehensively. The paper outlines the evidence on which Wood's position is based, responds to some of the criticisms that have been raised about the evidence and challenges for the alternative view, ie the new technology explanation.

By way of contrast we include, alongside the paper by Woods, a study by Anthony Courakis, Keith Maskus and Allan Webster of occupational employment and wage changes in the UK. It is largely an empirical paper, but in the tradition of Leamer (1993) the paper argues that the apportionment of blame for employment and wage changes between trade and technology is misplaced and inconsistent with trade theory. Where trade theory predicts that tradeables are characterized by perfectly elastic factor demands, then employment in tradeables will only change if factor supply, factor demand in non-tradeables and technology change. Further technological improvements do not necessarily lower employment, but will affect trade. In which case the employment effects of trade and technology are much less readily separable than much existing work suggests. The paper is therefore at odds with several of the other papers in this volume. But this serves to illustrate the unchartered and unresolved nature of many of the issues covered in this volume. This is a collection of papers concerned with an emerging research agenda, not a text summarizing the consensus from a completed programme of research!

The last two chapters, although only tangentially relevant to the main theme, contain some interesting results. Sinclair argues that a country in a monetary union may suffer welfare loss if she is required to accept an inflation rate which diverges from what she would have chosen in isolation. He finds that the long-run Phillips curve cannot be vertical in general because higher inflation may raise or reduce unemployment through its fiscal effect. Lahiri and Raimondos-Moller find that untied aid always benefits the recipient country but harms the donor country, and they derive sufficient conditions under which the donor country's employment increases with tied aid.

References

Chenery, H., Shishido, S. and Watanabe, T. (1962) 'The Pattern of Japanese Growth 1914–54', *Econometrica*, 30, 98–131.

Krueger, A. J. (1981) *Trade and Employment in Developing Countries* (Chicago: University of Chicago Press).

Leamer, E. E. (1993) 'Wage Effects of a US-Mexican Free Trade Arrangement' in Peter M. Garber (ed.) *The Mexico-US Free Trade Agreement* (Cambridge, Mass.: MIT Press).

2 Trade Liberalization and Unemployment: Policy Issues and Evidence from Chile

Alejandra Cox Edwards and
Sebastian Edwards*

INTRODUCTION

How to liberalize? This is a question that has haunted policy makers and has confused policy advisors. A particularly pressing issue concerns adjustment costs associated with trade liberalization. This issue has been at the center of discussions about the proper sequencing and speed of reform.[1] Does the order in which markets are reformed affect the outcome of the adjustment package? Should a country tackle the inflationary problem before dealing with market-oriented reforms, or should the opposite sequence be pursued? Which 'order' of liberalization will result in lower unemployment costs? Should the external sector be opened to foreign competition abruptly or gradually? How costly is trade liberalization if the labour market is still regulated and distorted? These questions are not only important from a purely economic point of view, but also from a political one. Often the sequence of reform will affect the political support for the reform process. While a particular sequence will generate support from certain groups – say exporters – it will alienate other groups, such as labour unions in protected sectors. In designing reform packages policy makers have increasingly tried to balance these political considerations with more technical ones.

The importance of the employment consequences of trade liberalization has not escaped the attention of the specialized media. For example, in a recent article on the future of the South African economy, *The Economist* points out:

8

[S]outh Africa has one of the most closed economies in the region . . . it keeps in place residual exchange controls that hamper foreign investment . . . Behind these [policies] . . . lie many things: *worries about unemployment*; a fear of markets . . . *[I]f unemployment is a worry, trade liberalization can be phased in over a number of years* . . . (Emphasis added; 12 August 1995, p. 11)

Economists have also understood that adjustment costs – and in particular unemployment – play an important role in determining the appropriate sequencing and speed of reform. In *The Wealth of Nations* Adam Smith argued that:

[t]o open the colony trade all at once . . ., might not only occasion some transitory inconvenience, but a great permanent loss . . . [T]he sudden loss of employment . . ., might alone be felt very sensibly (Vol. II, Ch. VII, pt. III, page 120).

This point has also been made repeatedly in the modern literature on the dynamics of reform. For instance, in their classical study on industrialization policies in the developing nations, Little, Scitovsky and Scott (1970) argued – mainly based on political economy considerations – that structural reforms should be carried out gradually. The reason for this policy advice was based on the role of adjustment costs and on the opposition to reforms that these costs can generate. According to Little *et al.*, faster reforms would result in larger short-term costs – especially unemployment and bankruptcy – and thus in stiffer political opposition. Along similar lines, Michaely (1982) has argued that in order to minimize the political opposition to trade reform it is necessary to reduce the short-run unemployment effects and other adjustment costs associated with these policies.

The same argument regarding political opposition can be made with respect to political support. Markets liberalization challenges all individuals to perform in an environment of new opportunities. Therefore, it is central to encourage economic agents to take risks and find out the potential pay-off of open markets. This adds one more dimension to the sequencing question: the need to open channels for the broad sharing of risks across the economy, in order to encourage business starts. Here is where labour market reforms are essential.

Stability and equity are desirable objectives for workers and for policy makers. In a market economy, stability in employment is achieved through abundant employment opportunities. This abundance also improves workers' negotiating power, because in such an environment they can leave a poorly paid job for a better one without the risk of experiencing long term unemployment. If an equitable system is one that rewards individuals in proportion to their contribution, an open system of representation in labour negotiations is a basic condition for equity. The evidence from Chile which we present here shows that unemployment duration is less linked to sources of job destruction in the 1980s (after the labour reforms) than in the 1970s. As strict job security rules were removed, and the costs of negotiating labour conditions at the plant level were lowered, employers' risks associated with job creation were lowered, making it easier for the unemployed to get back into jobs.

A key question, however, and one that until recently has received limited attention, refers to the actual effects of trade reforms on employment and unemployment. What does the historical experience show? Are the unemployment costs of trade liberalization as high as it is sometimes feared? And if so, what can be done – in terms of other policies, for example – to reduce them? The purpose of this paper is to address some of these issues from a policy, historical and empirical perspective.[2] We focus on what has arguably been one of the most dramatic trade liberalization episodes in modern times: the Chilean trade reform of the 1970s. In little more than three years a protective structure characterized by high and dispersed tariffs averaging more than 100 per cent, and quantitative restrictions (QRs) that covered virtually every import item, was replaced by a uniform tariff of 10 percent.[3] In particular, we use unemployment survey data for a number of years to analyze whether this trade liberalization reform had an impact on unemployment. The rest of the paper is organized as follows. The next section presents a simple diagrammatic framework for analysing the impact of trade liberalization on employment. We then survey some of the policy and empirical work on the relationship between trade reforms and labour market conditions. Subsequently we provide an overview of the Chilean liberalization reform, and of Chile's labour market behaviour during the second half of the 1970s. In turn, we present results from our own empirical analysis. Finally, we offer some concluding remarks and thoughts on directions for further research.

TRADE REFORM, LABOUR MARKET DISTORTIONS AND UNEMPLOYMENT: A DIAGRAMMATIC FRAMEWORK

The framework known as the Ricardo–Viner model with real wage rigidity can be used to provide a simple illustration of possible short-run employment consequences of tariff reform. In this model, capital is fixed to its sector of origin in the short-run; it can be reallocated slowly over time. In contrast to the textbook case with flexible prices and mobile factors of production, a tariff reduction in this more realistic setting can lower the equilibrium real wage rate required to maintain full employment. However, if for some reason the economy's labour market is distorted and exhibits downward rigidity of real wages – due to minimum wage laws or indexation clauses – the required reduction in the wage rate will not take place. Unemployment would result, in this case, as a consequence of this labour market imperfection.

Consider the case of a small country that produces and consumes three goods: importables (M), exportables (X), and non-tradeables (N). Households consume all three goods and maximize a utility function subject to an income constraint. Perfect competition prevails in the goods market. Firms maximize profits subject to existing technology and endowments of three factors of production: labour, capital and natural resources. In addition, the government imposes an import tariff, and presumably the tariff revenue is transferred back to consumers. Finally, the price of exportables is the numeraire.

The initial labour market equilibrium is illustrated in Figure 2.1. The horizontal axis measures total labour available in the economy, and the vertical axis depicts the wage rate in terms of exportables. Schedule L_T represents the demand for labour by the tradeable goods sector and is equal to the horizontal sum of the demand for labour by the exportables sector (schedule L_X), and the demand for labour by the importables sector. Demand for labour by the non-tradeable goods sector is shown by the schedule L_N. The initial equilibrium is characterized by full employment and a wage rate equal to w_0. At this point $O_T L_A$ labor is employed in the production of exportables, $L_A L_B$ in the production of importables, and $O_N L_B$ in the production of non-tradeables.

Assuming that in the short run only labour can move across sectors, although in the long run all three factors are mobile, Figure 2.2 illustrates the process of adjustment in the labour market. The reduction in the tariffs will result in a lower domestic price of importables, generating a downward shift of the L_T curve (with the L_X curve constant). The new L_T intersects the L_N curve at point R. However, the reduction

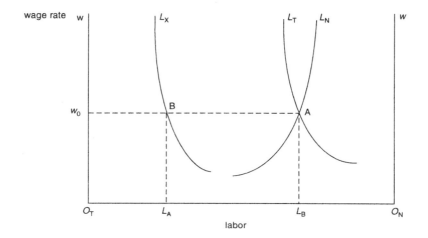

Figure 2.1 Standard model: labour market equilibrium

in the domestic price of importables will also cause a decline in the price of non-tradeables (relative to exports), shifting the L_N curve downward (by less than the shift in L_T). The final short-run equilibrium is reached at point S. At this point, the production of exportables has increased, with labour employed in this sector having increased by $L_A L_Q$.

Real wages have declined in terms of exportables (from w_0 to w_1 in Figure 2.2). Wages have also declined in terms of non-tradeables because the vertical distance between the L_N and L_N' curves is smaller than the reduction in w. In contrast, the real wage in terms of importables has increased because the domestic price of these goods fell by more than the decline in the nominal wage.

In the exportables sector, the real return to sector-specific factors has increased. However, the real return to fixed factors in the importables and non-tradeables sectors could either increase or decrease. The real return on the sector-specific factors allocated to the importables sector will decrease in terms of exportables and could either increase or decrease in terms of the other two goods (see Edwards, 1988).

To sum up, in the standard Ricardo–Viner model with wage flexibility, a tariff reduction will have the following short-run effects on production, prices, and factor rewards: (1) production of exportables will increase; (2) production of importables will decrease; (3) production of non-tradeables may increase or decrease; (4) prices of non-tradeables

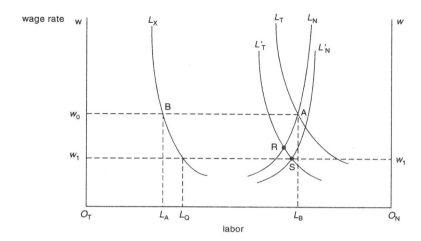

Figure 2.2 Standard model: effects of trade liberalization

will decrease; (5) wages will increase in terms of importables and decrease in terms of exportables and non-tradeables; (6) the real return to the sector-specific factors allocated to the exportables sector will increase relative to importables but could increase or decrease relative to the other goods; and (7) the real return to factors specific to the non-tradeables sector will increase relative to non-tradeable goods but either increase or decrease relative to the other two goods.

Although the dependent economy framework presented here provides a useful starting point for analyzing the way in which a trade reform affects the labour market, it has a number of shortcomings. Perhaps the most important one for this paper is the assumption of factor price flexibility. Many developing countries exhibit some kind of (real) wage rigidity. In the following sections we consider economy-wide and sector-specific wage rigidities, which are essential for understanding the relationship between liberalization and unemployment.

Economy-wide wage rigidities

Consider first the case of an economy-wide minimum wage. In order to simplify the diagram, this minimum wage is assumed to be expressed in terms of our numeraire (exportables). The results we present are fairly sensitive to this assumption. Edwards (1990) discusses in detail how using different price indexes to set the minimum wage will

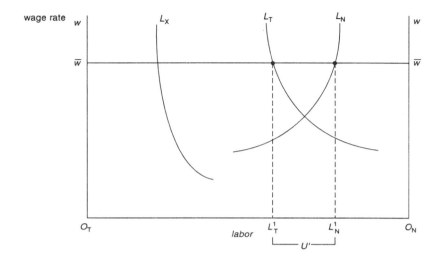

Figure 2.3   Economy-wide minimum wage: unemployment

affect the results. Nonetheless, the incorporation of an economy-wide minimum wage requires a modification of the diagram.

The nature of the initial labour market equilibrium is now captured by Figure 2.3. Demand for labour by the tradeable goods sector (L_T) is equal to the horizontal sum of the demand for labour by the exportables sector (L_X), and the demand for labour by the importables sector $(L_M,$ not shown). Demand for labour by the non-tradeables sector is given by the L_N schedule. If there is a minimum wage rate equal to $\bar{w}$, unemployment of magnitude U' will result; the amount of labour demanded by the non-tradeables sector is now determined by the minimum wage and is equal to $O_N L'_N$.

Figure 2.4 shows that when labour is the only mobile factor, and there is a minimum wage in real terms (expressed in terms of exportables), a tariff reduction will result in an increase in unemployment which is given by U''. As mentioned earlier, trade liberalization requires a decline in the (real) wage in order to maintain the previous level of employment. If institutional factors prevent this reduction, the necessary adjustment will occur via quantities, prompting a reduction in total employment. The extent of additional unemployment depends on: (1) the magnitude of the tariff reduction; (2) the magnitude of the fall in the price of non-tradeables, and; (3) the employment elasticities in the different sectors.

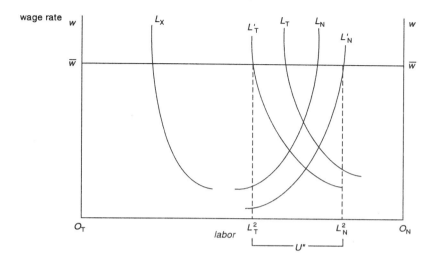

Figure 2.4 Economy-wide minimum wage: trade liberalization

Sector-specific wage rigidity

In most countries, real wage rigidity is not generalized. It usually affects a subgroup of sectors in the economy. To illustrate the implications of sector-specific wage rigidity, we briefly apply the ongoing diagrammatic apparatus to two cases, with zero unemployment and another with unemployment.

Case 1: Sector-specific wage rigidity with no unemployment

This configuration was recently used by Burda and Sachs (1987) to analyze the structure of unemployment in Germany. It is assumed that one sector, say non-tradeables, is subject to an above-equilibrium wage rate, and that the wage rate in the rest of the economy – the so-called uncovered sector – takes the level required to ensure full employment in the economy as a whole. The initial conditions under these assumptions are summarized in Figure 2.5. $\overline{W}_N$ is the minimum wage in the protected sector (the non-tradeables sector), and W_T is the wage rate in the uncovered (tradeables) sector. Employment in tradeables is equal to the distance $O_T A$, and employment in non-tradeables is equal to $O_N A$.

Under these conditions, and assuming that capital and natural resources

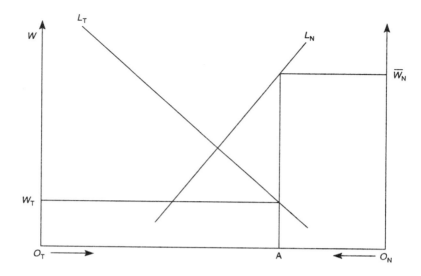

Figure 2.5   Sector-specific wage rigidity and full employment

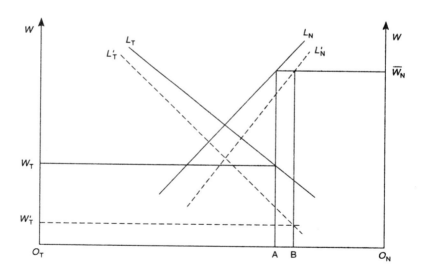

Figure 2.6   Sector-specific wage rigidity and trade liberalization

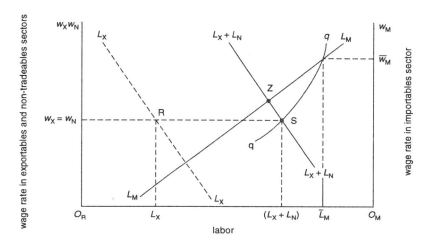

Figure 2.7 Sector-specific wage rigidity and unemployment

are sector-specific, a tariff reduction will increase the wage gap between the protected and the uncovered sectors, reduce employment in non-tradeables and importables, and increase employment and output in exportables (see Figure 2.6).

The wage differential $(W_T - \overline{W}_N)$ handicaps this approach, since full employment and an intersectoral wage differential can only be maintained if there are severe entry barriers to the protected non-tradeables sector. An elegant way of resolving this issue is by introducing a Harris–Todaro mechanism, which illustrates the dynamics of intersectoral labour migration. This concept is introduced below.

Case 2: Sector-specific minimum wages with unemployment

Consider the case with a binding minimum wage in the importables sector. Figure 2.7 is similar to Figure 2.5, but total labour employed in the importables sector is measured from the right-hand origin O_M. The wage rate $\overline{W}_M$ is the minimum wage enforced upon the importables sector; L_M represents employment in this sector. Curve qq is a rectangular hyperbola known as the Harris–Todaro locus, along which the following equation holds:

$$W_N = W_X = [L_M/(L_M + U)]\overline{W}_M, \qquad (1)$$

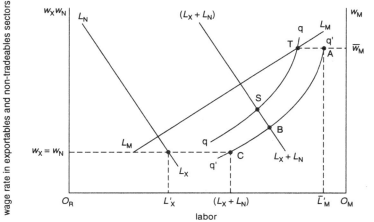

Figure 2.8   Sector-specific wage rigidity, unemployment, and trade
liberalization

where U is the equilibrium level of unemployment (Harris and Todaro, 1970; Harberger, 1971). In the absence of a minimum wage, equilibrium is attained at point Z. With a minimum wage, curve $(L_X + L_N)$ intersects with qq at S. The distance $O_R L_X$ is total employment in the exportables sector; the distance $L_X(L_X + L_N)$ is employment in non-tradeables; the distance $(L_X + L_N)\overline{L}_M$ is the initial equilibrium level of unemployment; and the distance $O_M \overline{L}_M$ is employment in the covered sector.

The short-run effects of a reduction in the price of importables are illustrated in Figure 2.8. As the price of importables declines, demand for labour in that sector shifts down. The new demand for labour in that sector (not drawn) will intersect $\overline{W}_M$ at point A. A new rectangular hyperbola q'q' passes through this point, and labour demanded by the importables sector is now reduced to $O_M \overline{L}'_M$.

What will happen to wages and employment in the uncovered sectors and to unemployment? Assuming that the price of non-tradeables remains constant, curve $(L_X + L_N)$ remains in its original position, and point B is the new equilibrium with a lower wage and higher employment in the uncovered sectors. However, as discussed above, the tariff reduction will reduce the price of non-tradeables and $(L_X + L_N)$ will shift down, but to a lesser extent than the decline in the price of importables. The final short-run equilibrium is then given by point C, the intersection a new $(L_X + L_N)'$ curve (not drawn) and the new q'q' rectangular hyperbola.

In sum, the post-liberalization equilibrium is characterized by: (1) lower employment in the covered sector (importables); (2) lower wages in the uncovered sectors, expressed in terms of exportables; (3) either higher or lower equilibrium unemployment; (4) either higher or lower employment in non-tradeables, and; (5) higher employment and production in exportables. In this setting, the level of unemployment is: $U = L_M(\overline{W}_M/W_N) - 1$. Since L_M declines while $(\overline{W}_M/W_N)$ goes up, it is not possible to know a priori the net effect on U. The impact on U depends on the elasticities of demand for labour in each sector.

Not surprisingly, a tariff reduction in the presence of a minimum wage with partial coverage generates a different outcome than that obtained in the case of an economy-wide minimum wage. First, under partial coverage, there is an increase in production and employment in exportables. Second, employment in non-tradeables may also increase. In the short-run case with a sectoral minimum wage, trade liberalization can result in a decline in the equilibrium level of unemployment, whereas it always increases under an economy-wide minimum wage. More importantly, this exercise illustrates an important finding: trade liberalization may generate nontrivial (short-run) unemployment problems.

What will happen in the long run in the presence of this type of sector-specific minimum wage? In the short-run, after the domestic price of importables falls, the real return to (sector-specific) capital will differ across sectors. A tariff reduction reduces the return to capital in the importables sector and by a lesser extent in the non-tradeables sector, and increases it in the exportables sector. This situation, characterized by sectoral differences in the real return to capital, cannot continue indefinitely. With time, capital will be reallocated, moving out of importables and into the other sectors. In terms of Figure 2.8, this means that L_M and qq will shift downward again (the resource-pull effect), while demand for labor in the uncovered sectors will shift upward. Moreover, these curves will shift so that the final outcome will be characterized by a higher equilibrium wage in the absence of wage rigidities.

The final long-run equilibrium must satisfy two conditions: the return to capital must be equalized across sectors, and the labour market must be in equilibrium in the sense that equation (1) must hold. As capital is reallocated, employment in the importables sector declines and employment in the exportables and non-tradeables sectors rises, as compared to the short-run levels depicted in Figure 2.8. Whether wages in the uncovered sectors will be higher or lower in the long run cannot be determined a priori. The long-run wage in these sectors depends on the elasticities of substitution and on the relationship between the slopes of L_M, qq and $(L_X + L_N)$.

TRADE REFORM AND LABOUR MARKET CONDITIONS:
ISSUES AND EVIDENCE

From a political economy perspective, higher unemployment is possibly the most feared adjustment cost associated with structural reform and trade liberalization. Historically, policy makers in a number of countries have postponed the opening of trade out of concern for potential labour market dislocations. Interestingly enough, however, until recently very few empirical studies had explicitly dealt with the employment effects of trade reforms.[4] The World Bank study on liberalization episodes in 19 countries directed by Michaely *et al.* (1991) argues that, even in the short run, the unemployment costs of reform have usually been small. The authors claimed that while industries that are negatively affected by the reform process lay off workers, expanding sectors will tend to create a large number of employment positions. In analyzing the employment consequences of trade reform, Michaely *et al.* distinguish between gross and net effects. The gross – or in their words 'disemployment' – effect is defined as the unemployment associated with the contraction of some industries after the trade liberalization reform is undertaken. The net effect, on the other hand, is defined as the total change in aggregate unemployment in the economy. Naturally, from an aggregate economic perspective the net effect is the most interesting one, because under most circumstances we would expect a reduction in the level of employment in those sectors that lose competitiveness, and an increase in employment in those sectors that, as a consequence of a reform, expand their level of activity.

In the Michaely *et al.* project, variants of the 'before' and 'after' method were used to assess the employment effects of trade reforms. In three of the case studies, however (Chile, Spain, and Yugoslavia) a method that attempted to control for the evolution of other economic variables – such as the terms of trade, fluctuations in economic activity and macroeconomic policies – was used. The authors of the Chile and Yugoslavia studies found that, when controlling for other factors, the *net* effect of liberalization on employment was positive: as a consequence of the liberalization program the aggregate rate of unemployment declined in these countries. For Spain, the results differed depending on which liberalization episode was considered. While in the first two liberalization attempts (1960–6) and (1970–4) aggregate unemployment increased after the trade reforms, in the third episode (1977–80) there was a *decline* in net unemployment after liberalization.[5] Regarding the other countries in the Michaely *et al.* study, unemployment increased *after* the following episodes[6]. Argentina in 1967–70 and 1976–80; Israel in 1952–5 and 1962–8; Indonesia in 1966–72; Korea in 1978–9; the Philippines in 1960–5; and Turkey in 1980–4. In most of these cases, however, the increase in unemployment was rather small, and could be attributed to factors different from the reform itself. These results led the directors of the project to conclude that 'by and large, liberalization attempts have *not* incurred significant transition costs by way of unemployment' (Michaely, *et al.*, Vol. 7, ch. 6, p. 80, emphasis added).

Undoubtedly, the Michaely *et al.* project constitutes the most ambitious attempt to deal with the link between structural reforms and the labour market. However, as is usually the case with a collection of multi-authored country studies, the empirical and historical analyses were uneven and, at times, somewhat unfocused.[7]

The link between trade liberalization and labour market adjustment has also been studied for the case of the Southern Cone of Latin America during the 1970s. In particular, in the case of the Chilean liberalization of 1975–9, it has been argued that the existence of labour distortions – including minimum wages and backward looking wage indexation – generated a segmented labour market, with a protected and an unprotected sector. This resulted in important wage rigidities that impaired the labour market's ability to adjust to the trade reform and other shocks. For example, Edwards and Cox Edwards (1991) have used a simple model to estimate that, as a result of existing labour market rigidities, the trade liberalization reform generated short-run unemployment in Chile of the order of 3.5 per cent of the labour force.[8]

A detailed study by Revenga (1994) on the Mexican experience with trade liberalization suggests that the drastic trade reform of 1985–8 had very modest costs in terms of aggregate unemployment. The aggregate national unemployment rate increased to 4.4 per cent in 1985, but it was down to 2.9 per cent by 1989.[9] Econometric analyses of Mexico's employment and wage behaviour at a more disaggregated level indicate that the significant – and rapid – trade liberalization in that country did not impact employment at the industry level, but had small effects at the firm level (Feliciano 1994, Revenga 1994). This suggests that while inefficient firms in a particular industry released workers, efficient ones tended to expand their level of employment in approximately the same amount. Interestingly enough the existing evidence shows that the skill composition of employment tended to change in Mexico after the reforms, with employment of more skilled workers expanding relative to that of unskilled ones. Revenga (1994) argues that Mexico's flexible labour market structure, where real wages were allowed to fluctuate significantly, explains why the trade reforms did not affect employment as many analysts had predicted.

A detailed firm level study of Morocco's experience with trade liberalization between 1984 and 1990 reached similar conclusions. Using a data set with 26 000 observations, Currie and Harrison (1994) found that changes in import tariffs and QR coverage had no significant effect on the total aggregate level of employment. However, in those specific industries that had been very heavily protected by the pre-reform trade regime – textiles, beverages and apparel – tariff reduction did generate a decline in employment. They also found that Morocco's trade reform had been associated with an increase in the use of both temporary workers and more skilled workers. As in the Mexican case, the authors attribute their findings to the fact that, in spite of the existence of legal restrictions, Morocco's labour market is de facto quite flexible, with a large percentage of the labour force earning less than the legally mandated minimum wage.

The results discussed above for Mexico and Morocco contrast with those obtained for the case of Uruguay, a country that traditionally has had severely rigid labour regulations. Rama (1994) used data for 1978–86 at the four digit level for the manufacturing sector to investigate how that country's trade reform had affected employment and wages. He found that the import tariff elasticity of employment was significantly positive, with a range between 0.38 and 0.51. From his empirical analysis of the Uruguayan case, Rama concludes that 'if labor market imperfections outlast . . . product market imperfections, . . . there may by problems during the transition if trade liberalization proceeds too quickly' (p. 122).

Overall, this evidence suggests that the effect of trade reforms on employment may depend on the institutional characteristics of the labour market. In fact, Edwards and Cox-Edwards (1994) show that in the case of competitive and undistorted labour markets, tariff reductions will have little, if any, effect on aggregate employment, and will tend to generate an increase in real wages.[10] If, however, the labour market is subject to binding policy-induced distortions such as minimum wages, or if it is characterized by uncompetitive practices, trade liberalization may have severe adjustment costs in the form of unemployment. Moreover, in countries with a highly regulated labour market, the liberalization of other sectors, in the presence of these labour distortions, may be counter-productive from a welfare point of view. This suggests that in countries where labour markets are highly distorted, a reform strategy that tackles these distortions early on would be advisable.

THE CHILEAN TRADE REFORM AND THE LABOUR MARKET: AN OVERVIEW

In September of 1973, after three years of a socialist administration led by President Salvador Allende, the military staged a coup and took over Chile's government.[11] One of the central policies of the military government was the opening up of international trade. In five years all quantitative impediments to trade were eliminated, and import tariffs were reduced from an average of more than 100 per cent to a uniform 10 per cent level. The trade reform was initially accompanied by a strongly depreciated real exchange rate that encouraged a frantic growth of nontraditional exports. What makes the Chilean experience particularly interesting, and at times difficult to interpret, is that at the same time as a major modernization reform was being undertaken an effort was made to control a 600 per cent inflationary process. In fact, many of the controversies that have surrounded the interpretation of the Chilean experience are due to the inability to convincingly separate the effects of the stabilization program from that of the reforms themselves (see Bosworth *et al.*, 1994).

In the late 1930s and early 1940s Chile embarked on an import substitution development strategy through the indiscriminatory imposition of tariffs, import quotas, and all sorts of regulations and controls. After some time, the tariff structure began to reflect benefits obtained by different pressure groups. By the late 1960s high and variable tariffs had become a permanent feature of the Chilean economy. At the time of the military coup in 1973 import tariffs averaged 105 per cent and were highly dispersed, with some goods subject to nominal tariffs of more than 700 per cent and others fully exempted from import duties. In addition to tariffs, a battery of quantitative restrictions were applied, including outright import prohibition, prior import deposits of up to

10 000 per cent and a distortive multiple exchange rate system consisting of fifteen different rates (see de la Cuadra and Hacchette, 1986).

The liberalization process

In October 1973 the Minister of Finance stated that Chile's 'best prospects for growth are in opening to international competition' (Mendez, 1979: pp. 63–64). Initially, however, the authorities had no clear idea on how far they wanted to go with this reform. In fact, not until late in 1977 – after Chile had withdrawn from the subregional integration bloc called The Andean Pact – was it determined that the final goal of the trade liberalization was the achievement of a uniform 10 per cent import tariff.

In December of 1977 the chief economic strategist, Minister de Castro, announced that the final goal was now to reduce tariffs to a *uniform* rate of 10 per cent by mid-1979. In explaining this new change in the tariff policy de Castro pointed out that the prevailing schedule with differentiated rates between 10 per cent and 35 per cent generated an unjustifiable discriminatory situation. In his speech he said, '[W]e have decided to eliminate the distortions generated by the discriminatory tariff structure and to establish a uniform tariff; in this way all activities producing for the domestic market will be on an equal footing regarding foreign competition' (Banco Central de Chile, *Boletín Mensual*, December 1977: p. 1960). Table 2.1 contains the itinerary of trade liberalization.

As can be seen from Table 2.1, the liberalization was somewhat abrupt. By June 1976 the average tariff was 33 per cent, significantly below the average tariff in the majority of developing countries. This achievement was particularly impressive, since all quantitative import restrictions had also been eliminated by that date. By June 1979 when the trade reform came to an end, all items, except automobiles, had a nominal import tariff of 10 per cent.

The trade liberalization effort impacted different manufacturing sectors in different ways. Table 2.2 contains data on the evolution of the rate of effective protection for eighteen industries within the manufacturing sector.[12] As the reforms progressed, both the level and dispersion of the effective rates of protection were reduced. By June 1979, the average effective tariff was 13.6 per cent, and the range between the highest and lowest effective tariffs was only six percentage points.

An important consequence of the reform was that it increased the level of effective protection granted to agriculture. Through the

Table 2.1 Itinerary of tariff liberalization
(percentages)

Date (m/d/yr)	Maximum tariff rates	% of items subject to maximum tariff	Tariff mode	% of items	Average nominal tariff
12/31/73	220	8.0	90	12.4	94.0
3/1/74	200	8.2	80	12.3	90.0
3/27/74	160	17.1	70	13.0	80.0
6/5/74	140	14.4	60	13.0	67.0
1/16/75	120	8.2	55	13.0	52.0
8/13/75	90	1.6	40	20.3	44.0
2/9/76	80	0.5	35	24.0	38.0
6/7/76	65	0.5	30	21.2	33.0
12/23/76	65	0.5	20	26.2	27.0
1/8/77	55	0.5	20	24.7	24.0
5/2/77	45	0.6	20	25.8	22.4
8/29/77	35	1.6	20	26.3	19.8
12/3/77	25	22.9	15	37.0	15.7
6/78[a]	20	21.6	10	51.6	13.9
6/79[a]	10	99.5	10	99.5	10.1

[a] During 1978 and the first half of 1979 the tariff schedule was linearly reduced.

Source: Ffrench-Davis (1981).

imposition of price controls on agricultural products and high import tariffs on inputs, most crops traditionally had a substantive negative rate of effective protection. In 1974, for example, the agricultural sector had a negative average rate of effective protection of 36 per cent. As a result of the reforms that eliminated this bias against agriculture, the sector experienced a drastic boom in Chile.[13]

The initial phases of the liberalization of international trade were supplemented (until 1979) by an active policy of assuring a competitive real exchange rate. In fact, the reduction of trade barriers and the deterioration of Chile's terms of trade after 1974 *required* a depreciation of the equilibrium real exchange rate. This new depreciated value of the real exchange rate was first achieved via the maxi-devaluation of October of 1973, and then was maintained by an active crawling exchange rate system, which lasted until January of 1978.[14] The importance assigned by the government to a 'depreciated' real exchange rate was clearly articulated by Pinochet in a 1976 speech (Mendez 1979: p. 195): 'We shall continue to encourage nontraditional exports. . . . The Minister of Finance will announce the manner in which the exchange

Table 2.2   Effective rates of protection in manufacturing sectors
(percentages)

Sector	1974	1976	1978	1979
Food stuff	161	48	16	12
Beverages	203	47	19	13
Tobacco	114	29	11	11
Textiles	239	74	28	14
Footwear	264	71	27	14
Timber products	157	45	16	15
Furniture	95	28	11	11
Paper products	184	62	22	17
Publishing	140	40	20	12
Leather products	181	46	21	13
Rubber products	49	54	26	15
Chemicals	80	45	16	13
Petroleum and coal	265	17	12	13
Nonmetallic minerals	128	55	20	14
Basic metals	127	64	25	17
Metallic industries	147	77	27	15
Nonelectrical machinery	96	58	19	13
Electrical machinery	96	58	19	13
Average	151.4	51.0	19.7	13.6
Standard deviation	60.4	15.7	5.3	1.7

Source: Aedo and Lagos (1984)

rate shall be established in order to guarantee a viable and permanent value for foreign currency.'[15] At the end of 1976 the real effective exchange rate was almost 150 more depreciated than in the third quarter of 1973.

In June 1976 and again in March 1977 the peso was revalued, in attempts to break inflationary expectations. In the second half of 1977, to compensate partially for the effects of the new rounds of tariff reductions, the rate of nominal devaluation with respect to the US dollar was once again increased.

In 1978, a significant change in the stabilization program took place, when the exchange rate became the main anti-inflationary instrument. The rate of devaluation was preset at a rate below ongoing inflation, and in 1979 it was completely fixed with respect to the dollar. Between 1978 and 1982, and partially as a consequence of the new exchange rate policy, a significant degree of real exchange rate overvaluation developed. This overvaluation became increasingly unsustainable, until in 1982 a major crisis erupted – see Edwards and Cox-Edwards (1991) for details.

Table 2.3 Unemployment and wages in Chile: 1970–83

Year	(1) Labor force (1000s)	(2) U (1000s)	(3) Open U rate (%)	(4) MEP (1000s)	(5) MEP (% of labor force)	(6) Real wages (1970 = 100)
1970	2 923.2	167.1	5.7			100.0
1971	2 968.8	112.8	3.8			125.4
1972	3 000.8	93.0	3.1			125.4
1973	3 037.0	145.8	4.8			86.0
1974	3 066.8	282.1	9.2			90.2
1975	3 152.9	425.6	13.5	41.7	1.3	88.7
1976	3 216.4	511.4	15.9	168.8	5.2	86.3
1977	3 259.7	462.9	14.2	187.1	5.7	96.6
1978	3 370.1	478.6	14.2	148.0	4.4	97.5
1979	3 480.7	480.3	13.8	128.4	3.7	98.7
1980	3 539.8	417.7	11.9	187.9	5.3	108.3
1981	3 669.3	400.0	10.9	171.2	4.7	115.7
1982	3 729.7	760.9	20.4	190.2	5.1	112.2
1983	3 797.5	706.3	18.6	391.6	10.3	n.a.

Notes and sources: *U* means unemployment. The minimum employment program (MEP) was a temporary palliative system created by the government in 1973 to alleviate the unemployment problem. The labour force and unemployment figures (columns 1, 2 and 3 refer to June of each year) were estimated by Castaneda (1992). Column 4 is based on Banco Central (1983). Column 5 corresponds to the quotient of column 4 divided by column 1. Column 6 was constructed using National Accounts data. See A. Edwards (1984, p. 85) for further details.

Labour markets, unemployment and trade reform

During the first few years of its rule, the military introduced some important reforms to the functioning of the labour market. In particular, union activity was severely curtailed, and the ability for firms to lay off workers was increased greatly. Also, social security taxes were reduced, and mandated wage indexation mechanisms to deal with inflation became generalized – the indexation mechanism forced employers to increase salaries in the amount of past accumulated inflation. From 1974 onwards, and in spite of the reforms aimed at adding 'flexibility' to Chile's labour market, unemployment became a very serious problem (see Figure 2.1 and Table 2.3).

A subject extensively debated in Chile's popular press at that time was the extent to which the process of tariff reduction 'contributed' to the unemployment problem. There is little doubt that as a result of the tariff reform a number of contracting and even disappearing manufacturing firms laid off a number of workers. On the other hand, firms from the rapidly expanding exporting sector increased employment, partially offsetting the negative effect. Moreover, some firms in the formerly protected industries were able to adjust successfully to the new circumstances, and after a transitional period were able, once again, to expand employment.

Trade liberalization reforms tend to affect labour market options through two channels. First, there is a natural adjustment period when laid off workers take time to start searching for work in a different, expanding sector. Second, in reality – and contrary to the simplest textbook case – physical capital is fixed in its sector of origin, making the expansion of production in a number of the exporting sectors somewhat sluggish. As additional investment takes place over time, is it possible to increase production and employment fully in these expanding sectors?

In the case of Chile, there have been controversies on what proportion of total unemployment can be attributed to the trade reforms, the stabilization program, the privatization processes or other policies. Edwards (1982), for example, estimated on the basis of a partial equilibrium model that an upper bound for the unemployment effect of the trade reform was 3.5 percentage points of the labour force, or 129 000 people, with the bulk of this unemployment located in the food, beverages, tobacco, textiles, and leather products subsectors (57 000 people). On the other hand, in a 1986 study, de la Cuadra and Hacchette calculated that the trade reform generated a reduction of employment in the manufacturing sector of approximately 50 000 workers. Even though these are not negligible numbers, they clearly indicate that an explanation for the bulk of unemployment should be sought elsewhere. In the next section we report results obtained from survey data on the effects of trade reform on unemployment between 1976 and 1981.

TRADE REFORM AND UNEMPLOYMENT: AN ANALYSIS BASED ON SURVEY DATA

Most analyses of labor market behavior during the Chilean reforms have been based on aggregate data. Because of this, it has been difficult to separate convincingly the effects of macro developments – including the stabilization program – from those stemming from microeconomic reforms, including the trade liberalization process. One notable exception is the work of Heindl (1985), who estimates flows of employment creation and destruction and shows how these increased in the mid to late 1970s. It is important to note than in 1978 there was a major reform to labor legislation eliminating 'just-cause' as a requirement for dismissal, and establishing a maximum severance compensation. The purpose of this reform was to increase the degree of flexibility of labor markets and to accommodate the dislocations introduced by the reforms. In this section we report results obtained from the analysis of the probability of becoming unemployed. Two basic questions were asked: first, does the sector of origin affect the probability of being unemployed? More specifically, are those workers originally employed in more 'deprotected' sectors more likely to become unemployed? Second, conditional on being unemployed, does the sector of origin affect the duration of unemployment? We argue that while the first question can only be answered tentatively, the data set allows us to answer the second question with greater precision.

The data set

The basic information used in the analysis comes from the University of Chile June unemployment surveys for the Greater Santiago Area (GSA). These contain information on wages received during the month of May and labor market participation during the week preceding the survey. The GSA represents about one third of the country's labor market, is predominantly urban, and with a concentration in services. Based on the same data for a longer time series. Figure 2.9 reports the evolution of the overall rate of unemployment. As can be seen, unemployment rates fluctuated around 7 per cent for men and 5 per cent for women during the 1960s, they fell between 1970 and 1973 and they climbed very fast between 1974 and 1976 to rates of the order of 15 per cent. They subsequently fell during the late 1970s and early 1980s, and in 1982 they climbed back to levels above 20 per cent. After 1982, there was a steady reduction of the unemployment rate to reach historical levels in the early 1990s. Unemployment rates are typically higher among the young and the less educated, and there is a relatively consistent shift upwards in all rates during the mid 1970s and the early 1980s.

Figure 2.10 takes the sample of unemployed that have lost jobs (as opposed to new entrants) and reports unemployment duration trends. Median unemployment duration rises from around 12 weeks to around 24 weeks in the mid 1970s, and then sharply up to 50 weeks in the early 1980s, to fall back to previous levels (12 weeks) in the early

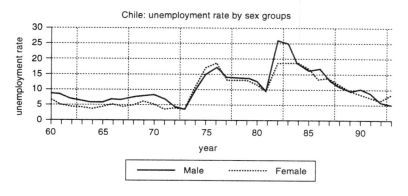

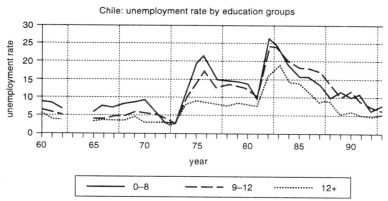

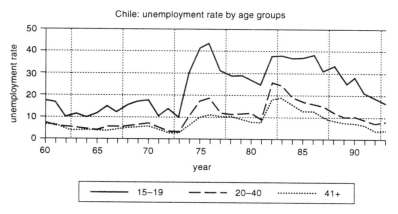

Figure 2.9

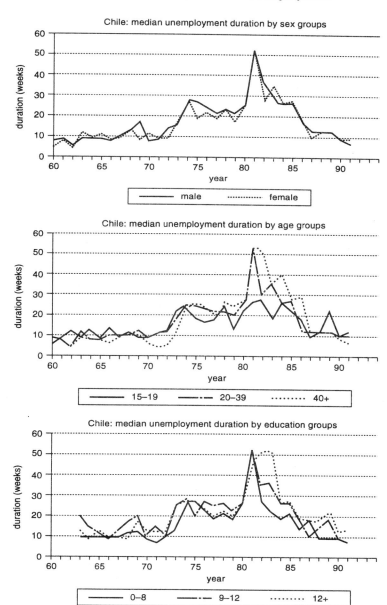

Figure 2.10

1990s. This evidence, along with the properties of the data, justifies our emphasis on the determinants of unemployment duration.

The GSA surveys allow us to identify personal characteristics for each individual in the sample. These include age, education, sex, placement in the household, labor force status during the reference week, including sector and occupation (for the employed and unemployed that lost jobs), and wages and income for the month of May. The surveys also ask those that are out of work about the sector of previous employment, and the number of weeks they have been unemployed. In short, the data set provides some useful information on incomplete unemployment spells, although the maximum number of unemployed weeks is censored at 99. Table 2.4 provides a summary of the data for 1976, 1979 and 1981. **Nemp** is a variable that takes the value of one if the individual is unemployed and zero if he/she in employed; **ex** is experience and is defined in years; **ye** is education and is also measured in years; **assets** refers to an estimate of the individual assets measured in current pesos, and is used as a proxy for the individual's reservation wage; **dhead** is a binary variable that captures whether the individual is a head of household; **dprox** is the degree of deprotection of sector x relative to the previous period with available data; and **sex** classifies individuals by male/female.

As pointed out above one would want to answer, at least, two questions: (a) with other things given, does the degree of deprotection affect the probability of being unemployed, and (b) with other things given, does deprotection affect the conditional probability of remaining unemployed – in other words, does deprotection affect unemployment duration? In principle, these questions can be addressed by estimating probit equations. In dealing with the first question the dependent variable is whether the individual in unemployed; in addressing the second question the dependent variable is the probability of an unemployed worker being unemployed more than 12, 24, 48 and 96 weeks, conditional on being unemployed at the time of the survey.

Both probabilities will be determined by individual characteristics as they determine individual supply prices, and also will depend on market conditions, as they affect wage offers (see, for example, Nickell 1979). The data set provides information on some of these variables, allowing us to include them in the analysis or to construct proxy indicators. For example, relatively high levels of personal assets or family income will tend to make individual supply prices rise, increasing unemployment duration. Likewise, in the empirical analysis, we can use the rate of unemployment for specific experience-schooling cells to

Table 2.4   Data set characteristics: 1976, 1979 and 1991

A.1976 Variable	Obs	Mean	Std.Dev.	Min	Max
nemp	4738	0.141	0.348	0	1
ex	4738	19.788	13.204	0	83
ye	4738	8.454	4.308	0	19
asset	4738	39.408	137.760	0	1998
dhead	4738	0.541	0.498	0	1
dpro76	4738	-0.010	0.196	-0.679	0.406
sex	4738	0.346	0.476	0	1

B.1979 Variable	Obs	Mean	Std. dev.	Min	Max
nemp	5373	0.125	0.331	0	1
ex	5373	18.870	13.302	0	71
ye	5369	9.197	4.125	0	19
asset	5373	258.735	895.369	0	12999
dhead	5373	0.496	0.500	0	1
dpro76	5373	-0.015	0.034	-0.109	0.053
sex	5373	0.354	0.478	0	1

C.1981 Variable	Obs	Mean	Std. dev.	Min	Max
nemp	5369	0.081	0.273	0	1
ex	6778	21.196	14.418	0	85
ye	6755	8.947	4.046	0	19
asset	7335	44.973	249.501	0	9000
dhead	7336	0.447	0.497	0	1
dpro76	7336	-0.004	0.015	-0.060	0.100
sex	7336	0.500	0.500	0	1

estimate market conditions. But the researcher cannot know how individuals adjust their supply price as market conditions change, and there are other important variables, such as 'motivation' that are unobservable. Another serious problem is that the variable 'sector of origin' is not an invariable individual characteristic for those in the sample.

Results

Using data on effective rates of protection, we created the following variables: pro74(s) = effective rate of protection in 1974 sector(s). The raw data are those reported in Table 2.2; for 1981 a flat value of

effective rate of protection of 10 per cent was considered. In the case
of agriculture we considered a rate of effective protection of −36 per
cent in 1974, −18 per cent in 1979, −13 per cent in 1979; and −5
per cent in 1981.

We then estimated indexes of deprotection in the following way:
dpro76(s) = [pro76(s) − pro74(s)]/[1 + (pro74(s))], where s is a particular sector of economic activity. We also estimated deprotection indexes for years 1979 and 1981. In each case the deprotection index
was defined as the *marginal* decline in the rate of effective protection.
In the case of nontradable sectors − services such as construction, the
public sector and education − we assigned a value of zero to the
deprotection index. Notice that deprotection is measured here as a negative number; the more negative the index, the higher the degree of
deprotection resulting from the trade liberalization reform.

We first analyse for 1976, 1979 and 1981 the probability of being
unemployed. In doing this we included only those individuals that had
lost their jobs and, thus, excluded those that had just joined the labor
force. The results obtained are presented in Table 2.5. As can be seen,
most of the coefficients are significant at conventional levels. These
results suggest that, at the margin, the probability of being unemployed
declines with experience and schooling − although the schooling coefficient is not significant in 1979 and only marginally so in 1981. Interestingly enough, and perhaps a bit surprising, those with lower assets
appear to have a larger probability of being unemployed. Heads of
households and males also appear as having a significant lower probability of being out of work.

More interestingly for our purpose, however, the degree of deprotection
seems to affect the probability of being unemployed positively. The
lower the deprotection − that is the larger dprox becomes − the lower
the probability of unemployment. As pointed out previously, however,
these results should be interpreted with care. The reason for this is
that, contrary to the other variables in the analysis, dprox is not an
invariable characteristic of the individual. In fact, it is possible that
the 'sector' variable means different things for different people in the
sample. To illustrate this, consider the following example: assume the
case of two individuals that lost their jobs in the textile sector 12
weeks ago. Assume further that while one of the individuals remains
unemployed, the other found work in the banking sector 3 weeks ago.
While for the first person the 'sector' will be 'textiles', for the second
it will be 'banking'. And yet, both lost their jobs from the same sector
at the same time.

Table 2.5   Estimated probability of being unemployed, 1976, 1979 and 1981

A.1976
Probit estimates

Number of obs = 4738
chi2(6) = 323.89
Prob>chi2 = 0.000
Log likelihood = −1761.6283   Psuedo R2 = 0.0842

nemp	Coef.	St. err.	t	$P> |t|$
ex	−0.005	0.002	−2.348*	0.019
ye	−0.074	0.007	−11.367*	0.000
asset	−0.005	0.001	−5.677*	0.000
dhead	−0.359	0.063	−5.740*	0.000
dpro76	−0.347	0.117	−2.955*	0.003
sex	−0.391	0.059	−6.644*	0.000
_cons	−0.049	0.080	−0.612	0.541

B.1979
Probit estimates

Number of obs = 5196
chi2(6) = 170.76
Prob>chi2 = 0.000
Log likelihood = −1560.269   Psuedo R2 = 0.0519

nemp	Coef.	St. err.	t	$P> |t|$
ex	−0.001	0.002	−0.545	0.586
ye	−0.054	0.007	−7.899*	0.000
asset	−0.000	0.000	−4.002*	0.000
dhead	−0.255	0.065	−3.946*	0.000
dpro79	−1.794	0.682	−2.630*	0.009
sex	−0.404	0.062	−6.522*	0.000
_cons	−0.545	0.086	−6.363*	0.000

C.1981
Probit estimates

Number of obs = 5196
chi2(6) = 170.76
Prob>chi2 = 0.000
Log likelihood = −1560.269   Psuedo R2 = 0.0519

nemp	Coef.	St. err.	t	$P> |t|$
ex	−0.003	0.003	−1.253	0.210
ye	−0.033	0.008	−4.192*	0.000
asset	−0.003	0.001	−4.105*	0.000
dhead	−0.099	0.073	−1.354	0.176
dpro81	−1.732	1.544	−1.122	0.262
sex	−0.254	0.070	−3.600*	0.000
_cons	−0.936	0.103	−9.099*	0.000

* Within 95% conf. interval.

One way of dealing with this issue is to define a sample where the 'sector' variable indeed becomes an invariable individual characteristic. This will be the case, for example, if we concentrate on those that are already unemployed, and analyse the conditional probability of remaining unemployed. We turn now to the analysis of this problem. Conditional on having lost their jobs and not found one, we examined the probabilities of staying unemployed beyond 12, 24, 48 and 96 months. We were particularly interested in testing the role of the tariffs reductions. To the extent that workers have sector-specific human capital, and the trade reform reduces incentives to produce in that sector, deprotection causes a depreciation in the value of human capital of those that were employed there, inducing them to stay in the unemployment ranks. But it also may be the case that trade reforms reduce the value of human capital accumulated by virtually every person in the labor market, especially among the most experienced, reducing the importance of original sector of employment in explaining unemployment duration.

The probit equations were of the following form:

$$\text{prob(unemp>24 weeks in 1976)} = f(ye, ex, asset, dpro76) \quad (2)$$

We experimented with a number of equations, analysed the determinants of unemployment and unemployment duration for men and women, and used different durations thresholds (12, 24, 48 and 96 weeks of unemployment duration). In a first stage, we used dummy variable to identify each sector, in a later stage we used the dpro76, dpro79 or dpro81 indexes in each of the respective years.

Tables 2.6 and 2.7 contain the basic results for 12 and 24 weeks duration. As can be seen, in general, unemployment duration increases with experience and schooling. Assets appear to have a positive sign in 1976 and 1981, although in the latter is not significant. Interestingly enough, it has a negative coefficient in 1979. Whether an individual is head of household appears to be important only in 1981, where the estimation suggests that heads of household have shorter unemployment spells. The sex variable does not appear to be important. In all regressions the deprotection index has a negative coefficient, and is significant at conventional levels in four of the six cases.

Table 2.6 Conditional probability of remaining unemployed for 12 or more weeks

A.1976
Probit estimates

Number of obs = 666
chi2(6) = 15.26
Prob>chi2 = 0.0184

Log likelihood = −334.85297

Psuedo R2 = 0.0223

Unemp12	Coef.	St. err.	t	P> |t|
ex	0.005	0.006	0.901	0.368
ye	0.025	0.017	1.408	0.160
asset	0.012	0.005	2.474*	0.014
dhead	0.002	0.148	0.017	0.987
dpro76	−0.395	0.265	−1.491	0.136
sex	0.066	0.131	0.505	0.614
_cons	427	0.177	2.412*	0.016

B.1979
Probit estimates

Number of obs = 500
chi2(6) = 25.89
Prob>chi2 = 0.0002

Log likelihood = −291.63544

Psuedo R2 = 0.0425

unemp12	Coef.	St. err.	t	P> |t|
ex	0.024	0.006	3.910*	0.000
ye	0.052	0.000	−1.725	0.085
asset	−0.001	0.000	−1.725	0.085
dhead	0.007	0.170	0.042	0.966
dpro79	−1.233	1.615	−0.764	0.445
sex	−0.046	0.148	−0.312	0.755
_cons	−0.270	0.205	−1.317	0.188

C.1981
Probit estimates

Number of obs = 327
chi2(6) = 18.64
Prob>chi2 = 0.0048

Log likelihood = −192.01443

Psuedo R2 = 0.0463

unemp12	Coef.	St. err.	t	P> |t|
ex	0.024	0.008	3.068*	0.002
ye	0.021	0.023	0.914	0.362
asset	0.001	0.002	0.300	0.765
dhead	−0.346	0.202	−1.709	0.088
dpro81	−8.673	3.410	−2.543*	0.011
sex	−0.192	0.180	−1.068	0.286
_cons	0.061	0.273	0.222	0.824

* Within 95% conf. interval.

Table 2.7   Conditional probability of remaining unemployed for 24 or more weeks

---

A.1976
Probit estimates

Number of obs = 666
chi2(6) = 8.81
Prob>chi2 = 0.1843

Log likelihood = −433.69495

Psuedo R2 = 0.0101

nemp	Coef.	St. Err.	t	P> |t|
ex	0.004	0.005	0.725	0.006
ye	0.016	0.016	1.016	0.310
asset	0.003	0.003	1.182	0.238
dhead	0.065	0.133	0.486	0.627
dpro76	−0.479	0.237	−2.020*	0.044
sex	0.029	0.118	0.246	0.806
_cons	−0.050	0.162	0.311	0.756

B.1979
Probit estimates

Number of obs = 500
chi2(6) = 25.17
Prob>chi2 = 0.003

Log likelihood = −330.38208

Psuedo R2 = 0.0367

nemp	Coef.	St. Err.	t	P> |t|
ex	0.017	0.006	3.071*	0.002
ye	0.042	0.017	2.437*	0.015
asset	−0.003	0.000	−1.096	0.274
dhead	0.076	0.161	0.475	0.635
dpro79	−3.884	1.543	−2.518*	0.012
sex	−0.101	0.142	−0.708	0.479
_cons	−0.545	0.197	−2.772*	0.006

C.1981
Probit estimates

Number of obs = 327
chi2(6) = 27.36
Prob>chi2 = 0.0001

Log likelihood = −212.97907

Psuedo R2 = 0.0603

nemp	Coef.	St. Err.	t	P> |t|
ex	0.037	0.008	4.808*	0.000
ye	0.041	0.022	1.849*	0.065
asset	0.002	0.002	0.749	0.454
dhead	−0.557	0.197	−2.832*	0.005
dpro81	−2.915	3.274	−0.890	0.374
sex	−0.072	0.174	−0.415	0.679
_cons	−0.749	0.266	−2.821*	0.005

* Within 95% conf. interval.

Table 2.8 Estimated probability and marginal contribution of deprotection of unemployed for 24 or more weeks

	1976	1979	1981
Estimated probability of unemployment for average individual	0.632	0.560	0.498
Marginal contribution of deprotection to male head of household probability	0.022	0.029	0.009
Marginal contribution of deprotection to male not head of household probability	0.024	0.030	0.009

CONCLUDING REMARKS

The results presented above provide preliminary evidence suggesting that, in the case of Chile's trade liberalization reform, once it is controlled for individual characteristics, the degree of deprotection tended to increase the probability of being unemployed and the conditional probability of remaining unemployed. The econometric results reported above can be used to investigate further the effect of deprotection on unemployment. Two particularly interesting questions refer to the estimated (conditional) probability for the 'typical' individual, and to the marginal effect of deprotection in each year on the (conditional) probability of unemployment. In Table 2.8 we present the estimated values for the case of conditional unemployment of 24 or more weeks. The estimated conditional probabilities of unemployment have been calculated for the average individual in the sample – that is for the individual with an average degree of education and experience and subject to the (sample weighted) average degree of deprotection. As can be seen, this conditional probability is very high in 1976, and declines quite significantly in the next few years: in 1976, for the average person already unemployed, the estimated probability of being out of work for 24 weeks or more is 0.632; it declines to 0.56 in 1979 and to 0.498 in 1981. The rest of the table contains the estimated marginal contribution of deprotection to the conditional probability of being unemployed for two groups of males; head of household and not head of household. What is particularly interesting about these estimates is their evolution through time. As can be seen, the marginal contribution of deprotection is quite similar in 1976 and 1979, and falls dramatically in 1981. This suggests that in the case of a preannounced (and presumably credible) reform, as firms have time to adjust to their new competition conditions the impact of reform on (conditional) unemployment duration becomes negligible.

All in all these results suggest that in the case of Chile's major trade reform, the degree of deprotection had a significant, although rather small and declining through time, effect on the probability of being unemployed. In a way this is not overly surprising given that throughout this period Chile maintained a fairly rigid minimum wage regulation. In fact, as Edwards and Cox Edwards (1991), among others, have argued, to the extent that there are wage rigidities in some sectors of the economy – the so-called 'protected' sectors – and physical capital is sector-specific, trade liberalization will tend to result in short term unemployment.

It is important to notice, however, that these results are subject to a number of data-imposed limitations. First, the data set refers exclusively to the urban Santiago area and, thus, does not capture the evolution of labor market forces in the rest of the country. In particular, this data set contains very few observations from the agricultural sector. Second, the definition of 'sector of unemployment' can be misinterpreted by those surveyed. Does it refer to the last remunerated employment, as we have interpreted it, or is it really the sector of preferred (future) employment? Third, there are no observed data on supply prices, and we have proxied them by the initial level of data. Fourth, there are no complete histories of employment and unemployment and, thus, it is not possible to investigate the determinants of being unemployed. This, indeed, has been the reason why we concentrated on the duration of unemployment. And, fifth, the analysis presented here does not permit us to estimate the total net effect on aggregate unemployment of the trade reforms

Although these limitations suggest that these results should be taken with a grain of salt, they are sufficiently robust to the equation specification, the threshold used to define duration and gender breakdown as to provide preliminary, but strongly suggestive evidence supporting the idea that in a setting with rigid wages deprotection will tend to increase the conditional probability of remaining unemployed.

Notes

* We thank Daniel Lederman for diligent research assistance.
1. In a simple textbook world these issues are trivial. The first best solution is to liberalize all markets instantaneously and simultaneously. In the real world, however, things are more complicated. Political constraints, externalities and adjustment costs make the simple textbook solution impractical or plainly incorrect.
2. In some of our previous work we have discussed theoretically the way in which trade liberalization affects employment and unemployment. In particular, we have analysed how the existence of different labor market distortions interact with trade liberalization. See, for example, Edwards (1988) and Edwards and Cox Edwards (1994). See also the recent survey by Agénor and Aizenman (1995) and the forthcoming book by Agénor and Montiel (1995).
3. On the Chilean reforms, including the trade liberalization effort, see Bosworth, *et al.* (1994) and Edwards and Cox Edwards (1991).
4. All major multi country studies on trade reform episodes analytically discussed labor market issues. However, they did not attempt to quantify the effects of tariff and QR changes on sectoral or aggregate employment and unemployment. The important study by Krueger (1981) analysed how different trade regimes affected labor creation over the long run.
5. See de la Dehesa, *et al.* (1991).
6. It is interesting to note that, in spite of their 'before and after' comparisons, almost every time unemployment does increase after the reform the authors tend to attribute it to causes other than the reform itself. For example, in the Argentine case they refer to overvaluation, in the Israeli episode they mention restrictive macro policies; in Korea they talk about recession and so on.
7. See Edwards (1995) for an evaluation of this study.
8. Edwards and Cox Edwards (1991) use a segmented labor market model to quantify the effects of the Chilean trade reform on unemployment. On this issue, see also Corbo *et al.* (1986) and Ramos (1986).
9. These data refer to the 'open' rate of unemployment.
10. This, of course, is the standard Stolper–Samuelson result under the assumption that in the country in question labor is the abundant factor.
11. On the Chilean experiment, see Edwards and Cox Edwards (1991) and Valdés (1995).
12. The effective rate of protection is a measure of the relative degree of inefficiency of domestic production relative to international production. A positive value means that domestic value added for that particular activity exceeds value added at international prices. The effective tariff for good

$i(\gamma_i)$ is computed in the form of $\gamma_i = (t_i - \sum a_{ij}t_j)/(1 - \sum a_{ij})$, where t_i is

the nominal tariff, a_{ij} is the input/output coefficient between input j and good I, and t_j is the nominal tariff on input j. Notice that if the good and *all* inputs have the same nominal tariff, then the effective and nominal rates of protection are the same ($\gamma_i = t_i$). It should be noted that from a general equilibrium perspective the usefulness of the concept of effective rates of protection is quite limited.

13. On the degree of effective protection in Chile's agriculture sector prior to the reforms, see, for example, Varas (1975).

14. The initial maxi-devaluation responded, in part, to the need to avoid an almost imminent balance of payments crisis. As the tariff process proceeded the crawling peg tried to (approximately) maintain the high level of the real exchange rate.

15. In fact, the exchange rate played a crucial role in the government's explanation of the negative effects of protectionism during the previous decades. For example, according to de Castro:

> The relatively forced industrialization of the country was obtained through various mechanisms. One of these was the foreign exchange rate policy. From 1939 on, the exchange rate was maintained artificially low. . . . The exporting sector lost all possibility to export because . . . [with a low] exchange rate . . . they could not manage to cover their local production costs. (Mendez 1979, p. 201)

References

Adeo, C. and Lagos L. F. (1984 'Protection Efectiva en Chile, 1974–1979', *Documents de Trabajo No. 94*, Instituto de Economica, Universidad Cotolica de Chile, 1984.

Agénor, P. and Aizenmann, J. (1995) 'Trade Liberalization and Unemployment', Working Paper No. 20, Research Department, International Monetary Fund.

Agénor, P. and Montiel, P. (1995) *Development Macroeconomics* (?: Princeton University Press).

Banco Central (1983), Banco Central de Chile, *Boletin Mensual*, several issues, 1983.

Bosworth, B., Dornbusch, R. and Labán, R. (1994) *The Chilean Economy: Policy Lessons and Challenges* (Washington, DC: The Brookings Institution).

Burda, M. and Sachs, J. (1987), 'Institutional Aspects of Unemployment in Germany,' NBER Working Paper (Cambridge, MA: National Bureau of Economic Research).

Castaneda, T. (1992) *Combating Poverty: Innovative Social Reforms in Chile during the 1980s*, San Francisco, California, ICS Press.

Corbo, V., De Melo, J. and Tybout, J. (1986) 'What Went Wrong in the Southern Cone', *Economic Development and Cultural Change*, 34 (3).

de la Cuadra, S. and Hacchetta, D. (1986) 'The Timing and Sequencing of a Trade Liberalization Policy: The Case of Chile' (Santiago, Chile, Universidad Católica).

Currie, J. and Harrison, A. (1994) 'Trade Reform and Labor Market Adjustment in Morocoo', Paper presented at the World Bank Labor Markets Workshop, Washington, DC, July 6–8.

de la Dehesa, G., Ruiz, J. and Torres, A. (1991) 'Spain's Three Liberalization Episodes', in Michael et al. (1991), vol. 6.

Edwards, A. (1984) *Three Essays on Labour Market in Developing Countries*,

PhD dissertation, University of Chicago, August 1984.

Edwards, S. (1982) 'Trade Liberalization, Minimum Wages and Employment in the Short Run: Some Reflections Based on the Chilean Experience', Working paper, UCLA.

Edwards, S. (1988) 'Terms of Trade, Tariffs, and Labor Market Adjustment in Developing Countries', *World Bank Economic Review*, 2, May.

Edwards, S. (1990) 'Structural Reforms and Labor Market Adjustment,' Working Paper, UCLA Dept. of Economics.

Edwards, S. (1995) *Crisis and Reform in Latin America: From Despair to Hope* (New York: Oxford University Press).

Edwards, S. and Cox Edwards, A. (1991) *Monetarism and Liberalization: The Chilean Experiment* (Chicago: University of Chicago Press).

Edwards, S. and Cox Edwards, A. (1994) 'Labor Market Distortions and Structural Adjustment in Developing Countries', in S. Horton, *et al.* (eds.) *Labor Markets in an Era of Adjustment*, Vol. 1 (Washington, DC: EDI Development Studies Series, World Bank).

Feliciano, Z. (1994) 'Workers and Trade Liberalization: The Impact of Trade Reforms in Mexico on Wages and Employment', mimeo, Harvard University.

Ffrench-Davis, R. (1981) 'Intercambio y Desarrollo', *Trimestre Economico Lecturas 38*, Fondo de Cultura Economica.

Harberger, A. C. (1971) 'On Measuring the Social Opportunity Cost of Labor', *ILO Review*, 103: pp. 559–79.

Harris, J. and Todaro, M. P. (1970) 'Migration, Unemployment and Development: A Two-Sector Analysis', *American Economic Review*, 60: 126–42.

Heindl, E. (1985) 'Un modelo para la determinación de flujos y parámetros dinámicos en el mercado de trabajo', *Estudios de Economía* 12 (1).

Krueger, A. (1981) *Trade and Employment in Developing Countries* (Chicago: University of Chicago Press).

Little, I., Scitovsky, T. and Scott, M. (1970) *Industry and Trade in Some Developing Countries* (Oxford: Oxford University Press).

Mendez, J., (ed.) (1979) *Chilean Economic Policy* (Santiago, Chile: Calderón).

Michaely, M. (1982) 'The Sequencing of a Liberalization Policy: A Preliminary Statement of Issues', mimeo, Washington, DC, The World Bank.

Michealy, M., Choksi, A. and Papageorgiou, D. (eds.) (1991) *Liberalizing Foreign Trade* (New York: Basil Blackwell).

Nickell, S. (1979) 'Estimating the Probability of Leaving Unemployment', *Econometrica*, 47, November.

Rama, M. (1994) 'The Labor Market and Trade Reform in Manufacturing', in M. Connolly and J. de Melo (eds.) *The Effects of Protectionism on a Small Country: The Case of Uruguay* (Washington, DC: World Bank, Regional and Sectoral Studies).

Ramos, J. (1986) *Neoconservative Economics in the Southern Cone of Latin America, 1973–1983* (Baltimore: Johns Hopkins University Press).

Revenga, A. (1994) 'Employmentand Wage Effects of Trade Liberalization: The Case of Mexican Manufacturing', Paper presented at the Seminar on Labor Markets in Developing Countries in Washington, DC, World Bank, July.

Valdés, J. (1995) *Pinochet's Economists: The Chicago School in Chile* (New York: Cambridge University Press).

Varas, J. (1975) 'El impacto de una liberalización del comercio en el sector agricola chileno [A Trade Liberalization and the Agricultural Sector in Chile]', *Cuadernos de Economía*, 12, August.

3 Lessons for Policy Reform in Light of the Mexican Experience[1]

Anne O. Krueger

INTRODUCTION

After the widely-publicized 'debt crisis' in the early 1980s, policy makers concerned with development came to recognize that accumulating debt had been but the symptom of deeper problems of flawed economic policy. In many countries, policy 'reform' programs were adopted. In some instances, these were undertaken tentatively, and efforts at reform were reversed at the first sign of difficulty. In other cases, reforms addressed some critical policy issues such as unrealistic exchange rates and quantitative restrictions on imports, but failed to tackle the fundamental issues concerning property rights and the role of the state in economic activity. In only a few cases did policy makers go beyond these immediate and pressing issues to attempt to alter the relative role of the market and of the state in the economy.

Of those cases, Mexico was in the forefront.[2] After announcing inability to service her debt without support in 1982, there had followed a 3–5 year period of 'traditional' adjustment, in which quantitative controls on trade had been strengthened, the banks were nationalized, and monetary and fiscal policy had been fairly restrictive to reduce the size of the prospective fiscal deficit. By the mid-1980s, however, the authorities became convinced that: (a) the earlier build-up of debt and the debt crisis had been the result of their own policies and not the fault of the rest of the world;[3] (b) the stabilization policies that had been pursued since 1982 had successfully reduced the current account deficit but there had been no pick-up in economic growth; and (3) without altering the underlying economic policies, prospects for future Mexican growth would be poor indeed.

By the late 1980s and early 1990s, the Mexicans were in the vanguard of policy reform. They had not only dismantled virtually all quantitative restrictions, reduced the highest tariff rate to 25 per cent, greatly depreciated the real exchange rate to accommodate the shift, and transformed the 'primacy' fiscal deficit into a surplus, but they had also begun to remove regulations and government controls over major segments of economic activity. To cite just a few: transportation was deregulated; price controls over a variety of commodities were reduced; the old Ejido system of collective land ownership was amended; and, most striking of all, privatization of a large number of state enterprises was undertaken.

Finally, and most visibly of all, the Mexican authorities negotiated entry into the North American Free Trade Agreement, signifying their commitment to the maintenance of an open economy and of the new, restrained, role of government in the economy. Foreign debt as a percentage of exports had fallen sharply, from its peak of 423 per cent in 1986 to 205 per cent in 1993, and interest payments on outstanding foreign debt fell from 40.4 per cent of export (of goods and services) earnings in 1982 to 10.9 per cent in 1993.[4] To a degree, this reduction was accomplished by transforming external debt to internal debt, which peaked in 1991. By the early 1990s, Mexican economic growth had resumed, albeit at relatively sluggish rates of 3–4 per cent annually, against a rate of population growth of around 2 per cent per annum (see Table 3.1) Interestingly, and partly associated with the large capital inflows, savings as a percentage of GDP fell continuously after 1987, from 22.0 in that year to 15.8 per cent in 1994 (see Table 3.2), while investment – financed in part by capital inflows – rose from 19.2 per cent of GDP in 1987 to 23.5 per cent in 1994.

There ensued several years in which there were large capital inflows into Mexico, as foreign investors saw these policy changes as portending a prosperous future for the Mexican economy. However, in December 1994, after a 15 per cent devaluation which failed to stem demands for foreign exchange for purposes of capital flight, a major financial crisis ensued. The peso, which had traded at 3.45 pesos per US dollar the preceeding month, was trading at 5.32 pesos per US dollar at the end of December, 1994 (a 54 per cent depreciation), and subsequently depreciated to a low of 6.8 pesos per dollar in March before recovering somewhat.[5]

This dramatic decline caught the attention of the financial community policy makers, and the academic community alike. Diagnoses of what had happened ranged all the way from blaming a series of unfortunate circumstances in 1994 (political assassinations, the Chiapas revolt, the presidential election, and concern about political stability) to assertions

Table 3.1   Mexican real variables, 1980–94.

	Real GDP (1990 pesos, bn)	Merchandise Exports	Imports (US $, bn)	Current account balance
1980	593.7	15.5	18.9	−10.8
1981	640.9	20.1	23.9	−16.1
1982	636.8	21.2	14.4	−6.3
1983	610.2	22.3	8.6	5.4
1984	631.7	24.2	11.3	4.2
1985	647.6	21.7	13.2	1.1
1986	624.0	16.0	11.4	−1.7
1987	635.4	20.7	12.2	4.0
1988	643.6	20.5	20.3	−2.4
1989	664.8	22.8	25.4	−5.8
1990	694.9	26.8	31.3	−7.5
1991	720.2	26.9	38.2	−14.9
1992	740.0	27.5	48.2	−24.4
1993	745.2	30.0	48.9	−23.4
1994	771.2	34.6	58.9	−28.8

Source: International Monetary Fund, *International Financial Statistics*, 1995 yearbook and April 1996.

that policy reforms in Mexico had fundamentally failed. In between, economists' diagnoses included the view of Sachs *et al.* (1995) that, once capital outflows had increased, the Mexican authorities failed to allow a rise in interest rates and ran down reserves instead, thereby leaving them vulnerable, and Harberger's (1995) attribution of the difficulties to the excess spending associated with the 1994 election and other negative shocks without the accompanying changes in exchange rate policy that would have been necessary to offset them. Some economists (Dornbusch and Werner, 1994; Krueger and Barahona, 1991) had for several years argued that exchange rate policy (to be described below) was inappropriate, and that December 1994 was simply the denouement.

However, all agreed that, by December, the exchange rate had to be altered. But there was less agreement among economists as to what had gone wrong and why policies had to change. In part for that reason, the proposal by the American administration to provide a large line of credit to Mexico was highly controversial.

In the light of the visibility of the Mexican policy reforms, an understanding of what went wrong and why is especially important. In this

Table 3.2 Mexican government budget balance, national savings and gross domestic investment (as a percentage of GDP)

	Budget balance/GDP*	Savings/GDP	Gross domestic investment/GDP
1980	−7.5	22.2	27.1
1981	−14.1	21.4	27.4
1982	−16.9	22.4	22.9
1983	−8.6	24.7	20.7
1984	−8.5	22.5	20.0
1985	−9.6	22.5	21.1
1986	−15.9	18.2	18.3
1987	−16.1	22.0	19.2
1988	−12.5	19.3	20.4
1989	−5.6	18.8	21.4
1990	−4.0	19.2	22.6
1991	−1.5	17.8	22.4
1992	0.5	16.1	23.3
1993	na	15.8	21.7

* Financial balance series used. Figures for 1991 and 1992 are preliminary.

Sources: The budget data is from Banco de Mexico *The Mexican Economy* (1994), table 34. The savings data is from OECD *Economic Outlook* (June 1995), annex table 27. The investment data is calculated from IBRD *World Tables* (1995), country page.

paper, I first review the Mexican policies with regard to the exchange rate (and its use as a nominal anchor). Then, I attempt to show why a nominal anchor exchange rate policy is in most circumstances fundamentally flawed. A final section then evaluates the lessons from the Mexican experience for policy reform in developing countries.[6]

MEXICAN EXCHANGE RATE POLICIES

As already mentioned, by the mid-1980s, Mexican policy makers began to abandon their approach of the early 1980s. In the early years after the onset of the debt crisis, quantitative restrictions had restrained imports, and domestic producers within Mexico remained as protected as they had earlier been. Policies of import-substitution, which had been followed throughout the preceding three decades, were not initially challenged. There was some restructuring of public sector enterprises and some deregulation starting in 1985.

Table 3.3   Mexican nominal and real exchange rates, 1980 to 1995

	Wholesale price index (1990=100)	Nominal exchange rate per US $	Real exchange rate (1980=100)	Nominal interest rate (%)
1980	0.7	0.0230	100.0	20.63
1981	0.9	0.0245	93.6	29.57
1982	1.4	0.0564	140.8	43.62
1983	2.9	0.1201	146.4	54.70
1984	4.9	0.1678	123.0	48.36
1985	7.6	0.2569	122.0	59.48
1986	14.3	0.6118	149.8	84.68
1987	33.6	1.3782	147.0	97.24
1988	69.8	2.2731	121.3	63.65
1989	81.1	2.4615	118.8	36.29
1990	100.0	2.8126	114.0	31.24
1991	120.5	3.0184	101.7	17.10
1992	136.7	3.0949	92.5	15.68
1993	148.8	3.1156	86.8	15.46
1994	158.9	3.3751	89.2	13.26
1995	221.1	6.4194	126.2	39.18

Notes: 1) Nominal exchange rates are new pesos per US dollar for the period average.
2) The real exchange rate was calculated between the peso and US dollar (with which Mexico does more than 70 per cent of her trade). The real exchange rate was calculated as the nominal exchange rate times the US producer price index divided by the Mexican wholesale price index.

Source: International Monetray Fund, *International Financial Statistics*, 1995 year book and April 1996.

By 1987, however, major economic problems were re-emerging. Inflation reached an annual rate of 135 per cent in that year (see Table 3.3), and the government budget swung once again into huge deficits (16 per cent of GDP in 1986 and 1987, and 12.5 per cent in 1988 – see Table 3.2). This time, the authorities undertook a 'maxi devaluation, with the exchange rate moving from 0.6118 pesos per dollar at the end of 1986 to 1.378 pesos dollar at the end of 1987.

Thereafter, the program to contain inflation was combined with other policy reform efforts. To control inflation, the government budget deficits were sharply reduced, going from 16 per cent of GDP in 1987 to

5.6 per cent in 1989, 4 per cent in 1990, 1.5 per cent in 1991, and reaching surplus in 1992. Simultaneously, each year the Mexican government negotiated a 'pact' with the labor unions, under which the amount by which minimum wages would be increased was set. As part of the pact, the government committed itself to the maximum it would permit the nominal exchange rate to alter during the course of the coming year. This amount was generally proportionally less than the expected rate of inflation, so that the result was real appreciation of the currency.

The defense given for this policy was that, without assurances given to the labor unions about the extent of the likely change in the exchange rate, they would have been unable to reach agreement, nominal wage increases would have been larger, and difficulties in bringing down inflation would have been even greater.[7]

This policy resulted in, or was equivalent to, a 'nominal anchor' exchange rate policy. This is a policy under which the amount, if any, by which the exchange rate is permitted to depreciate is less than the differential in inflation rates between the country adopting the policy and the rest of the world. The result is real appreciation, on a purchasing power parity basis, for as long as the policy is maintained.

It is generally accepted among macroeconomists that, in the context of a high inflation, efforts to bring the rate of price increase back to more acceptable levels will necessitate an anchor for prices – either the money supply or the exchange rate. The use of the exchange rate as a nominal anchor was defended as necessary in Mexico because of the pressure that would otherwise result on wage increases; in other circumstances, the argument has been that during periods of falling inflation, it is not possible to know what the demand for real money balances is, so the monetary authority should adopt the nominal anchor regime instead.[8]

Attention returns to the properties of a nominal anchor exchange rate policy below. For present purposes, the salient fact is that the Mexican real exchange rate appreciated significantly *vis-à-vis* the US dollar from 1987 until its devaluation and subsequent depreciation in 1994 and 1995 (see Table 3.3). On a purchasing power parity basis (that is, adjusting for the differential between US and Mexican inflation rates), the real price of a US dollar fell from 146.4 in 1987 (on an index with 1980 = 100) to an average of 89.2 in 1994. At the end of the first quarter in 1995, it stood once again near 140.

During the period during which real appreciation was continuing, several phenomena made it difficult to provide a definitive analysis to the question of whether the peso was overvalued. The Mexican authorities could and did point out that the greatly depreciated real exchange rate of 1986 and 1987 had been abnormal, and that, therefore some real appreciation wa warranted.[9] Growth of export earnings also appeared satisfactory to some analysis.[10] Those believing the exchange rate was already overvalued in the early 1990s pointed to the large liberalization of trade that had taken place in the late 1980s, which would in itself have warranted some degree of real depreciation of the exchange rate.[11] Since there had not been a recent period in which trade was anywhere near as free, with imports receiving such low protection, as in the late 1980s, it was difficult to judge the appropriateness of the real exchange rate.

Examining then instead the behaviour of real variables, those believing that the exchange rate was more or less appropriate argued that there had to be some real appreciation to accommodate the large capital inflows which continued into 1994. Those who instead believed the exchange rate to be already overvalued pointed to the capital inflows as responsive, rather than autonomous with respect, to exchange rate policy.

The heart of the issue is thus clear: was the 'nominal anchor' policy as practiced by Mexico building in the seeds of its own destruction? Or was exchange rate policy appropriate, with the events of 1994 simply the result of negative shocks? If that was the case, policies through at least the end of 1993 were presumably sustainable in the absence of those shocks. Related to this are two subsidiary questions: why did domestic savings fall as they did after 1987, and if exchange rate policy was unrealistic, what accounted for the large capital inflows, (see Table 3.5) which were sustained until 1994?

THE NOMINAL ANCHOR LITERATURE

A search of the macroeconomic literature on stopping high inflation reveals that the nominal anchor policy is defended as an anti-inflation tool, although it is recognized that the exchange rate will generally become increasingly appreciated during the process while inflation is slowing down.[12]

Much of the argument for use of the exchange rate as a nominal anchor relies on the law of one price: once the rate of exchange rate change is known, agents know what the rate of increase in the domestic price of tradeable goods will be. That knowledge, in turn, induces behaviour which will slow down the rate of increase in the price of non-traded goods. If inflation is inertial, bringing down inflationary expectations will increase the demand for real money balances. Since that demand will be shifting, it will be impossible for the monetary authority to know what policies should be pursued with respect to the money supply, whereas they can accommodate demand under a nominal anchor policy.[13]

A major difficulty in analysing nominal anchor exchange rate policies arises from the fact that such policies are clearly not sustainable indefinitely: by construction, a nominal anchor policy is one in which the rate of currency depreciation is below the domestic rate of inflation by more than the world rate of inflation. Such a policy would imply continuing real appreciation if carried out indefinitely, and all analysts therefore recognize that the nominal anchor exchange rate policy must be temporary.

How temporary it must or should be, however, is not well understood. In the Mexican case, for example, the nominal-anchor exchange rate policy endured until 1994 and ended only with strong speculative selling after the devaluation (see Table 3.3).

Important questions arise regarding the determinants of the length of time under which such policies are sustainable, and when the bubble will end. While greater understanding of these issues is urgently needed, that issue is not addressed in this paper. Rather, it is assumed that inflation has an inertial component, that a nominal anchor exchange rate policy is pursued, and that investors base their behaviour on the assumption that the policy will continue.

Several empirical regularities of economies relying on nominal anchors have been pointed out by Rabelo and Vegh (1995).[14] These include: (1) slow convergence of the inflation rate to the rate of devaluation; (2) initially expanding economic activity after stabilization in contrast to the conventional stabilization programs, in which economic activity initially contracts; (3) the relative price of non-traded goods rises; (4) real wages increase as measured in traded goods; (5) ambiguous behaviour of the real interest rate; (6) a significant increase in the real money balances in the economy; (7) a deterioration in the current account of the balance of payments; (8) a large fiscal adjustment in programs that are successful in reducing the rate of inflation; and (9) a real estate boom.

While they point to some basic mechanisms at work (including the rising relative price of non-tradeables to tradeables as a consequence of nominal anchor policy), they note that no model accounts for the observed responses in these high-inflation economies.

Table 3.4   Mexican public sector debt and debt indicators

	External debt (US$, m)	External debt/GNP (percentage)	Interest/ exports (percentage)	Internal debt* (new pesos, bn)
1980	57 378	30.3	27.3	0.4
1981	78 215	32.5	35.2	0.8
1982	86 019	52.5	40.4	1.8
1983	92 964	66.4	34.8	3.6
1984	94 822	57.1	34.7	5.9
1985	96 875	54.9	34.4	9.0
1986	100 889	82.9	29.6	15.0
1987	109 469	82.1	23.5	29.5
1988	99 213	60.3	21.9	66.6
1989	93 838	47.3	19.7	99.4
1990	106 026	44.9	13.8	128.1
1991	115 362	41.2	14.7	131.1
1992	113 423	35.5	12.7	89.6
1993	118 028	35.5	10.9	61.8

* The 1993 figure is preliminary.

Sources: All data is from the IBRD *World Debt Tables 1994–5* (1995), country page, except the domestic debt which is from Banco de Mexico *The Mexican Economy*, (1994), table 44.

NOMINAL ANCHOR POLICIES AS A DISTORTION IN RATES OF RETURN BETWEEN DOMESTIC AND FOREIGN INVESTORS

What has not been taken into account in these analyses is the fact that a nominal anchor policy is, in effect, a distortion, in the same sense that a tariff imposes a distortion: foreign investors are offered a higher real rate of interest in the domestic economy than are domestic residents. Indeed, the normal assumption that the risk-adjusted real return on assets must be the same domestically as internationally (due to capital flows) cannot be made when analysing a nominal anchor policy. This follows immediately from the fact that foreigners can take foreign exchange, convert it into domestic currency for a period of time, receive the domestic interest rate, and then reconvert to foreign currency at the preannounced exchange rate. As long as the rate of depreciation of the currency is less than the domestic rate of inflation, the real interest rate received by foreigners must be above that received by

Table 3.5 Mexican international accounts

	International reserves[a] (US$, m)	Portfolio investment (US$, m)
1980	4 175	42
1981	4 971	1 160
1982	1 778	921
1983	4 794	−653
1984	8 019	−756
1985	5 679	−984
1986	6 674	−816
1987	13 692	−397
1988	6 327	121
1989	6 749	298
1990	10 217	−3 985
1991	18 052	12 138
1992	19 171	19 206
1993	25 299	28 355
1994	6 278	7 574
1995.1[b]	6 940	−7 827
1995.2[c]	10 070	n.a.

Notes
[a] The figures for 1994 onward are for reserves excluding gold. Gold reserves, by this stage, account for only one percent of total reserves.
[b] First quarter.
[c] Second quarter.

Sources: IBRD *World Debt Tables*, (1994–5), country page, figures up to 1993. IMF *International Financial Statistics*, (1994 and August 1995), country page, figures from 1994 onward.

domestic residents. Seen in this light, it is clear that the nominal anchor exchange rate policy builds in a distortion which biases the allocation of resources towards non-traded goods.

But that is only the beginning of the analysis. Consider first the returns to domestic residents. Assume that tradeable goods prices are constant in world markets. The nominal return on investment in tradeable goods will equal the constant-price-of-tradeables marginal product of capital minus the rate of depreciation of the currency. Since that rate is, by construction, less than the rate of inflation, the nominal rate of return adjusted by the change in the overall price level will be less than the constant-price return. For non-traded goods, the opposite will be the case. If domestic returns on capital are equalized between tradeables and home goods, then exchange rate policy constitutes a 'domestic distortion' reallocating resources toward home goods and away from tradeables. If investors anticipate maintenance of a nominal exchange-rate anchor policy,[15] the anticipated return on investment in home goods will be greater than it would be at constant terms of trade between home and traded goods.

Turning then to foreigners, foreign real rates of return will equal the domestic real rate of return plus the rate of real currency appreciation, and must, therefore, lie above the rates of return available to domestic investors. If the real rate of return to foreign investors in the nominal-anchor country is equal to the real rate of return they expect in the rest of the world, returns to domestic investors in that country must lie below the world real rate of return. If, instead, the real rate of return to domestic investors equals the world rate, foreigners must earn a premium over the world real rate in the amount of the rate of real currency appreciation.[16]

Such a policy must be dynamically unstable: the high real rate of return received by foreigners induces a capital inflow, which increases the interest-and-profit remittances owed to foreigners, while simultaneously investment is skewed away from tradeable goods which could expand foreign exchange earnings. Consumers find foreign goods increasingly relatively cheaper and bias their consumption in that direction, while producers bias their production toward home goods.

Stated in yet another way, foreigners are subsidized in their domestic investments in the amount of the rate of real currency appreciation. Over time, that subsidy must mount, while there is no counterpart generation of earnings to finance it. The accumulation of debt due to fiscal deficits in the 1980s built up debt-servicing obligations which could not be sustained; in the 1990s, a nominal anchor policy could build up the interest-and-profits obligations to foreigners.

That this happened in Mexico can be seen from Tables 3.6 and 3.7. Table 3.6 provides estimates of the nominal returns to American holders of Mexican or US treasury bills over the 1988 to 1994 period. The return to American holders of Mexican T-bills was the Mexican T-bill rate less the rate of currency depreciation. As can be seen, in every year until 1994, Americans purchasing T-bills at the beginning of the year and holding them until the end could earn double digit rates of return, contrasted with single digit rates of return for US T-bills.[17] Since US inflation rates were single digit and below T-bill rates, real returns to US holders of either asset were positive, although returns on Mexican T-bills were greater until 1994.

Table 3.6 Nominal and real returns to US holders of US and Mexican treasury bills (percentage)

	Mexican treasury bill rate	Depreciation of peso	US return on Mexican T-bills	US treasury bill rate
1988	69.1	3.2	63.9	6.7
1989	45.0	15.8	25.2	8.1
1990	34.8	11.5	20.9	7.5
1991	19.3	4.3	14.4	5.4
1992	15.6	1.4	14.0	3.5
1993	15.0	−0.3	15.3	3.0
1994	14.1	71.4	−33.4	4.3

Notes: 1) Peso depreciation is from year's end to year's end.
2) US return on Mexican T-bills is the nominal rate on Mexican T-bills adjusted by the rate of peso depreciation.

Source: International Monetary Fund, *International Financial Statistics*, 1995 yearbook and April 1996, country pages.

Table 3.7 Real returns to Mexican nationals from holding US or Mexican treasury bills for one year (percentage)

	Nominal returns to Mexicans holding		Mexican inflation rate	Real returns to Mexicans holding	
	US T-bills	Mexican T-bills		US T-bills	Mexican T-bills
1988	10.1	69.1	51.7	−27.4	11.5
1989	25.2	45.0	19.7	4.6	21.1
1990	19.9	34.8	29.9	−7.7	3.8
1991	9.9	19.3	18.8	−7.5	0.4
1992	4.9	15.6	11.9	−6.2	3.3
1993	2.7	15.0	8.0	−4.9	6.5
1994	78.8	14.4	7.1	66.9	6.5

Notes: 1) The Mexican inflation rate is the percentage change in consumer prices measured December to December.
2) Nominal returns to Mexican holders of US T-bills were calculated as the nominal interest rate in US dollars adjusted by the rate of peso depreciation. Real returns are adjusted by the Mexican inflation rate.

Source: International Monetary Fund, *International Financial Statistics*, 1995 yearbook and April 1996.

Table 3.7 provides estimates of the real returns to Mexican nationals from holding US or Mexican T-bills for each year. The first two columns give the nominal returns from the two assets. The third column gives the Mexican inflation rate. The last two columns then give the real returns. As can be seen, Mexican nationals could not earn positive returns in either asset in all years; and their real return on Mexican T-bills was far below the return received by US nationals. Thus, whereas Americans could receive a 15 per cent real return from holding Mexican T-bills in 1993, Mexicans holding those same assets received a real return of only 6 per cent. The incentive for everyone to get out of pesos before the devaluation is also obvious.

One last calculation is of interest. Suppose two American investors had each invested $1 on 1 January 1988, reinvested their interest earnings, and withdrawn their money on 31 December 1994 (after the peso devaluation). Suppose further that one had purchased pesos on 1 January 1988 while the other had purchased US treasury bills. The American investor in US T-bills would have received a real return of 12 per cent over the 7 years; the American investor in Mexican T-bills would have received a real return of 92 per cent – even after losing in the December devaluation and subsequent depreciation of the peso.[18]

If a nominal anchor exchange rate policy is seen as a distortion, one can also explain several of the empirical regularities noted by Rebelo and Vegh (1955). The rise in the relative price of non-tradeables, as they themselves point out, is a direct result of continuing inflation under a nominal-anchor-exchange-rate policy. Real wages may increase as measured in traded goods, but decline in terms of non-traded goods as relative prices of tradeables and non-tradeables change. Expansion of economic activity in the shorter term can come about as a result of the expansion in investment in non-tradeables, especially if foreign capital inflows are directed toward those activities.

The ambiguous behaviour of the real interest rate is not necessarily a consequence of the distortion between domestic and foreign returns, although varying degrees of responsiveness of capital inflows to the high real return for foreign investors might explain differences between countries. That real money balances increase may be the direct result of the nominal anchor policy providing assurance, at least in the short run, that domestic currency will retain its purchasing power over traded goods.[19]

The deterioration of the current account that follows adoption of nominal anchor policies has too many explanations: appreciation of the real exchange rate is sufficient in all interpretations of the policy. The capital inflow itself may be regarded as the cause; alternatively, increased spending as a result of trade liberalization or increased real balances may lead to the same result. The real estate boom may be seen as part of the increased attractiveness to foreigners of domestic non-traded assets yielding earnings streams rising rapidly in nominal terms.

Not on the Rebelo and Vegh list, but intriguing, is the behaviour of domestic savings and investment. Clearly, to accommodate a current account deficit, domestic investment must exceed domestic savings. But in Mexico, and in some other countries pursuing nominal anchor policies, domestic savings fell while domestic investment remained constant or increased as a percentage of GDP.[20] As was noted above (see Table 3.2), Mexican savings fell sharply as a percentage of GDP while investment maintained its former level.[21] This phenomenon would be explicable if real returns to domestic savers were sufficiently low as to discourage domestic savings. As can be seen from the data in Table 3.7, that may have been the case, as the real domestic deposit rate appears quite low. In addition, the relaxation of the credit constraint that accompanied liberalization may also have encouraged additional consumption.

CONCLUSIONS

There remains a great deal that is not well understood about the process of policy reform, and responses to it. In the macroeconomic domain, a central question is why inflation persists, albeit at declining rates, once a stabilization program is undertaken.[22] Yet, the fact is that it does, and many countries have resorted to a nominal anchor exchange rate policy in the hopes of speeding up the deceleration of inflation. Where inflation is seen as a major problem, this policy is obviously attractive. Indeed, Brazil and Argentina are currently employing versions of a nominal-anchor policy, and the Mexican authorities have announced their intention to resume a nominal anchor exchange rate policy.[23]

To date, macroeconomists have analysed a nominal anchor exchange rate policy from the vantage point of inflation, analysing it without regard to the distortion between domestic and foreign returns on investment that it creates. Carefully specifying a model in which to analyse such a distortion is difficult, both because of the unsustainability of a crawling peg policy and because it is not evident (at least to this author) how to specify initial conditions (with regard to desired and actual capital stocks, in particular) in traded and home goods. Nonetheless, it is straightforward to demonstrate that there *is* a distortion between returns earned by foreign and domestic owners of domestic assets under a nominal anchor exchange rate policy. That distortion is equivalent to a subsidy on foreign capital invested in the domestic economy, or equivalently a tax on domestic capital owners. The high real return earned by foreigners should be viewed as incurring future obligations in much the same way as mounting debt was analysed in the 1980s, and enough has been said to raise questions as to the wisdom of these policies.

Clearly, much more work needs to be done by international economists in analysing the properties of nominal anchor exchange rate regimes. To the extent that there remain puzzles regarding the evolution of the Mexican peso in 1994 and 1995, those puzzles should concern the timing of events and not their existence. Since all observers could have known that the nominal anchor exchange rate policy was not indefinitely sustainable, the real question is why they chose to exit in 1994, rather than either sooner or later. An answer to that question, however, awaits further research.

Notes

1. Department of Economics, Stanford University. I am indebted to John Black and Vittorio Corbo for valuable comments and suggestions on an earlier draft of this manuscript and to Roderick Duncan and Chonira Aturupane for helpful discussions and research assistance.
2. Chilean economic reforms had progressed further, of course, and Chilean economic growth by the late 1980s was sufficiently impressive to influence policy makers elsewhere. Turkey, too, had undertaken substantial changes in policy in the early 1980s and experienced rapid growth against the tide of the 'lost decade' for most developing countries. Generally, however, the rapid growth countries were those in East and Southeast Asia, where reforms had largely taken place much earlier.
3. Mexico had been an oil exporter in the 1970s and thus experienced a major improvement in her terms of trade. In addition, new oil deposits had been discovered, so that Mexico's dollar value of export earnings had grown more rapidly than those of any other developing country in the 1970s. However, the debt/export ratio had remained virtually unchanged, as spending kept pace with the rapid growth of export earnings.
4. See Table 3.4 for the underlying data. Estimates of debt/export ratios are sensitive to changes in the real exchange rate; for that reason, debt as a percentage of export earnings is often preferred as an indicator. The two measures move in the same direction in Mexico's case.
5. Tracing the evolution of the exchange rate through 1995 would serve little purpose. Suffice it to say that the rate of inflation accelerated to reach

over 50 per cent for the year, and that the peso depreciated further before the end of 1995.

6. The traditional Mexican political structure has been undergoing significant changes at the same time as the policies discussed below have been pursued. There is little doubt that politics significantly influenced the timing of the exchange rate crisis; it is arguable, however, that given the exchange rate policy that was being followed, and the commitment to continuing it, a crisis would in any event have occurred. The discussion in this paper addresses only the economic issues arising from exchange rate policy, and does not attempt to grapple with the deeper questions associated with political reforms in Mexico.

7. See Aspe (1993) for a statement, and defense, of these policies. See also OECD (1992).

8. See the next section for further discussion. Vegh (1992) has a good discussion of this point.

9. The real exchange rate had reached the same levels in 1982 and 1983 after the initial debt crisis – see Table 3.3.

10. See the OECD (1992, pp. 182–3) analysis, wherein in July 1992 the OECD advocated pegging the peso to the US dollar (without any prior devaluation), believing that the 'fundamentals' were appropriate. Loser and Kalter (1992), writing for the International Monetary Fund, also implicitly accepted the realism of the peso exchange rate in 1992: '. . . The authorities have been successful . . . In the process the peso appreciated in real terms at a time when the balance of payments strengthened, helped by a process of external liberalization and reform that the authorities pursued . . .' (p. 1)

11. See also the econometric estimates of Krueger and Barahona (1991), and those of Dornbusch and Werner (1994).

12. Sachs *et al.* (1995) believe that, despite the increasingly appreciated real exchange rate, the policy is warranted: 'The panic surely did not have to happen, even in the face of adverse shocks. Countries like Mexico, Israel, Turkey, and others that have used the exchange rate as a nominal anchor in the initial stages of disinflation, tend to arrive at a situation of current account deficit and real appreciation in the later stages of stabilization. Other countries have succeeded in adjusting to these conditions without precipitating a panic. The key is to make the adjustment early enough, while reserves are still plentiful and while there is little short-term dollar-denominated debt . . .' (p. 2).

This defense does not provide a rationale for the use of a nominal anchor in the first place, and overlooks the tendency for capital inflows to be *induced* by the nominal anchor policy.

13. The most carefully developed models of this position are from Bruno (1989) and Bruno and Fischer (1990). Their models show the possibility of two equilibrium rates of inflation for the same fiscal deficit because of the changing real money demand as inflationary expectations alter. In their model, therefore, use of a nominal anchor *may* enable an economy to shift from the high-inflation equilibrium to a lower-inflation equilibrium even at an unchanged fiscal deficit.

14. See Rebelo and Vegh (1995) for a survey of the various theories in the

      macroeconomic literature. They count 13 'major exchange-rate-based stabilizations' in the past thirty years.

15. Whether such a policy is credible over the longer term is doubtful for reasons spelled out later in this chapter.
16. One possibility, which is not considered here, is that investment in tradeables might show a sufficiently low real rate of return that it would be unprofitable (this could happen, for example, if the real wages were maintained constant in terms of home goods prices), while investment in home goods continued to show a real rate of return at or above the international real return.
17. To be sure, part of this real return was surely compensation for the risk that the exchange rate regime would alter.
18. Much of the gain was front-loaded, as nominal and real interest rates were falling in Mexico. Of course, an investor getting out of Mexican assets before December 1994 would have done even better.
19. Stated another way, given a nominal-anchor policy expected to be sustained in the short run, domestic residents will choose between holding domestic and foreign currency based on the interest rate differential. Since domestic residents must take into account the future depreciation of foreign currency if they choose it as a store of value, domestic money becomes more attractive as long as the nominal-anchor policy is expected to prevail.
20. Vittorio Corbo has pointed out that investors who are nervous about the sustainability of policies may prefer portfolio investment to direct investment; investment may consequently be sustained despite uncertainties resulting in lower savings rates.
21. Sachs *et al.* (1995) cite Banco de Mexico data showing public savings *rising* from 1989 to 1994 from 3.1 to 5.0 per cent of GDP (with higher percentages in between, peaking at 7.5 in 1991), and private savings falling from 12.4 per cent of GDP in 1989 to a low of 7.3 per cent of GDP in 1973. Private savings less private investment changed from minus 0.9 per cent of GDP in 1989 to minus 9.6 per cent of GDP in 1992, and minus 8.4 per cent of GDP in 1994. The current account deficit rose from 2.6 per cent of GDP in 1989 to 7.9 per cent of GDP in 1994. Thus, more than the entire swing in the current account balance was accounted for by the swing in the private savings–investment balance.
22. As noted above, there are also major questions regarding the determinants of the time at which investors' expectations will switch and the unsustainable policy will have to be reversed.
23. *Wall Street Journal*, September 19, 1995.

References

Aspe, P. (1993) *Economic Transformation the Mexican Way* (Cambridge: MIT Press)
Bruno, M. (1989) 'Stopping High Inflation', *Econometrica*, March.
Bruno, M. and Fischer, S. (1990) 'Seigniorage, Operating Rules, and the High Inflation Trap', *Quarterly Journal of Economics*, May.

Dornbusch, R. and Werner, A., (1994) 'Mexico: Stabilization, Reform and No Growth', *Brookings Papers on Economic Activity*, I.

Harberger, A. C. (1995) 'Mexico's Exchange Rate Crisis', mimeo, April.

Krueger, A. O., and Barahona, P. (1991) 'The Mexican Program of Trade and Exchange Rate Reform', *Quantum*, Monterrey, Mexico (in Spanish; mimeographed English version available on request).

Loser, C. and Kalter, E. (1992) *Mexico: The Strategy to Achieve Sustained Economic Growth*, International Monetary Fund Occasional Paper 99, Washington DC, September.

OECD, 1992. *Economic Surveys: Mexico* (Paris: OECD).

Rebelo, S. and Vegh, C. (1995) 'Real Effects of Exchange Rate-Based Stabilization: An Analysis of Competing Theories', National Bureau of Economic Research Working Paper No. 5197. July.

Sachs, J., Tornell, A. and Velasco, A. (1995) 'Lessons from Mexico', manuscript, Center for International Affairs, Harvard, March.

Vegh, C. (1992) 'Stopping High Inflation', International Monetary Fund *Staff Papers*, September.

4 International Trade, Deindustrialization and Labour Demand: An Input–Output Study for the UK (1979–90)

Mary Gregory and Christine Greenhalgh[1]

INTRODUCTION

During the past 25 years deindustrialization has been a particularly striking feature of the UK labour market. The process of employment loss in manufacturing accelerated during the period from 1979–90, often dubbed 'The Thatcher era'. The absolute and relative loss of employment in UK manufacturing has variously been attributed (see, for example, Green, 1989) to:

(a) loss of market share due to import penetration by both European and Asian competitors, that is, real deindustrialization;
(b) corporate restructuring and the 'contracting-out' of service activities to specialist providers, that is, notional deindustrialization;
(c) labour-saving technical progress in manufacturing which, *ceteris paribus* on the level of final demand, results in job losses, that is, deindustrialization of employment, not output.

Understanding which of these processes has contributed most directly to the disappearance of manufacturing jobs is crucial to assessing the nature of UK deindustrialization. An earlier analysis by Rowthorn and Wells (1987) distinguished between 'positive' deindustrialization, typified by rising productivity in manufacturing coupled with real income growth, and 'negative' deindustrialization, arising from industrial failure and the loss of markets.

The analysis of Wood (1994) has recently rekindled the debate about the relative importance of internal and external factors affecting employment. Wood argues that advanced economies with high costs will inevitably lose market share in the production of standard manufactures using well-known technology. These countries have to concentrate their production in skill- and innovation-intensive sectors in which low labour cost countries have comparative disadvantage in international trade.

Sachs and Shatz (1994) have estimated the impact of trade on employment in the US and conclude that the rising import penetration in less skill-intensive products has been a significant influence on the level and skill structure of US manufacturing employment over the period 1978–90. The further issue of the impact of trade on growing earnings inequality in the US, a feature also present in the UK labour market but not in all European countries, has recently been surveyed by Burtless (1995). Both trade and skill-biased technical change are seen as having played a role in these trends, with the majority of researchers assigning the larger impact to technology.

In the analysis which follows we seek to identify the nature of deindustrialization in the UK during the Thatcher era, using the information about inter-industry purchases and final demands for both domestic and imported products embodied in the input–output tables for 1979, 1985 and 1990. Was it a necessary and relatively benign consequence of productivity growth in manufacturing and the reorganization of work within the economy? Or was it an alarming indicator of loss of international competitiveness in traded manufactured goods?

Precisely how the process of increased global competition has its impact on the sectoral pattern of output and employment is made complex by the roundabout nature of both production and trade. Loss of market share through trade can be decomposed into:

(d) import penetration in intermediate goods, causing a reduction of the proportion of total value added achieved in the UK;
(e) the loss of final goods markets, effectively moving the entire production process abroad.

In innovative sectors the former may be the dominant source of job loss if only a limited subset of the stages of production can be sourced abroad, whereas for mature products the latter may be expected, taking abroad all the jobs except management and administration of the corporate headquarters. The Wood hypothesis can thus be framed for empirical testing as the twin expectations that:

(f) there will be differential trade loss by sector with more rapid pen-
     etration of final goods markets in the least technologically dynamic
     sectors;
(g) the domestic share of value added will diminish more rapidly over
     time for standard technology commodities.

In the first part of the paper we analyse the changes in industrial gross
output over the Thatcher era, presenting results on the relative contributions of rising final demand, import penetration, and technical change.
The methodology for this analysis, originally developed by Chenery in
his classic study of the growth of Japan, involves decomposition of
the change in sectoral gross output into components arising from domestic final demand, exports, import penetration in final and intermediate use, and changes in inter-industry input purchases. Technical change
is identified through the Leontief coefficients, which are affected both
by changes in business organization including 'contracting-out' and by
the impact of new process technology on the level and mix of input
purchases.

   In the second part of the paper we investigate the changing nature
of labour demand arising from the documented restructuring of industry and trade. By examining the changing labour requirements of different
sectors we can extend the above decomposition of changes in output
into a parallel analysis of the sources of change in employment income. We distinguish changes in employment income attributable to
changing output patterns from those due to labour-saving productivity
gains.

SOURCES OF CHANGE IN GROSS OUTPUT

We start from the approach pioneered by Chenery and associates for
the analysis of patterns of economic growth (Chenery *et al.*, 1962;
Chenery and Syrquin, 1975) and applied by, among others, Postner
and Wesa (1983) to Canada, Feldman *et al.* (1987) to the US, Skolka
(1989) to Austria, and Sakurai (1995) to eight OECD countries.

   The balance equation for the flow of domestic output can be written
as:

$$X = W^{d} + F^{d} + E \tag{1}$$

where X denotes the vector of sectoral gross outputs, W^{d} and F^{d} are the vectors of flows to domestic intermediate and final use, and E represents the vector of exports by sector. Under the standard Leontief assumptions, notably that each sector's requirements for inputs are in fixed proportion to its gross output, this gives the basic input–output solution for sectoral gross outputs:

$$X = (I - A^{\mathrm{d}})^{-1} \{F^{\mathrm{d}} + E\} \qquad (2)$$

where A^{d} is the matrix of input–output coefficients from domestic suppliers and I is the identity matrix.

Imports are typically handled within this framework in one of two ways. In line with national accounts conventions they may be allocated exclusively to final demand, where they are competitive with home produced goods. On this approach the analysis is often conducted in terms of net exports. Alternatively, imports may be treated as intermediate purchases, complementary to other intermediate goods as inputs in production. Again invoking the fixed proportions assumption, requirements for imports form an auxiliary relationship alongside equation (2). However, the input–output tables for the UK are unusually extensive, providing information on both final and intermediate use of imported commodities, with in addition intermediate use presented as the full matrix of inter-industry purchases. The information on imported commodities thus replicates that for home-produced goods. This allows us to make a significant extension to the more familiar approaches, expressing gross output as:

$$X = (I - hA)^{-1} \{fF + E\} \qquad (3)$$

where A is the matrix of input–output coefficients from all sources, F is the vector of total final demand, h and f are the domestic supply ratios in intermediate and final demand respectively, hA is the element-by-element product of the two matrices h and A, and fF the element-by-element product of the two vectors f and F. This formulation develops a further channel for potential import penetration. The Leontief assumption requires proportional use of all inputs (complementarity), but imports and home-produced intermediate goods are competitive in supplying them, as in supplying final demand.

Relationship (3) holds for any point in time, with X, A, F, E, h and f indexed accordingly. Differencing this relationship and rearranging terms, the change in gross output between any two periods, subscripted 0 and t, can be decomposed as:

$$\Delta X = X_t - X_0$$
$$= (I - h_t A_t)^{-1} \{f_t F_t + E_t\} - (I - h_0 A_0)^{-1} \{f_0 F_0 + E_0\}$$
$$= Rf(\Delta F) + R(\Delta E) + R(\Delta f)F + R(\Delta h)W + Rh(\Delta A)X \qquad (4)$$

where Δ denotes the change over the period, $W = AX$ is the intermediate absorption vector and $R = (I - hA)^{-1}$ is the Leontief inverse matrix. By this means the change in sectoral gross output can be allocated among the changes in domestic final demand (ΔF), the change in exports (ΔE), changing import penetration in final demand (Δf) and in intermediate use (Δh), and technical change as reflected in the Leontief coefficients, ΔA.

While the decomposition is exact, it is not unique. Alternative variants may be derived from combinations of year 0 and year t values for the weighting factors R, f, F, W, h and X attached to each source of change. This issue is examined further in Appendix 1. Non-uniqueness has not been a source of difficulty in our analysis. The estimates of alternative variants have coincided quite closely, particularly at the aggregated level, causing no ambiguities in interpretation. The results which we report are an average of Paasche- and Laspeyres-based variants.

TECHNOLOGY AND EMPLOYMENT

Since employment is a major focus of interest we extend the basic input–output model to include an employment sector. Employment may change because the level and composition of output changes, or because the employment-intensity of production changes, even if output itself does not. The purpose here is to quantify the relative contribution of each of these sources to total employment change.

Total labour requirements are given by:

$$L = lX \qquad (5)$$

where L is the vector of sectoral employment levels and l is the vector of employment coefficients per unit of gross output (expressed as a diagonal matrix). Differencing (5) over time gives:

$$\Delta L = l_t X_t - l_0 X_0$$
$$= l(\Delta X) + (\Delta l)X \qquad (6)$$

Equation (6) decomposes the change in employment into the part attributable to the change in sector gross outputs at constant labour use, $l(\Delta X)$, and the part attributable to the change in labour use per unit of output, $(\Delta l)X$. Again, the alternative variants are discussed in Appendix 1, and we report an average of the Paasche and Laspeyres forms. Combining (6) with the decomposition of output change in (4) allows the allocation of employment change across the various sources of output change on the one hand and labour requirements per unit of output on the other.

The analysis is based on the years 1979, 1985, and 1990. The focus on these three years was dictated primarily by the availability of detailed input–output tables on the same industrial classification. Fortunately, the cyclical position of the macroeconomy was also reasonably similar in the three years, while the subdivision in mid-decade separates the period of exchange rate overvaluation of the early 1980s from the more competitive later years. We used commodity by commodity rather than industry by industry tables, and aimed to retain as much disaggregation as possible, consistent with ensuring comparable sectoral definitions for each year. Both the commodity basis and the high degree of disaggregation provide a closer fit with the Leontief assumptions of a homogeneous product within each sector and a common sectoral technology. A total of 87 sectors have been used in the analysis. All data have been double-deflated to 1985 prices. Further details on data sources and adjustments are given in Appendix 2.

A particular feature of note is that as our measure of employment income or labour use, L, we use real employment income generated in the production of gross output. Employment income measures the outlay on labour from the employer's perspective, implicitly combining a head-count of workers and hours with earnings levels. The elements of L, employment income by sector in nominal terms, are obtained directly from the input–output tables. Our measure of real employment income revalues these at constant 1985 hourly earnings, using data from the New Earnings Survey (see Appendix 2).

All the statistical analysis was performed at the maximum level of disaggregation retained in the sectoral definitions, but the results for the 87 industries have been re-aggregated to six sectors for tabulation here. These groupings of sectors into six major categories were designed to highlight the contrasts between manufacturing and services, high technology and standard technology and more traded and less traded commodities. A listing of the 87 sectors and the six-way groupings is given in Appendix 2.

Table 4.1   Levels of gross output by major sector

Sector	Gross output (£m1985)		
	1979	1985	1990
I Primary and extractive	94 653	109 562	136 124
II High tech manufacturing	94 189	96 892	108 647
III Other manufacturing	129 561	113 273	120 942
IV Financial services	30 642	70 807	115 755
V More tradeable services	30 536	24 702	34 231
VI Less tradeable services	177 221	179 179	221 700
Total	556 802	594 415	737 399

Sector	Percentage distribution		
	1979	1985	1990
I Primary and extractive	17.0	18.4	18.5
II High tech manufacturing	16.9	16.3	14.7
III Other manufacturing	23.3	19.1	16.4
IV Financial services	5.5	11.9	15.7
V More tradeable services	5.5	4.2	4.6
VI Less tradeable services	31.8	30.1	30.1
Total	100.0	100.0	100.0

RESULTS: CHANGING ECONOMIC STRUCTURE

The most dramatic feature of the changing structure of gross output in Britain was the enormous rise in real supply of financial services (Table 4.1). This growth occurred both during the recession of the early 1980s and in the boom of the latter half of the decade. The level of gross output produced in this sector rose by a factor of 3.8, thus causing its share of gross output to treble in 11 years from 5.5 per cent in 1979 to 15.7 per cent in 1990. In total the growth in financial services contributed 47 per cent of the growth of gross output.

Somewhat surprisingly the early Thatcher years, which were dominated by recession, produced as high an absolute rate and a faster proportional rate of growth in gross output of financial services than did the later boom years. High technology manufactures grew more slowly than total output in both recession and recovery, hence declining as a share of output. Other manufactures first slumped and then revived, but this performance caused a substantial fall in output share particularly during the recession.

Table 4.2 Decomposition of change in gross output

	Term 1 Domestic final demand	Term 2 Exports	Term 3 Home share in final demand	Term 4 Home share in intermediate demand	Term 5 Leontief coefficients	Row sum Total change
£m1985						
1979–90	146 394	36 170	–34 705	–1 644	34 382	180 598
1979–85	37 676	20 199	–23 734	–3 841	7 313	37 614
1985–90	106 967	14 350	–10 741	3 669	28 740	142 984
Percentages of gross output in initial year						
1979–80	26.3	6.5	–6.2	–0.3	6.2	32.4
1979–85	6.8	3.6	–4.3	–0.7	1.3	6.8
1985–90	18.0	2.4	–1.8	0.6	4.8	24.1

Decomposition of the changes (Table 4.2) reveals that over the whole period rising domestic final demand, exports and the changing Leontief coefficients were positive influences for output growth, and the falling home share in the final markets was a negative influence, whilst the home share in intermediate markets hardly changed. Growth of domestic final demand (Term 1) made the largest contribution to the growth of gross output. The extra output generated by rising exports (Term 2) was broadly cancelled out by the loss of home share in final demand (Term 3) during the whole period. Rising import penetration in intermediate goods (Term 4) caused very small output losses, whilst the more roundabout nature of UK production (Term 5) was positive in its impact.

There were some differences between the periods of recession and recovery: during 1979–85, when the pound was substantially above its fundamental equilibrium exchange rate for much of the time, import penetration was more rapid. However in the second half of the Thatcher era, despite the return to parity in exchange rates, the potentially beneficial effect of export market growth was still largely negated by rising import penetration in final goods.

The most striking feature of the sectoral contributions (Table 4.3) is the positive contribution of the Leontief technology coefficient of financial services (Sector IV Term 5), which stands out as having risen dramatically. Barker (1989) has also identified these changes for 1979–84 and stresses the role of inter-industry demands for financial services. Despite the rapid incorporation of new and expanding financial

Table 4.3 Decomposition of change in gross output by major sector

1979–90 as percentage of gross output 1979

Sector	Term 1 Domestic final demand	Term 2 Exports demand	Term 3 Home share in final demand	Term 4 Home share in intermediate demand	Term 5 Leontief coefficients	Row sum Total sector change	Sector change £m1985
I Primary and extractive	36.4	3.1	-1.1	6.2	-0.7	43.8	41 471
II High tech manufacturing	17.0	20.6	-14.9	-5.3	-2.0	15.4	14 458
III Other manufacturing	11.2	4.7	-8.4	-7.0	-7.2	-6.7	-8 618
IV Financial services	72.9	10.3	-4.5	9.6	189.5	277.8	85 112
V More tradeable services	22.4	-9.2	-6.5	2.0	3.5	12.1	3 695
VI Less tradeable services	29.5	4.2	-3.0	1.7	-7.3	25.1	44 479
Total	26.3	6.5	-6.2	-0.3	6.2	32.4	180 598

1979–85 as percentage of gross output 1979

Sector	Term 1 Domestic final demand	Term 2 Exports demand	Term 3 Home share in final demand	Term 4 Home share in intermediate demand	Term 5 Leontief coefficients	Row sum Total sector change	Sector change £m1985
I Primary and extractive	8.9	7.0	-0.7	2.7	-2.2	15.8	14 910
II High tech manufacturing	4.8	8.5	-10.3	-1.5	1.4	2.9	2 703
III Other manufacturing	0.8	0.7	-4.3	-3.1	-6.6	-12.6	-16 287
IV Financial services	9.2	12.6	-5.5	4.2	110.5	131.1	40 165
V More tradeable services	2.5	-7.6	-9.9	1.1	-5.2	-19.1	-5 834
VI Less tradeable services	11.3	1.8	-1.7	-1.5	-8.8	1.1	1 958
Total	6.8	3.6	-4.3	-0.7	1.3	6.8	37 614

Table 4.3 continued

1985–90 as percentage of gross output 1985

Sector	Term 1 Domestic final demand	Term 2 Exports	Term 3 Home share in final demand	Term 4 Home share in intermediate demand	Term 5 Leontief coefficients	Row sum Total sector change	Sector change £m1985
I Primary and extractive	22.8	-3.6	0	1.6	3.5	24.2	26 561
II High tech manufacturing	13.4	11.5	-6.3	-3.1	-3.3	12.1	11 756
III Other manufacturing	10.1	4.2	-3.8	-3.6	-0.2	6.8	7 669
IV Financial services	31.1	-0.6	-0.1	6.1	27.0	63.5	44 947
V More tradeable services	21.8	-2.6	6.0	2.7	10.6	38.6	9 529
VI Less tradeable services	16.8	2.0	-1.0	2.2	3.7	23.7	42 521
Total	18.0	2.4	-1.8	0.6	4.8	24.1	142 984

Table 4.4 Change in sector gross output from final demand

1979–90 £m1985

Sector	Change in sector gross output (direct + indirect) originating with:					Change in gross output
	Consumers' expenditure	Government expenditure	GDFCF	Inventory change	Exports	
I Primary and extractive	14 159	3 941	20 370	194	2 808	41 471
II High tech manufacturing	1 825	-401	133	-3 114	16 015	14 458
III Other manufacturing	-4 884	-750	2 069	-3 982	-1 071	-8 618
IV Financial services	40 482	11 281	17 163	-98	16 284	85 112
V More tradeable services	6 404	533	-653	-150	-2 439	3 695
VI Less tradeable services	34 886	8 492	-858	-621	2 580	44 479
Total	92 871	23 097	38 224	-7 771	34 177	180 598

1979–85 £m1985

Sector	Change in sector gross output (direct + indirect) originating with:					Change in gross output
	Consumers' expenditure	Government expenditure	GDFCF	Inventory change	Exports	
I Primary and extractive	-330	1 017	7 900	-739	7 063	14 910
II High tech manufacturing	1 099	727	-3 041	-3 317	7 234	2 703
III Other manufacturing	-7 599	-1 719	-681	-2 760	-3 529	-16 288
IV Financial services	18 728	510	7 360	-188	13 754	40 165
V More tradeable services	-1 083	-1 049	-1 220	-214	-2 269	-5 834
VI Less tradeable services	842	8 315	-3 551	-649	-2 999	1 958
Total	11 657	7 802	6 767	-7 866	19 254	37 613

Table 4.4 *continued*

1985–90 £m1985

Sector	Change in sector gross output (direct + indirect) originating with:					Change in gross output
	Consumers' expenditure	Government expenditure	GDFCF	Inventory change	Exports	
I Primary and extractive	14 489	2 924	12 470	933	–4 255	26 561
II High tech manufacturing	726	–1 128	3 174	203	8 780	11 756
III Other manufacturing	2 715	968	2 750	–1 222	2 458	7 669
IV Financial services	21 753	10 771	9 803	90	2 529	44 947
V More tradeable services	7 486	1 582	567	64	–170	9 529
VI Less tradeable services	34 044	177	2 693	27	5 580	42 521
Total	81 214	15 295	31 458	95	14 923	142 984

services into the economic structure, these purchases only helped to offset other input savings and import market losses during the early 1980s. However in the boom the changing composition and sourcing of demand for intermediate goods and services contributed a substantial positive element amounting to one-fifth of the now rapid growth of gross output.

Some of the growth of demand for financial services undoubtedly reflects the contracting-out of services previously carried out within firms, which we denoted above as notional deindustrialization. However it seems likely there were also genuine rises in intermediate demands of firms for services from banks and insurance groups, as manufacturers increased the financing and insurance service components of their products and as they drew more frequently on specialist advisers in conducting their businesses in the volatile recession and recovery years. Note that the rise in inter-industry demand for services was not uniform across all years and for all types of services: there were falling producer requirements for less tradeable private and public services in the first period (Table 4.3 Term 5).

Changing patterns of final demands (Table 4.3 Term 1) were also important in sustaining the upsurge in output of financial services in the boom, when demand for financial services increased much faster than that for all other commodities, in contrast with Barker's (1989) study. The origins of the growth in demand for the gross output of financial services also vary through time. The components of domestic final demand can be disaggregated using the conventional macroeconomic identity (Table 4.4). These demands arose disproportionately in the private sector including exports in the first sub-period and in the public sector in the second.

RESULTS: TESTING THE WOOD HYPOTHESIS

In considering the expected channels of impact of global competition identified as (d) to (g) above, our first pointer is the behaviour of imports in final and intermediate goods markets. Table 4.5 reveals a sharp contrast between the overall effect of import penetration in these two routes for supplies of imports. From 1979 to 1990 the home share of intermediate supply remained broadly constant at around 80 per cent whereas the home share of final goods fell by over 5 per cent to reach a low of 86 per cent in 1990. Between sectors there were important differences, with manufacturing losing share in both intermediate and

Table 4.5 Home share in output by major sector (percentages)

1979

Sector	Final demand	Intermediate demand	Total expenditure
I Primary and extractive	94.1	73.5	82.8
II High tech manufacturing	82.3	74.4	79.3
III Other manufacturing	86.3	77.4	81.5
IV Financial services	94.2	93.3	93.9
V More tradeable services	90.3	74.9	82.2
VI Less tradeable services	98.2	97.0	97.9
Total	91.6	79.8	86.6

1985

Sector	Final demand	Intermediate demand	Total expenditure
I Primary and extractive	96.2	83.3	89.9
II High tech manufacturing	72.9	69.4	71.6
III Other manufacturing	82.3	73.2	77.6
IV Financial services	96.9	97.0	97.0
V More tradeable services	73.8	77.5	75.8
VI Less tradeable services	97.2	95.6	96.9
Total	88.6	81.4	85.7

1990

Sector	Final demand	Intermediate demand	Total expenditure
I Primary and extractive	96.4	81.7	89.0
II High tech manufacturing	67.1	60.3	64.8
III Other manufacturing	76.8	68.4	72.3
IV Financial services	97.1	97.0	97.0
V More tradeable services	81.1	87.7	84.9
VI Less tradeable services	96.1	97.0	96.3
Total	86.2	81.0	84.0

final goods markets to a similar degree, whilst services were gaining share in intermediate markets. Sectors which increased their home share of intermediate supply included (of course) oil and gas (I), as well as financial and other services (IV, V).

This evidence underlines the view that the UK frequently lost entire manufacturing production processes to its competitors as well as losing segments of supply chains to intermediate suppliers. Comparing high-technology and mature manufacturing, there seems at first sight not to be very strong support for the Wood hypothesis, as the home shares for high technology were initially the lowest of all the six sectors and also fell more rapidly than those of mature manufactured products. The home share of final goods for the high technology sector fell dramatically from 82 per cent to 67 per cent in this 11 year period.

However we must also note that the rates of intra-industry trade between advanced industrial countries, which had risen rapidly in the 1970s, were continuing to rise in this period at different rates by sector. Thus any differential rates of import growth must be compared with the growth in exports before concluding that the high technology sector had clearly lost comparative strength. As seen above in Table 4.3, although the favourable contribution of exports (Term 2) was in total negated by rising imports (Terms 3 + 4), these trends were not identical for every sector. In particular there is evidence of faster growth in exports for the high technology sector than for mature manufactures. Although the high technology sector was losing ground on the balance of net trade during the early 1980s recession and barely keeping pace during the whole period, the manufacturing trade balance of standard goods fared much worse in both recession and recovery. These facts point to a more rapid expansion of intra-industry trade in the high-technology field, whilst the export evidence also provides some support for the Wood hypothesis.

The performance of selected high technology sectors is illustrated in Table 4.6, where it can be seen that within this group there was considerable variation both in overall performance and in the gross output decomposition, reflecting different patterns of growth of demand, of net trade and of inter-industry trade. Three areas of strength in gross output, pharmaceuticals, aerospace and electronic equipment, display a variety of orientations, with aerospace drawing its impetus from extremely rapid export growth, in contrast with the more equal importance of foreign and domestic demand for the other two strongly growing industries. Mechanical engineering and motor vehicles are both large industries which faced problems during much of the period, but with the automobile sector recovering well in the later years. The interesting contrast is between the large loss of net trade for engineering contrasting with the gain for the vehicles sector, a pattern which generates very different growth rates in gross output despite the very similar rates of growth in final demand for these two sectors.

Some further information can be gained from the examination of

Table 4.6 Decomposition of output growth: selected high technology sectors 1979–90

Sector	Term 1 Domestic final demand	Term 2 Exports	Term 3 Home share in final demand	Term 4 Home share in inter- mediates	Term 5 Leontief coefficients	Row sum Total sector change
23 Pharmaceuticals	47.9	38.8	−19.5	6.9	−12.7	61.5
36 Mech engineering	6.7	−2.8	−12.8	0.6	1.8	−6.5
40 Electronic equip	44.4	46.1	−38.5	−9.6	9.5	51.9
41 Motor vehicles	8.9	10.3	−1.4	−1.1	−1.4	15.3
43 Aerospace	2.7	167.1	−43.0	16.9	2.9	146.6
All high tech mfg	17.0	20.6	−14.9	−5.3	−2.0	15.4

Table 4.7 Value added by major sector

Total value added

Sector	Value added (£m1985)			Ratio to gross output		
	1979	1985	1990	1979	1985	1990
I Primary and extractive	48 132	51 530	43 448	0.509	0.470	0.319
II High tech manufacturing	40 871	35 097	37 363	0.434	0.362	0.344
III Other manufacturing	38 072	29 093	34 604	0.294	0.257	0.286
IV Financial services	21 525	44 208	49 241	0.702	0.624	0.425
V More tradeable services	16 231	13 483	18 364	0.532	0.546	0.536
VI Less tradeable services	140 804	130 798	148 641	0.795	0.730	0.670
Total	305 635	304 208	331 660	0.549	0.512	0.450

Value added from exports

Sector	Value added (£m1985)			Ratio to gross output generated by exports		
	1979	1985	1990	1979	1985	1990
I Primary and extractive	10 599	17 451	6 508	0.542	0.656	0.291
II High tech manufacturing	18 471	17 951	20 355	0.424	0.353	0.341
III Other manufacturing	12 055	9 137	11 361	0.295	0.244	0.285
IV Financial services	5 324	13 319	10 151	0.702	0.624	0.425
V More tradeable services	5 868	5 155	5 010	0.429	0.451	0.445
VI Less tradeable services	15 205	9 927	12 506	0.714	0.543	0.524
Total	67 522	72 941	65 890	0.461	0.440	0.364

ratios, levels and trends in value added (Table 4.7). Before proceeding to the detailed results it may be noted that on our estimates the growth of value added, 8.5 per cent over the period 1979–90, is significantly lower than the official figures, and more in line with the recent estimates, for manufacturing only, by Stoneman and Francis (1994). The ratio of value added to gross output was always lower in mature than high technology manufactures and lower in both types of manufactures than for primary goods and services. These manufacturing value added ratios were falling from 1979 to 1990 (peak to peak), thus not supporting the Wood view that low value added manufacturing product markets would tend to be lost first to cheaper Third World competitors. However in the late 1980s boom the value added ratio of mature manufactures increased and that of high-technology goods fell less sharply, perhaps indicating the beginning of new trends with the recent expansion of output from new Asian suppliers.

Certainly the balance between manufacture and service activity has shifted towards the service sectors which had higher value added per unit of gross output. Thus across the whole economy the Wood phenomenon of movement towards sectors with higher value added is observed. However the rapidly expanding financial services sector experienced a fall in its value added ratio, particularly during the boom. This suggests there was greater domestic competition and decreasing marginal productivity, as new service products were developed and new entrants arrived in the market. Furthermore the absolute levels of value added in the exported services were volatile and decreasing in the more tradeable service sector V and in the largest service sector VI.

RESULTS: TECHNOLOGY AND THE DEMAND FOR LABOUR

The real employment income measures, which mirror levels and changes in total person-hours of work demanded at constant 1985 real wages (see Appendix 2), are presented in Table 4.8. The net changes in employment demand for the whole economy are well-known, but what is striking is the uniformity of the shake-out across sectors with only financial services increasing its overall labour demand between 1979 and 1990. The net fall of 5.4 per cent reflects dramatic compositional changes in the structure of employment across the sectors which were particularly severe in the initial Thatcher years. During the period to 1985 labour requirements fell by more than 11 per cent overall but by more than 20 per cent in primary and manufacturing sectors and even the rapid rise in demand during the boom did not succeed in restoring labour demand to 1979 levels.

Table 4.9 contains the first decomposition of the employment change, as denoted in equation (6) above, which reveals the measured impact of changing technology and business organization on the demand for labour. As expected the positive effects of rising gross output are

Table 4.8 Employment income by major sector

Sector	Employment income £m1985		
	1979	1985	1990
I Primary and extractive	22 787	18 631	17 893
II High tech manufacturing	33 802	28 731	25 881
III Other manufacturing	28 543	22 815	22 534
IV Financial services	19 306	24 641	31 983
V More tradeable services	11 855	9 784	9 748
VI Less tradeable services	102 547	89 972	98 927
Total	218 840	194 573	206 967

Percentage distribution

Sector	1979	1985	1990
I Primary and extractive	10.4	9.6	8.6
II High tech manufacturing	15.4	14.8	12.5
III Other manufacturing	13.0	11.7	10.9
IV Financial services	8.8	12.7	15.5
V More tradeable services	5.4	5.0	4.7
VI Less tradeable services	46.9	46.2	47.8
Total	100.0	100.0	100.0

Ratio to gross output

Sector	1979	1985	1990
I Primary and extractive	0.241	0.170	0.131
II High tech manufacturing	0.359	0.297	0.238
III Other manufacturing	0.220	0.201	0.186
IV Financial services	0.630	0.348	0.276
V More tradeable services	0.388	0.396	0.285
VI Less tradeable services	0.579	0.502	0.446
Total	0.393	0.327	0.281

dramatically counterbalanced by the job-shedding effect of decreasing labour input requirements per unit of gross output. Labour-saving in the whole period through technological change and factor substitution amounted to more than one third of the 1979 level of labour demand and it proceeded apace in both slump and boom.

The changing labour requirements may be compared with the effect of import penetration (Table 4.10). If the home shares of both final and intermediate goods had remained constant at 1979 levels, labour demand (also at 1979 technology) would have increased by a further

Table 4.9   Decomposition of change in employment income

1979–90 Due to:	Change in gross output	Change in employment income ratio	Change in gross output	Change in employment income ratio
Sector	£m1985	£m1985	percent of gross output 1979	
I Primary and extractive	6 573	−11 467	28.8	−50.3
II High tech manufacturing	4 903	−12 824	14.5	−37.9
III Other manufacturing	−756	−5 253	−2.6	−18.4
IV Financial services	38 571	−25 893	199.8	−134.1
V More tradeable services	2 528	−4 635	21.3	−39.1
VI Less tradeable services	22 974	−26 593	22.4	−25.9
Total	74 793	−86 666	34.2	−39.6

1979–85 Due to:	Change in gross output	Change in employment income ratio	Change in gross output	Change in employment income ratio
Sector	£m1985	£m1985	percent of gross output 1979	
I Primary and extractive	1 322	−5 477	5.8	−24.0
II High tech manufacturing	1 446	−6 517	4.3	−19.3
III Other manufacturing	−3 270	−2 458	−11.5	−8.6
IV Financial services	19 642	−14 307	101.7	−74.1
V More tradeable services	−1 957	−114	−16.5	−1.0
VI Less tradeable services	2 991	−15 566	2.9	−15.2
Total	20 173	−44 439	9.2	−20.3

1985–90 Due to:	Change in gross output	Change in employment income ratio	Change in gross output	Change in employment income ratio
Sector	£m1985	£m1985	percent of gross output 1985	
I Primary and extractive	4 193	−4 932	22.5	−26.5
II High tech manufacturing	3 012	−5 862	10.5	−20.4
III Other manufacturing	2 247	−2 528	9.8	−11.1
IV Financial services	14 030	−6 687	56.9	−27.1
V More tradeable services	4 670	−4 706	47.7	−48.1
VI Less tradeable services	17 779	−8 823	19.8	−9.8
Total	45 932	−33 538	23.6	−17.2

4.4 per cent. Thus on this evidence the impact of changing process technology on total labour demand far exceeded (by a factor of 9) the direct impact of market losses from import penetration. These results mirror the balance of findings of US studies surveyed in Burtless (1995). Of course these figures reflect measured changes but do not necessarily reveal the underlying causes of change; as argued strongly by Courakis *et al.* (1995), technological choices cannot realistically be deemed to be independent of the competitive effects of globalization of markets.

Comparing terms and sectors in Table 4.10 we note that, as expected, the labour-shedding impact of new technology was relatively more important in primary and manufacturing sectors than in services, but the pervasive and persistent impact of labour-saving technology is evident from the considerable similarity across sectors in the degree of labour saving which was achieved in both slump and boom. The loss of jobs through import penetration initially exceeded the employment-creating effect of exports but the net trend reversed in the boom. In the whole period the employment impact of changes in trade patterns was weakly positive (Terms 2 + 3 + 4) whereas these same terms in the gross output decomposition (Tables 4.2 and 4.3) were in sum neutral. This underlines the view that trade was not job-destroying on average even though the commodity composition of trade was shifting away from standard manufactures and towards financial services.

CONCLUSIONS

The evidence we have extracted shows that all of the explanations for deindustrialization, namely import penetration, contracting-out and labour-saving technology, have contributed in varying degrees to the changing level and composition of output and employment in Britain during the Thatcher era. The findings suggest that although import penetration in final goods markets was substantial it was on average balanced by growth in exports. The more productive use of labour by firms was considerably more powerful than any loss of markets in directly reducing labour demand in all sectors of the economy throughout the 1980s.

However the growth of the financial services sector was very strong throughout the period, reflecting changes in business organization and in product composition. Rising labour use due to the expanding scale of this sector largely offset the labour shedding effects of technology in all sectors. Even so the total real demand for labour in 1990 was

Table 4.10 Decomposition of change in employment income by sources of output change

1979–85 Sector	Term 1 Domestic final demand	Term 2 Exports	Term 3 Home share in final demand	Term 4 Home share in intermediate demand	Term 5 Leontief coefficients	Row sum Total sector change	Employment income ratio change
Due to:			as percentage of employment income in 1979				
I Primary and extractive	31.5	1.1	-1.0	4.5	-7.2	28.8	-50.3
II High tech manufacturing	14.8	17.5	-13.9	-2.6	-1.4	14.5	-37.9
III Other manufacturing	12.6	5.4	-9.2	-6.5	-4.9	-2.6	-18.4
IV Financial services	52.4	7.4	-3.2	6.9	136.3	199.8	-134.1
V More tradeable services	22.6	-2.8	-6.5	2.5	5.6	21.3	-39.1
VI Less tradeable services	26.8	2.6	-2.1	1.6	-6.4	22.4	-25.9
Total	25.6	5.2	-5.1	0.7	7.7	34.2	-39.6

1979–85 Sector	Term 1 Domestic final demand	Term 2 Exports	Term 3 Home share in final demand	Term 4 Home share in intermediate demand	Term 5 Leontief coefficients	Row sum Total sector change	Employment income ratio change
Due to:			as percentage of employment income in 1979				
I Primary and extractive	8.8	1.2	-0.9	-0.5	-2.9	5.8	-24.0
II High tech manufacturing	4.7	7.5	-9.8	-0.2	2.1	4.3	-19.3
III Other manufacturing	2.1	0.0	-5.2	-2.9	-5.5	-11.5	-8.6
IV Financial services	7.2	9.8	-4.2	3.3	85.8	101.7	-74.1
V More tradeable services	2.2	-3.8	-9.1	1.6	-7.4	-16.5	-1.0
VI Less tradeable services	12.4	1.0	-1.4	-1.3	-7.9	2.9	-15.2
Total	8.5	2.4	-3.8	-0.7	2.8	9.2	-20.3

Table 4.10 continued

1985–90 Sector	Term 1 Domestic final demand	Term 2 Exports	Term 3 Home share in final demand	Term 4 Home share in intermediate demand	Term 5 Leontief coefficients	Row sum Total sector change	Employment income ratio change
	as percentage of employment income in 1985						
I Primary and extractive	22.8	−0.3	0.1	3.0	−3.1	22.5	−26.5
II High tech manufacturing	12.7	10.1	−6.4	−2.0	−3.8	10.5	−20.4
III Other manufacturing	10.7	5.8	−4.2	−3.6	1.1	9.8	−11.1
IV Financial services	27.9	−0.5	−0.1	5.5	24.2	56.9	−27.1
V More tradeable services	23.1	−0.6	3.6	3.4	18.2	47.7	−48.1
VI Less tradeable services	14.0	1.4	−0.8	2.2	2.9	19.8	−9.8
Total	16.5	2.7	−1.7	1.4	4.6	23.6	−17.2

below that of 1979. The evidence for structural shifts arising from the pressure of international competition, pushing the UK in the direction of sectors with higher value added and/or using advanced technology, generally supports the expected pattern for a high cost advanced economy, but there are some contrary indicators, not least the finding of strongly rising imports and low value added share in high technology products.

APPENDIX 1: DECOMPOSITION OF THE CHANGE IN OUTPUT AND EMPLOYMENT

The change in gross output between period 0 and period t is:

$$\Delta X = X_t - X_0$$
$$= (I - h_t A_t)^{-1} \{f_t F_t + E_t\} - (I - h_0 A_0)^{-1} \{f_0 F_0 + E_0\} \qquad (A1)$$

Since this involves the discrete-time representation of a process of continuous change a range of variants can be derived and their economic interpretation argued – the familiar 'index number problem' reviewed in a related context by Martin and Evans (1981).

Adopting a Paasche-type approach, (A1) can be expressed as:

$$\Delta X = R_t f_t(\Delta F) + R_t(\Delta E) + R_t(\Delta f)F_0 + (R_t - R_0)[f_0 F_0 + E_0] \qquad (A2)$$

$$= R_t f_t(\Delta F) + R_t(\Delta E) + R_t(\Delta f)F_0 + R_t(\Delta h)A_0 X_0 + R_t h_t(\Delta A)X_0 \qquad (A3)$$

where $R_t = (I - h_t A_t)^{-1}$, $R_0 = (I - h_0 A_0)^{-1}$, $R_0(f_0 F_0 + E_0) = X_0$, and the expansion of the final term in (A2) uses the property that for any matrices P and Q then $(P^{-1} - Q^{-1}) = -P^{-1}(P - Q)Q^{-1}$.

The comparable expression on a Laspeyres approach is:

$$\Delta X = R_0 f_0(\Delta F) + R_0(\Delta E) + R_0(\Delta f)F_t + R_0(\Delta h)A_t X_t + R_0 h_0(\Delta A)X_t \qquad (A4)$$

Similarly the change in employment can be decomposed as:

$$\Delta L = l_t X_t - l_0 X_0 = l_t \Delta X - (\Delta l)X_0 \qquad (A5)$$

and

$$\Delta L = l_t X_t - l_0 X_0 = l_0 \Delta X - (\Delta l)X_t \qquad (A6)$$

Inevitably, the numerical results differ between the two variants of the decomposition. However, the differences do not affect the overall pattern of the results, particularly at the level of the six aggregated groups reported here. For the decomposition of output therefore we report the average of equations (A3) and (A4), and for employment income the average of the equations (A5) and (A6).

APPENDIX 2: DATA SOURCES AND ADJUSTMENTS

INPUT–OUTPUT TABLES

Input–output tables for the UK are available for 1979, 1984, 1985 and 1990 (BSO 1983; CSO 1988; CSO 1989; CSO 1994). All are at current prices only, and are based on the 1980 Standard Industrial Classification. We have used the tables for 1979, 1985 and 1990. Although the 1985 tables are essentially an update of the benchmark tables for 1984, the miners' strike of 1984–5 introduced distortions into purchases of materials and fuels over that period. New estimates adjusting for this were made for 1985. 1985 has the further advantages of being a base year for constant price output series, and cyclically more comparable with 1979 and 1990.

For 1979 both industry × industry and commodity × commodity tables are available, but for the later years only the commodity × commodity basis is available, and this has been used throughout. It is also the preferable basis, corresponding more closely to the homogeneous product and common technology assumptions of input–output analysis. In addition to the commodity × commodity flow matrix for domestically produced goods we have used the commodity flow matrix for imported commodities, along with the vectors of final demands for home-produced and imported commodities for each year.

Although the tables for the three years are based on the same Standard Industrial Classification they contain minor differences in the level of commodity aggregation: 100 sectors in 1979, 102 in 1985 and 123 in 1990. A maximum of 97 sectors comparable across the three years could be achieved through direct aggregation. This was further reduced to 87 by the limited availability of sectoral output-price deflators, particularly within the engineering sectors. Of the 87 sectors on which the analysis is based 9 are in primary commodities or utilities, 67 in manufacturing, 10 in marketed services and 1 public administration. A full listing of the 87 sectors is appended.

CONVERSION TO CONSTANT PRICES

The 87-sector current-price data from CSO were deflated to a common 1985 price basis by sector-specific deflators for home-produced and imported commodities separately. For the 76 primary and manufacturing sectors, including construction, we were able to use producer price indices and import average value indices which had been compiled by Oxford Economic Forecasting with assistance from CSO.

To derive deflators for the 11 categories of domestically produced and imported services a more piecemeal approach had to be adopted. For domestic output of the three categories of financial services, other (mainly private sector) services and public services, we derived implicit deflators from the CSO current and constant price net output data given in the Blue Book. (For the public sector this required the weighted aggregation of deflators from the subheadings within this sector). Although formally these implicit deflators relate to net output CSO indicate that many of the indicators used in the construction of the constant price series for the net output are in practice gross output measures (CSO 1985).

Similar implicit price deflators are available for distribution, hotels and catering, which we distinguish as two sectors, and for transport and communications, where we distinguish six separate sectors. Our overall approach was to refine these to the more disaggregated level which we required. We first adopted the two more aggregated deflators as interim estimates for each of the two and six constituent sectors respectively. For the eight disaggregated sectors this completed the 87-sector vector of their inter-industry purchases at constant prices. The addition of sectoral employment income and gross profits, deflated as described below, gave an interim estimate of constant-price gross output for each sector, derived as the column-total of its purchases. Juxtaposed with the current-price valuation of gross output this measure provided our final estimate of the implicit deflator for domestic output in each of the eight sectors.

For import average value indices for the service sectors we could obtain no sector-specific information. The implicit price index for imports of services from the Pink Book was therefore applied to each of the 11 service sectors for which imports were recorded.

DEFLATION OF EMPLOYMENT INCOME AND PROFITS

Employment income generated in each sector was converted to a 'constant 1985 price' basis by revaluing at 1985 sectoral hourly earnings. The method developed is analogous to the deflation of gross output. The quantity units of employment, or weights, in each sector were the total person-hours worked there in 1985 by up to six groups: full-time manual and non-manual workers, male and female, and part-time female manual and non-manual workers. Sector-specific data on hourly earnings for each of the six groups from the New Earnings Survey provided the 'price relative'. Combining these gave the index of earnings change for each sector, which was then used to deflate employment income. Our measure of real employment income thus represents the employment income generated in each sector, revalued at 1985 earnings per person-hour in that sector.

Gross profits in each sector were deflated by the GDP implicit deflator.

THE SIX-SECTOR AGGREGATION

All the calculations have been performed at the 87-sector level, with the results then aggregated for presentation to six broad sectors. These sectors comprise:

I   Primary and extractive industries, utilities and construction: sectors 1–4, 6–9, 76
II   High technology manufacturing: sectors 17–26, 31–44, 72.
III Other manufacturing: sectors 5, 10–16, 27–30, 45–71, 73–75.
IV   Financial services: sector 85.
V   More tradeable services: sectors 81–84.
VI   Less tradeable services: sectors 77–80, 86–87.

INPUT–OUTPUT SECTORS

1	Agriculture, horticulture	45	Oils and fats
2	Forestry, fishing	46	Slaughtering
3	Coal and solid fuel	47	Milk
4	Oil and gas extraction	48	Fruit, vegetables and fish
5	Mineral oil processing	49	Grain and starch
6	Electricity, nuclear fuel	50	Bread and biscuits
7	Gas	51	Sugar
8	Water supply	52	Confectionery
9	Metal ore extraction	53	Animal feed
10	Iron and steel	54	Miscellaneous foods
11	Aluminum	55	Alcoholic drink
12	Other non-ferrous	56	Soft drink
13	Stone, clay, sand, gravel	57	Tobacco
14	Structural clay	58	Woollen and worsted
15	Cement, concrete, asbestos	59	Cotton
16	Glass and ceramics	60	Hosiery
17	Inorganic chemicals	61	Textile finishing
18	Organic chemicals	62	Carpets
19	Fertilizers	63	Jute and miscellaneous textile
20	Synthetic resins, plastic, rubber	64	Leather
21	Paints, dyes, inks	65	Footwear
22	Specialized chemicals	66	Clothing and fur
23	Pharmaceuticals	67	Household textiles
24	Soap and toiletries	68	Timber and wood
25	Chemical products	69	Furniture
26	Man-made fibres	70	Paper and board
27	Metal castings	71	Paper and board products
28	Metal doors and windows	72	Printing and publishing
29	Metal packaging	73	Rubber products
30	Metal goods	74	Plastics processing
31	Machine tools	75	Other manufacturing
32	Engineers' tools	76	Construction
33	Process machinery	77	Distribution and repairs
34	Mining and construction	78	Hotels, catering
35	Power transmission	79	Rail transport
36	Other mechanical engineering	80	Road transport
37	Insulated wires and cables	81	Sea transport
38	Industrial electrical equipment	82	Air transport
39	Domestic electric appliances	83	Transport services
40	Other electrical and electronic equipment	84	Post and telecommunications
41	Motor vehicles	85	Finance, insurance, professional services
42	Shipbuilding and repairing	86	Other services
43	Aerospace equipment manufacturing and repairing	87	Public administration, domestic services
44	Other vehicles		

Notes

1. Data for this analysis was obtained from the CSO and Oxford Economic Forecasting. Christine Greenhalgh benefited from the Oxford University teaching buyout scheme, which released her from 25 per cent of teaching duties during 1994–5. Finance for research assistance was obtained from the Institute of Economics and Statistics. Computing help was supplied by Andrew Farlow and Ian Sue Wing. Gavin Cameron was helpful in respect of the classification of industries by technology groups. Further work by the authors is currently being financed by the Leverhulme Trust's research programme: *The Labour Market Consequences of Technical and Structural Change.*

References

Barker, T. (1989) 'Sources of Structural Change for the UK Service Industries', paper presented to the Ninth International Conference on Input–Output Techniques, Hungary, September.

Burtless, G. (1995) 'International Trade and the Rise in Earnings Inequality', *Journal of Economic Literature*, vol. XCXXIII, June, pp. 800–816.

Business Statistics Office (BSO) Department of Industry (1983), *Input–Output Tables for the United Kingdom, 1979*, Business Monitor PA 1004 (London: HMSO).

Central Statistical Office (CSO) (1985) *UK National Accounts: Sources and Methods*, 3rd. edition (London: HMSO).

Central Statistical Office (CSO) (1988) *Input–Output Tables for the United Kingdom 1984* (London: HMSO).

Central Statistical Office (CSO) (1989) *Input–Output Tables for the United Kingdom 1985* (London: CSO).

Central Statistical Office (CSO) (1994) *Input–Output Tables for the United Kingdom 1990* (London: CSO).

Chenery, H., Shishido, S. and Watanabe, T. (1962) 'The Pattern of Japanese Growth 1914–54', *Econometrica*, vol. 30, no. 1, pp. 98–131.

Chenery, H. and Syrquin, M. (1975) *Patterns of Development: 1950–1970* (Oxford: Oxford University Press).

Courakis, A., Maskus, K. and Webster, A. (1995) 'Globalisation, Productivity Growth in Manufacturing and UK Labour Markets', paper for the Tokyo Club annual meeting, September.

Feldman, S., McClain, D. and Palmer, K. (1987) 'Sources of Structural Change in the United States 1963–78: An Input–Output Perspective', *Review of Economics and Statistics*, vol. LXIX, no. 3, August, pp. 503–510.

Green, F. (ed.) (1989) *The Restructuring of the British Economy*, (Hemel Hempstead: Harvester Wheatsheaf).

Martin, J. and Evans, J. (1981) 'Notes on Measuring the Employment Displacement Effects of Trade by the Accounting Procedure', *Oxford Economic Papers*, vol. 33 no. 1, pp. 154–164.

Postner, H. and Wesa, L. (1983) *Canadian Productivity Growth: An Alterna-*

tive (Input–Output) Analysis (Ottawa: Economic Council of Canada).

Rowthorn, R. and Wells, J. (1987) *Deindustrialisation and Foreign Trade: Britain's Decline in a Global Perspective* (Cambridge: Cambridge University Press).

Sachs, J. and Shatz, H. (1994) 'Trade and Jobs in US Manufacturing', *Brookings Papers on Economic Activity*, vol. 1, pp. 1–84.

Sakurai, N. (1995) 'Structural Change and Employment: Empirical Evidence for 8 OECD Countries', *OECD Science Technology and Industry Review*, no. 15, pp. 133–175.

Skolka, J. (1989) 'Input–Output Structural Decomposition Analysis for Austria', *Journal of Policy Modeling*, vol. 11 no. 1, pp. 45–66.

Stoneman, P. and Francis, N. (1994) 'Double Deflation and the Measurement of Output and Productivity in UK Manufacturing', *International Journal of the Economics of Business*, vol. 1 no. 3, pp. 423–437.

Wood, A. (1994) *North-South Trade, Employment and Inequality* (Oxford: Clarendon Press).

5 The Impact of Import Penetration on Unemployment in UK Manufacturing

Jitendralal Borkakoti*

INRODUCTION

The relationship between international trade and domestic unemployment has received serious attention only in recent years, partly because of economic recession, triggered by two oil crises (1973 and 1980) and partly because of observed deindustrialization in matured Western economies when, under both circumstances, workers and capitalists alike clamour for protection against import competition. There is an association between depression and deindustrialization as both create unemployment, although the former is cyclical and hence a medium-term phenomenon while the latter is essentially a long-term phenomenon as it involves structural change.

A comprehensive study[1] of the process of deindustrialization in the United States has been carried out by Bluestone and Harrison (1982). Taking deindustrialization as 'creative destruction' they report that, during the period 1969–76, private investment in new plants created about 25 million jobs in America while, during the same period, business bankruptcies or private business disinvestments led to a loss of 22 million jobs so that the economy had a net gain of jobs: a consequence of the economic upheavals of the period. This reflects the dynamic nature of the US economy. During the period 1980–5, the UK manufacturing sector shrunk by 28 per cent in terms of net employment while the comparable figures for the US, France and Germany are in single digits (for example, 6 per cent for the US).

A notable study by Lawrence (1983) begins by asserting five sources of structural change in the US economy and the propositions put forward are intuitively appealing and are general enough to be true of any developed economy. These sources of structural change are the following: (1) the secular decline of the share of manufactured products in consumption expenditure; (2) relatively more rapid growth of productivity in the manufacturing sector, which partially explains the relative fall in manufacturing employment; (3) high output elasticity of demand for manufactured goods so that an economic depression disproportionately causes loss of jobs; (4) shifts in the preference of the US consumers; and (5) shifts in the pattern of US trade specialization as a result of changes in comparative advantage caused primarily by changes in the relative factor endowments in the rest of the world. These are long-run phenomena, but there are also short-run factors such as changes in exchange rates which affect the US trade competitiveness. It is clear that trade is only one of several sources which may affect unemployment although casual inspection of data reveals that the countries which have increased their world-share of manufacturing exports during the seventies have done well in terms of having relatively lower levels of unemployment in the eighties. As Krueger (1980a, 1980b) points out, one should not think in terms of 'causal' relationship between imports and unemployment (because macroeconomic variables will have profound effect on the latter). However, the impact of 'trade competitiveness' on employment or unemployment is a legitimate concern. This chapter attempts to analyse the impact of import penetration on recent unemployment in the UK manufacturing sector by using some established statistical methods and also to estimate the impact of the UK trade competitiveness on employment. Numerous studies of this kind have been done for the US while studies for the UK are sparse.

THEORETICAL BACKGROUND

Theoretical models in the area of trade and unemployment find a way out of the straitjacket of full employment by replacing the standard neo-classical assumptions with some alternative assumptions which can 'generate' unemployment. Within the Walrasian price-adjustment structure, this is accomplished by assuming one of the following: fixed coefficient Leontief technology (Melvin, 1985), exogenously specified minimum or wage rigidity (Brecher, 1947a, 1974b); Lefeber, (1969: Srinivasan and Bhagwati, 1975; and others), sector-specific factors of production (Batra and Pattanaik, 1971; Neary, 1982, 1985; and others), or implicit contracts in the labour market (Matusz, 1986). These models

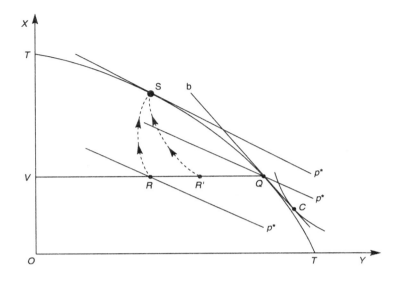

Figure 5.1

first demonstrate how unemployment may be increased or decreased by free trade, and then proceed to discuss policy issues concerning tariff, subsidy, and so on. Furthermore, there are a few interesting contributions (Bhagwati, 1982; Lapan, 1976; Mussa, 1982; and others) dealing with the theoretical issues of sectoral adjustment, that is, issues involving an economy's response to changing comparative advantage and the concommitant transformation which allows the 'senescent' sectors to decline and encourages the 'nascent' sectors to develop. A survey or a critical appraisal of these theories is beyond the scope of the present paper. However, the fundamental issue can be discussed by using Figure 5.1 where TT is the long-run production-possibility curve with Q and C respectively as production and consumption points. Now let the relative price of imports fall to p*. If both factors are sector-specific, as in Batra and Pattanaik (1971), admittedly an extreme assumption, then in the short-run unemployment will be created in the importable goods sector. If the importable goods sector consists of firms which could be ordered according to the degree of increasing efficiency, then the least efficient firms will go bust, output will fall, and unemployment will be created. The firms which can compete at the new world price will survive and will determine the position of the production point R along QV in Figure 5.1. The market will direct physical capital and human capital towards producing relatively more· of the exportable so that R will move to point S in the long run[2]. However, with government intervention, in terms of adjustment policies, it is possible that fall of output and unemployment in the importable goods sector could be substantially less, as illustrated by point R.

A MACROECONOMIC VIEW OF DEINDUSTRIALIZATION

The sharp decline of the share of the UK manufacturing in the GDP during the 1980s is revealed in Figure 5.2 and the consequent fall of manufacturing employment is shown in Figure 5.3. The fall in manufacturing employment is more drastic than that in total employment. Simultaneously, there has also been a deficit in the manufacturing trade balance. Figure 5.4 illustrates the merchandise trade balance as a percentage share of GDP, which shows a sharp deterioration between 1980 and 1989. Furthermore, it is often argued, the relatively high real exchange rates in the early 1980s have contributed significantly towards the deterioration of the merchandise trade balance. The real effective exchange rates have been high from 1979 to 1986 (see Figure 5.5).

As has already been pointed out, international trade is only one of several factors which can contribute towards this observed deindustrialization. A recent macro study of the US economy by Krugman and Lawrence (1993) shows that value added in the manufacturing sector and manufacturing employment respectively accounted for 25 per cent of GDP and 27.3 per cent of total employment in 1970, and these figures respectively dropped to 18.4 per cent and 11.4 per cent in 1990. Arguing that the net effect of simultaneous growth of exports and imports needs to be estimated in order to assess the impact of trade on deindustrialization, Krugman and Lawrence (1993) show that trade deficits cannot have been the main cause of the declining importance of manufacturing. The share of manufacturing in GDP fell by 6.6 per cent between 1970 and 1990 while, during the same period, manufacturing trade balance as share of GDP deteriorated by only 1.6 per cent. The prime cause is found to be a shift in domestic expenditure from manufacturing to services and construction. This shift in domestic expenditure on manufactured goods, according to Krugman and Lawrence (1993), is not caused by a fall in actual consumption of these goods, but by a significant fall in the manufacturing prices relative to those of services, caused primarily by productivity growth in manufacturing.[3]

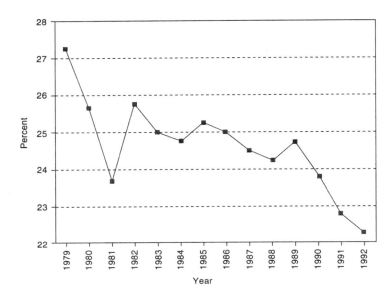

Figure 5.2   UK share of manufacturing in GDP (%)

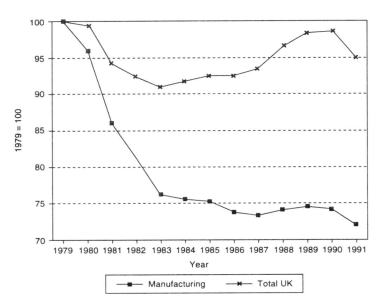

Figure 5.3   Total UK and manufacturing employment 1979=100

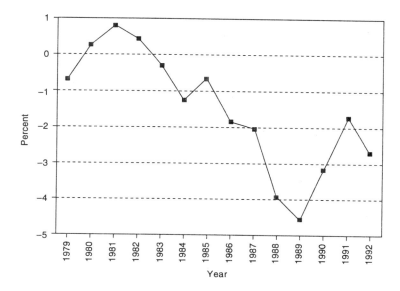

Figure 5.4 UK share of merchandise trade balance in GDP (%)

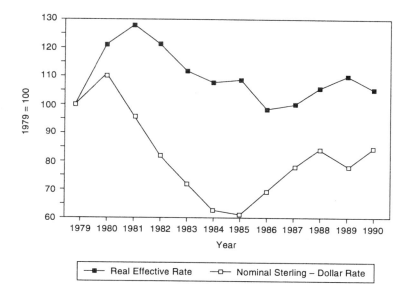

Figure 5.5 UK exchange rates 1979 to 1990

In terms of the degree of 'openness', one would expect the impact of net deficits in manufacturing trade on deindustrialization in the UK to be different from that in the US. The degree of openness[4] in 1990 is 41 per cent in the UK while it is only 16 per cent in the US. The share of manufacturing in GDP fell by 8 per cent between 1980 and 1990 in the UK while, during the same period, manufacturing trade balance as share of GDP deteriorated from 0.31 per cent to -3.2 per cent recording a deterioration by about 1100 per cent. Thus, there seems to be some prima facie evidence that the role of trade in the UK deindustrialization is relatively more significant than in the US.

IMPORT PENETRATION AND REVEALED COMPARATIVE ADVANTAGE

It seems appropriate to begin by estimating import penetration in the manufacturing sectors, and also by measuring sectoral revealed comparative advantage since the former and the latter are indirectly related. We use two measures[5] of import penetration: gross import penetration (GIP) which is defined as the ratio of imports to apparent consumption and net import penetration (NIP) which is defined as the ratio of net imports to apparent consumption. The idea that NIP is relatively more indicative of the impact of international trade (see, for example, Cable 1977 and Krugman and Lawrence 1993) emanates from the proposition that the domestic country's exports will also suffer because exports from the rest of the world (ROW) will inevitably compete successfully against the domestic country's exports if ROW has succeeded in exporting more to the domestic country. This likely effect, that exports may fall while imports increase, is not picked up by GIP which simply measures rise in import levels. Grossman (1986) also argues that it is inappropriate to identify import competition with the volume of imports, which is an endogenous variable determined by domestic and foreign demand and supply. Lastly, revealed comparative advantage (RCA) is measured by trade balance as a ratio of the sum of exports and imports. It is, thus, clear that RCA is positive whenever NIP is negative.

Table 5.1a presents GIP in percentage terms for 1979–80, 1984–5 and 1989–90 when the percentage measures are computed from two-year annual averages (see, for example, Luttrell 1978) in order to reduce the probability of single-year figures being unrepresentative. Next to the column of the GIP figures is the column of the sectoral employment

Table 5.1a Gross import penetration of selected manufacturing sectors

SITC	Description	GIP (%) 1979–80	% of labour force 1979–80	GIP (%) 1984–85	% of labour force 1984–85	GIP (%) 1989–90	% of labour force 1989–90
3112	Food	17.69	8.09	17.99	8.99	17.78	10.23
313	Beverages	7.85	1.68	10.14	1.44	14.42	1.5
314	Tobacco	6.25	0.55	6.47	0.48	5.13	0.29
321	Textiles	28.55	4.09	37.65	3.28	42.32	3.39
322	Wearing apparel	26.95	7.9	32.38	6.06	41.40	5.95
323	Leather & products	35.67	0.45	43.46	0.41	50.07	0.39
324	Footwear	27.63	1.04	39.98	0.97	45.82	1.0
331	Wood products	29.62	1.78	33.12	1.7	33.13	1.87
332	Furniture & fixtures	9.79	1.86	15.12	1.93	15.16	2.54
341	Paper & products	26.38	3.08	32.17	2.93	35.13	3.19
342	Printing & publishing	4.30	4.18	5.41	5.65	5.69	6.55
351	Industrial chemicals	28.22	3.33	35.06	10.8	42.21	3.1
3522	Drugs & medicines	11.72	1.11	17.34	1.26	18.61	1.59
3529	Chemical products, nec	22.54	1.34	33.57	1.4	34.36	1.65
355	Rubber products	14.37	1.52	23.76	1.27	28.21	1.35
356	Plastic products	11.25	2.38	15.60	2.52	15.38	3.59
361	Pottery, china, etc.	11.47	1.04	14.73	0.97	18.12	1.13
362	Glass & products	19.91	0.86	29.42	0.74	27.73	0.91
369	Non-metallic products, nec	3.40	2.15	4.80	2.13	7.14	2.46
371	Iron & steel	16.11	3.65	17.56	2.15	23.53	2.0
372	Non-ferrous metals	46.07	1.17	44.88	0.9	46.65	0.91
381	Metal products	12.24	7.27	16.65	6.22	18.79	7.05
3825	Office & computing machinery	72.29	0.7	87.20	0.88	77.20	1.17
3829	Machinery & equipment, nec	23.23	14.93	31.08	12.81	35.39	13.14
3832	Radio, TV & communications equipment	23.21	5.09	32.21	5.47	44.13	5.64
3839	Electrical apparatus, nec	18.70	4.36	29.58	4.21	32.84	4.49
3841	Shipbuilding and repairing	16.98	1.92	5.18	1.64	6.79	1.38
3842	Railroad equipment	2.98	0.72	3.11	0.59	8.82	0.4
3843	Motor vehicles	33.73	7.08	41.40	5.3	45.65	5.6
3844	Motorcycles & bicycles	67.40	0.17	67.77	0.1	80.22	0.07
3845	Aircraft	51.50	2.92	44.68	3.2	50.83	3.59
3849	Transport equipment, nec	4.35	0.05	6.29	0.07	9.09	0.08
385	Professional goods	62.42	1.54	98.45	1.53	88.89	1.81

Source: OECD Stan Database (1994)

as a percentage of the total manufacturing employment. It emerges clearly that GIP has increased over the years in almost all manufacturing sectors. Considering the sectors which show a value of GIP greater than 20 per cent, we find that there are 16 manufacturing sectors (out of a sample of 33 sectors) employing 57 per cent of the manufacturing work force in 1979–80, 19 sectors employing 64 per cent of the

Table 5.1b   Net import penetration of selected manufacturing sectors

SITC	Description	NIP (%) 1979–80	% of labour force 1979–80	NIP (%) 1984–85	% of labour force 1984–85	NIP (%) 1989–90	% of labour force 1989–90
3112	Food	11.45	8.09	11.56	8.99	10.29	10.23
313	Beverages	−7.28	1.68	−5.77	1.44	−5.29	1.5
314	Tobacco	−1.21	0.55	−1.26	0.48	−3.76	0.29
321	Textiles	6.43	4.09	16.33	3.28	17.00	3.39
322	Wearing apparel	10.47	7.9	16.63	6.06	24.62	5.95
323	Leather & products	3.61	0.45	8.48	0.41	14.86	0.39
324	Footwear	17.11	1.04	30.45	0.97	35.42	1.0
331	Wood products	27.23	1.78	30.87	1.7	31.37	1.87
332	Furniture & fixtures	1.65	1.86	7.60	1.93	8.59	2.54
341	Paper & products	19.44	3.08	24.53	2.93	25.26	3.19
342	Printing & publishing	−3.07	4.18	−2.39	5.65	−1.46	6.55
351	Industrial chemicals	−8.31	3.33	−5.10	10.8	0.01	3.1
3522	Drugs & medicines	−20.87	1.11	−21.44	1.26	−16.96	1.59
3529	Chemical products, nec	−17.28	1.34	−9.81	1.4	−11.09	1.65
355	Rubber products	−8.02	1.52	−0.66	1.27	0.88	1.35
356	Plastic products	2.11	2.38	5.76	2.52	7.01	3.59
361	Pottery, china, etc.	−28.21	1.04	−21.74	0.97	−14.27	1.13
362	Glass & products	2.34	0.86	9.58	0.74	11.51	0.91
369	Non-metallic products, nec	−3.13	2.15	−0.32	2.13	2.20	2.46
371	Iron & steel	2.72	3.65	−0.61	2.15	−1.50	2.0
372	Non-ferrous metals	14.31	1.17	14.28	0.9	16.40	0.91
381	Metal products	−7.59	7.27	−2.10	6.22	3.56	7.05
3825	Office & computing machinery	11.46	0.7	18.48	0.88	13.62	1.17
3829	Machinery & equipment, nec	−17.99	14.93	−9.20	12.8	−3.09	13.14
3832	Radio, TV & communications equipment	2.70	5.09	10.14	5.47	10.93	5.64
3839	Electrical apparatus, nec	−5.96	4.36	4.62	4.21	6.15	4.49
3841	Shipbuilding and repairing	−15.19	1.92	−16.32	1.64	−6.26	1.38
3842	Railroad equipment	−16.23	0.72	−14.51	0.59	−0.32	0.4
3843	Motor vehicles	1.45	7.08	16.11	5.3	19.58	5.6
3844	Motorcycles & bicycles	38.83	0.17	39.74	0.1	58.47	0.07
3845	Aircraft	−9.58	2.92	−18.98	3.2	−26.39	3.59
3849	Transport equipment, nec	−13.04	0.05	−2.52	0.07	1.73	0.08
385	Professional goods	−25.15	1.54	−16.01	1.53	−12.60	1.81

Source: OECD Stan Database (1994)

manufacturing work force in 1984–5, and 20 sectors employing 61 per cent in 1989–90. Considering the sectors which show a value of GIP greater than 30 per cent, we find that there are 7 sectors employing 14 per cent in 1979–80, 16 sectors employing 58 per cent in 1984–5, and 17 sectors employing 57 per cent of the manufacturing work force in 1989–90. Considering the sectors which show a value of GIP greater than 40 per cent, we find 5 sectors employing 7 per cent in 1979–80, 7 sectors employing 12 per cent in 1984–5, and 12 sectors employing 33 per cent of the total manufacturing work force in 1989–90. The steady deterioration over the years in terms of gross import penetration is apparent. Table 5.1b presents NIP in percentage terms. NIP is positive (indicating comparative disadvantage) in 16 out of 33 sectors employing 49 per cent of the total manufacturing labour force in 1979–80. It can be seen in Table 5.1b that the same 16 sectors continued to suffer from import penetration till 1984–85 when these sectors employed only 46 per cent of the total manufacturing work force. By 1989–90, the number of manufacturing sectors showing positive NIP values rose to 20 sectors which employed 65 per cent of the manufacturing work force. Thus the NIP values once again confirm the steady deterioration of UK manufacturing competitiveness. The general picture that emerges from the GIP and NIP figures demonstrates reasonably well that import penetration in the UK manufacturing sector is significant and fairly deep in some sectors (for example, wearing apparel, footwear and wood products).

Table 5.2 presents the estimates of revealed comparative advantage for the years 1979–80, 1984–85 and 1989–90. It is a measure of the UK deindustrialization that 21 sectors (out of 33 sectors), employing 65 per cent of the manufacturing work force, exhibit comparative disadvantage in 1989–90 while only 16 (employing 50 per cent of manufacturing labour) did so in 1979–80. Revealed comparative advantage consistently deteriorated throughout the period from 1979–80 to 1989–90 in many sectors which include not only the senescent industries like textiles (321), leather & products (323), and footwear (324) but also the nascent industries like radio, TV & communication equipment (3832), motor vehicles (3843) and electrical apparatus (3839). Lastly, we note that RCA is more closely associated with NIP than GIP. The correlation coefficient between NIP (GIP) and RCA is -0.86 (-0.31), -0.88 (-0.28) and -0.86 (-0.25) respectively for the years 1979–80, 1984–5 and 1989–90.

Table 5.2   Revealed comparative advantage of selected manufacturing sectors

SITC	Description	RCA (%) 1979–80	% of labour force 1979–80	RCA (%) 1984–85	% of labour force 1984–85	RCA (%) 1989–90	% of labour force 1989–90
3112	Food	−47.84	8.09	−47.35	8.99	−40.74	10.23
313	Beverages	31.67	1.68	22.17	1.44	15.51	1.5
314	Tobacco	8.81	0.55	8.87	0.48	26.81	0.29
321	Textiles	−12.68	4.09	−27.69	3.28	−25.14	3.39
322	Wearing apparel	−24.11	7.9	−34.55	6.06	−42.31	5.95
323	Leather & products	−5.33	0.45	−10.82	0.41	−17.43	0.39
324	Footwear	−44.83	1.04	−61.52	0.97	−63.02	1.0
331	Wood products	−85.07	1.78	−87.29	1.7	−89.91	1.87
332	Furniture & fixtures	−9.18	1.86	−33.59	1.93	−39.57	2.54
341	Paper & products	−58.34	3.08	−61.59	2.93	−56.14	3.19
342	Printing & publishing	26.33	4.18	18.06	5.65	11.40	6.55
351	Industrial chemicals	12.84	3.33	6.78	10.8	−0.01	3.1
3522	Drugs & medicines	47.09	1.11	38.21	1.26	31.30	1.59
3529	Chemical products, nec	27.71	1.34	12.75	1.4	13.90	1.65
355	Rubber products	21.83	1.52	1.36	1.27	−1.58	1.35
356	Plastic products	−10.36	2.38	−22.62	2.52	−29.52	3.59
361	Pottery, china, etc.	55.14	1.04	42.45	0.97	28.25	1.13
362	Glass & products	−6.24	0.86	−19.46	0.74	−26.18	0.91
369	Non-metallic products, nec	31.52	2.15	3.27	2.13	−18.17	2.46
371	Iron & steel	−9.23	3.65	1.72	2.15	3.08	2.0
372	Non-ferrous metals	−18.38	1.17	−18.91	0.9	−21.32	0.91
381	Metal products	23.68	7.27	5.94	6.22	−10.46	7.05
3825	Office & computing machinery	−8.61	0.7	−11.85	0.88	−9.67	1.17
3829	Machinery & equipment, nec	27.92	14.93	12.89	12.81	4.19	13.14
3832	Radio, TV & communications equipment	−6.18	5.09	−18.67	5.47	−14.13	5.64
3839	Electrical apparatus, nec	13.74	4.36	−8.48	4.21	−10.33	4.49
3841	Shipbuilding and repairing	30.90	1.92	61.20	1.64	31.54	1.38
3842	Railroad equipment	73.13	0.72	69.96	0.59	1.75	0.4
3843	Motor vehicles	−2.20	7.08	−24.15	5.3	−27.30	5.6
3844	Motorcycles & bicycles	−40.46	0.17	−41.47	0.1	−57.33	0.07
3845	Aircraft	8.51	2.92	17.52	3.2	20.61	3.59
3849	Transport equipment, nec	60.00	0.05	16.67	0.07	−10.53	0.08
385	Professional goods	16.77	1.54	7.52	1.53	6.62	1.81

Source: OECD Stan Database (1994)

IMPACT OF NIP ON SECTORAL EMPLOYMENT

We now use NIP ratios to estimate unemployment, *ceteris paribus*, due to an increase in import penetration. The method[6], which was originally introduced by Luttrell (1978) and adapted here, involves estimating what the sectoral employment would be in, say, the time period $t + n$, if import penetration changed, say, between t and $t + n$, and then finding the difference between the estimated and actual employment. If L^*_{t+n} is the estimated employment of a sector, then $\alpha L_{t+n} = L^*_{t+n}$ where L_{t+n} is actual employment and $\alpha = (1 - \mathrm{NIP}_t)/(1 - \mathrm{NIP}_{t+n})$, noting that NIPs are fractions. It is evident that $\alpha = 1$ if $\mathrm{NIP}_t = \mathrm{NIP}_{t+n}$ so that $L^*_{t+n} = L_{t+n}$. In this case, the impact of import penetration is zero. If, however, $\mathrm{NIP}_{t+n} > \mathrm{NIP}_t$, then $\alpha > 1$ so that $L^*_{t+n} > L_{t+n}$. The meaning is simple and clear. Holding other things constant, L^*_{t+n} would have been the level of employment at time $t + n$ if there were no increase in import penetration. Then, $\Delta L_m = L^*_{t+n} - L_{t+n}$, is a measure of change in employment at time $t + n$ due solely to import penetration between period t and $t + n$. If there is actual unemployment, the change in employment, namely, $\Delta L = L_{t+n} - L_t$, is negative. Now the share of ΔL_m in $-\Delta L$ will measure the 'contribution' of import penetration to unemployment during the considered period. Here the term 'unemployment' is used to mean 'job losses' in the manufacturing sector. An unemployed industrial worker may find a job, say, in the service sector, in which case the person will no longer be unemployed.

Using NIP, we have estimated the contribution of import penetration to sectoral unemployment for two periods: one from 1979–80 to 1984–5 and the other from 1984–5 to 1989–90. The results are presented in Tables 5.3a and 5.3b, respectively for the former and the latter period. In Table 5.3a, L^* is the estimated employment in 1984–5, had there been no import penetration, during the period from 1979–80 to 1984–5, L is the actual employment in 1984–5, ΔL_m is the pure impact of import penetration during the period such that $\Delta L_m = L^* - L$, and ΔL, is the actual unemployment obtained from the difference between 1984–5 actual employment and 1979–80 actual employment. Consider the food industry (sector 3112) in 1984–5 where ΔL_m is 0.6 thousand, so that out of 58.6 job losses ($-\Delta L$) , only 0.6 thousand are accounted for by an increase in net import penetration. On the other hand, consider machinery and equipment (sector 3829) in 1989–90 where job losses due to import penetration register 37.2 thousand out of total job losses of 54.3 thousand during the period from 1984–5 to

Table 5.3a   Impact of net import penetration on sectoral employment
(1000s) (1979–80 to 1984–85)

		Employment as % of total	Estimated L^*	Actual L	ΔL_m	ΔL
3112	Food	9.27	479.25	478.65	0.60	−58.6
313	Beverages	1.42	77.54	76.45	1.09	−35.1
314	Tobacco	0.47	25.29	25.30	−0.01	−11.2
321	Textiles	4.94	195.26	174.60	20.66	−97.1
322	Wearing apparel	4.37	346.38	322.55	23.83	−202.25
323	Leather & products	0.45	23.17	22.00	1.17	−7.75
324	Footwear	0.97	61.26	51.40	9.86	−17.6
331	Wood products	1.72	95.16	90.40	4.76	−27.65
332	Furniture & fixtures	2.08	109.58	102.95	6.63	−20.3
341	Paper & products	3.07	166.31	155.80	10.51	−48.85
342	Printing & publishing	5.92	302.65	300.65	2.00	22.95
351	Industrial chemicals	3.02	592.66	575.10	17.56	353.7
3522	Drugs & medicines	1.21	66.93	67.25	−0.32	−6.6
3529	Chemical products, nec	2.06	79.83	74.75	5.08	−14.3
355	Rubber products	1.36	72.49	67.55	4.94	−33.25
356	Plastic products	2.71	139.24	134.05	5.19	−23.9
361	Pottery, china, etc.	0.89	54.61	51.85	2.76	−17.5
362	Glass & products	0.79	42.66	39.50	3.16	−17.6
369	Non-metallic products, nec	2.42	116.42	113.25	3.17	−29.45
371	Iron & steel	3.63	110.47	114.25	−3.78	−128
372	Non-ferrous metals	1.31	48.13	48.15	−0.02	−29.3
381	Metal products	6.21	348.80	331.00	17.80	−151.8
3825	Office & computing machinery	1.11	50.88	46.85	4.03	0.4
3829	Machinery & equipment, nec	13.06	736.79	681.90	54.89	−310
3832	Radio, TV & communication equipment	5.07	315.63	291.50	24.13	−46.6
3839	Electrical apparatus, nec	5.46	249.29	224.40	24.89	−65.05
3841	Shipbuilding and repairing	1.47	86.70	87.55	−0.85	−39.95
3842	Railroad equipment	0.53	32.02	31.55	0.47	−16.25
3843	Motor vehicles	4.76	331.75	282.40	49.35	−187.55
3844	Motorcycles & bicycles	0.09	5.63	5.50	0.13	−5.75
3845	Aircraft	2.86	157.03	170.50	−13.47	−23.65
3849	Transport equipment, nec	0.05	3.91	3.55	0.36	0.1

Source: OECD Stan Database (1994)

1989–90. If we accept the premises of the statistical method, then the impact of import penetration seems to be quite a significant factor in explaining job losses in 21 sectors out of a total of 33 sectors for the period from 1979–80 to 1984–5, and in 14 sectors out of 33 sectors between 1984–5 and 1989–90.

Table 5.3b   Impact of net import penetration on sectoral employment (1000s) (1984–85 to 1989–90)

		Employment as % of total	Estimated L^*	Actual L	ΔL_m	ΔL
3112	Food	9.42	481.63	488.55	−6.92	9.9
313	Beverages	1.33	71.98	71.65	0.33	−4.8
314	Tobacco	0.25	13.37	13.70	−0.33	−11.6
321	Textiles	4.76	163.31	162.00	1.31	−12.6
322	Wearing apparel	4.24	314.32	284.20	30.12	−38.35
323	Leather & products	0.38	19.94	18.55	1.39	−3.45
324	Footwear	0.95	51.26	47.60	3.66	−3.8
331	Wood products	1.92	90.00	89.35	0.65	−1.05
332	Furniture & fixtures	2.79	122.77	121.45	1.32	18.5
341	Paper & products	3.13	153.79	152.30	1.49	−3.5
342	Printing & publishing	6.42	315.77	312.90	2.87	12.25
351	Industrial chemicals	2.89	155.51	147.95	7.56	−427.15
3522	Drugs & medicines	1.38	79.01	76.10	2.91	8.85
3529	Chemical products, nec	2.04	78.09	79.00	−0.91	4.25
355	Rubber products	1.28	65.30	64.30	1.00	−3.25
356	Plastic products	3.41	173.55	171.25	2.30	37.2
361	Pottery, china, etc.	0.77	57.58	54.05	3.53	2.2
362	Glass & products	0.74	44.35	43.40	0.95	3.9
369	Non-metallic products, nec	2.13	120.27	117.25	3.02	4
371	Iron & steel	2.79	94.81	95.65	−0.84	−18.6
372	Non-ferrous metals	1.09	44.50	43.40	1.10	−4.75
381	Metal products	6.32	356.30	336.55	19.75	5.55
3825	Office & computing machinery	1.45	52.52	55.65	−3.13	8.8
3829	Machinery & equipment, nec	13.43	664.80	627.60	37.20	−54.3
3832	Radio, TV & communication equipment	4.42	271.69	269.30	2.39	−22.2
3839	Electrical apparatus, nec	0.51	217.95	214.45	3.50	−9.95
3841	Shipbuilding and repairing	1.26	72.19	65.95	6.24	−21.6
3842	Railroad equipment	0.37	21.80	19.10	2.70	−12.45
3843	Motor vehicles	5.11	278.73	267.20	11.53	−15.2
3844	Motorcycles & bicycles	0.06	5.15	3.55	1.60	−1.95
3845	Aircraft	3.27	161.30	171.35	−10.05	0.85
3849	Transport equipment, nec	0.07	3.76	3.60	0.16	0.05
385	Professional goods	3.59	89.07	86.45	2.62	86.45

Source: OECD Stan Database (1994)

RELATIVE IMPACT OF DEMAND, PRODUCTIVITY AND IMPORTS ON UK MANUFACTURING EMPLOYMENT

It is deemed useful to carry out an empirical analysis in order to decompose the relative effects of demand, labour productivity and imports by using the standard accounting-identity method. Studies using this method include Frank (1977), Krueger (1980a, 1980b), and Lawrence (1983) on the United States, Cable (1977) on the United Kingdom, and Wolter (1977) on West Germany. These studies have found that the contribution of labour productivity to changes in employment is much more significant than that of import competition. The method begins with the following accounting identities:

$$C_{it} = Q_{it} + M_{it} - X_{it} \tag{1}$$

$$Q_{it}/L_{it} = A_{it} \tag{2}$$

where, for the sector i at time period t, C = domestic consumption, Q = domestic output, X = exports, M = imports, L = employment, and A = average productivity of labour. Define $S_{it} = Q_{it}/C_{it}$, so that S is the ratio of domestic output to consumption, and substitute for Q_{it} in (2) to get:

$$L_{it} = S_{it} \, C_{it}/A_{it} \tag{3}$$

Note *en passant* that $S = (1 - \text{NIP})$ as discussed in note 6. Now, if A_{it}, C_{it} and S_{it} all grow at constant continuous rates, then the growth rates of these variables can be related to the growth rate of L_{it} by logarithmically differentiating (3) with respect to time, so that the following is obtained:

$$\dot{L}/L = \dot{C}/C + \dot{S}/S - \dot{A}/A \tag{4}$$

Equation (4) shows that $\hat{L}$ the rate of growth of employment is accounted for by $\hat{C}$ the rate of growth of apparent consumption, $\hat{S}$ the rate of growth of the ratio of output in consumption, and $\hat{A}$ the rate of growth of labour productivity. This seems cogent but there may be problems with this method. Martin and Evans (1981) have commented that accounting identities are arbitrary, and different identities may yield different results. Furthermore, from the mathematical point of view, the system of equations (1) and (2) is a mixed multiplicative-additive system which causes 'interaction problems'. The accounting identity method, as concluded by Martin and Evans (1981), neglects cross effects of the variables[7], the effects of other variables, and changes in time. Grossman (1982), on the other hand, objects to the interpretation of changes in the average product of labour as reflecting 'technological progress', and, using Hicks-neutral technological progress in a CES production function, demonstrates that average labour productivity is independent of the technological-progress parameter.

Despite these caveats, we have carried out a similar study covering two periods, from 1979–80 to 1984–5 and from 1984–5 to 1989–90, and the results respectively are presented in Tables 5.4a and 5.4b. In both tables, the sum of $\hat{C}$, $\hat{S}$ and $-\hat{A}$ give $\hat{L}$. These rates of growth are calculated from real variables by using the standard formula[8]. A negative sign of $\hat{S}$ indicates that the share of output in consumption has decreased. This must be interpreted as an increase in net import penetration. First note that $\hat{L}$ for the first period is, in general, significantly higher than that in the second period. Regarding $\hat{S}$, we should note that 25 sectors (out of a sample of 30 sectors in Table 5.4a), employing 90 per cent of the manufacturing work force, suffered from penetration during the period from 1979–80 to 1984–5 while 24 sectors employing 79 per cent of the manufacturing work force, as can be seen from Table 5.4b, suffered from import penetration during the period from 1984–5 to 1989–90. During the period from 1979–80 to 1984–5, $\hat{S}$ is high for a few sectors, namely footwear (324), electrical apparatus (3839), motor vehicles (3843) and transport equipment (3849). More than half the percentage points of $\hat{L}$ are contributed by $\hat{S}$ in footwear. What one should look for is the contribution of $\hat{S}$ to the percentage points of $\hat{L}$. Figures 5.6 and 5.7 give a visual picture of $\hat{L}$ and $\hat{S}$. During the period from 1984–5 to 1989–90, it is clear from Table 5.4b that the impact of import penetration has significantly decreased, and the impact of demand has significantly increased, so that $\hat{C}$ accounts for a significant fall in unemployment rates, as compared to those in the previous period. It is not easy to draw clear cut conclusions regarding the impact of import penetration. If it is reasonable to assume that the impact of import penetration is severe when $\hat{S}$ accounts for more than one-fifth of the percentage points of $\hat{L}$, then the impact of import penetration is severe in 12 out of 30 sectors during the period from 1979–80 to 1984–5 and only in 7 out 30 sectors during the period from 1984–5 to 1989–90. This reveals that the severity of import penetration is significantly lower in the latter period as compared to the former period.

AN ECONOMETRIC APPROACH

Econometric models, somewhat inexplicably, are rare in this area. There seems to be only one contribution by Kierzkowski (1980), who derives

Table 5.4a   Estimated impact of demand, imports and labour productivity on UK manufacturing employment (from 1979–80 to 1984–85)

SITC	Description	% of labour force	$\hat{C}$	$\hat{S}$	$-\hat{A}$	$\hat{L}$
3112	Food	10.65	−1.349	−0.044	−0.911	−2.304
313	Beverages	1.70	−3.240	−0.252	−4.092	−7.584
314	Tobacco	0.56	−1.263	0.027	−6.275	−7.511
322	Wearing apparel	7.18	−2.139	−1.488	−6.262	−9.889
323	Leather & products	0.49	−3.491	−1.009	−1.478	−5.978
324	Footwear	1.14	−2.792	−3.545	0.551	−5.786
331	Wood products	2.01	−3.791	−1.085	−0.382	−5.258
332	Furniture & fixtures	2.29	−0.331	−1.280	−1.999	−3.610
341	Paper & products	3.47	−0.944	−1.383	−3.162	−5.489
342	Printing & publishing	6.69	1.590	−0.125	3.647	5.112
3522	Drugs & medicines	1.50	1.155	0.192	−3.265	−1.918
3529	Chemical products, nec	1.66	0.507	−1.245	−2.792	−3.530
355	Rubber products	1.50	−5.725	−1.374	−0.730	−7.829
356	Plastic products	2.98	0.147	−0.772	−2.689	−3.314
361	Pottery, china, etc.	1.15	−1.322	−0.947	−3.597	−5.866
362	Glass & products	0.88	−2.937	−1.530	−2.888	−7.355
369	Non-metallic products, nec	2.52	−1.144	−0.549	−2.965	−4.658
371	Iron & steel	2.54	−6.445	0.628	−9.413	−15.230
372	Non-ferrous metals	1.07	−6.902	−0.073	−2.308	−9.283
381	Metal products	6.37	−2.769	−1.029	−3.777	−7.575
3825	Office & computing machinery	1.04	11.808	−1.716	−9.702	0.390
3829	Machinery & equipment, nec	15.18	−3.658	−1.466	−2.318	−7.442
3832	Radio, TV & communication equipment	6.49	5.922	−1.612	−7.352	−3.042
3839	Electrical apparatus, nec	4.99	−0.469	−2.082	−2.549	−5.100
3841	Shipbuilding and repairing	1.95	−3.091	0.228	−4.714	−5.577
3842	Railroad equipment	0.70	−7.988	−0.259	0.274	−7.973
3843	Motor vehicles	6.28	−0.865	−3.177	−6.277	−10.319
3844	Motorcycles & bicycles	0.12	−9.586	−0.526	−3.777	−13.889
3845	Aircraft	3.79	−0.882	1.733	−3.489	−2.638
3849	Transport equipment, nec	0.08	2.468	−1.934	0.086	0.620

Source: OECD Stan Database (1994)

a model from partial equilibrium analysis and regresses employment on wage rate, income, capital–labour ratio and export–import ratio, using times series data for five sectors. This is a labour-theoretic approach to analyse the impact of trade on employment. Hine and Wright (Chapter 6 in this volume) have made an interesting contribution in

Table 5.4b Estimated impact of demand, imports and labour productivity on UK manufacturing employment (from 1984–85 to 1989–90)

SITC	Description	% of labour force	$\hat{C}$	$\hat{S}$	$-\hat{A}$	$\hat{L}$
3112	Food	11.16	1.063	0.331	−0.983	0.411
313	Beverages	1.64	1.750	−0.116	−2.959	−1.325
314	Tobacco	0.31	−0.481	0.485	−13.054	−13.050
322	Wearing apparel	6.49	3.453	−1.923	−4.065	−2.535
323	Leather & products	0.42	0.050	−1.405	−2.068	−3.423
324	Footwear	1.09	3.693	−1.347	−3.880	−1.534
331	Wood products	2.04	4.053	−0.037	−4.258	−0.242
332	Furniture & fixtures	2.77	7.601	−0.185	−3.910	3.506
341	Paper & products	3.48	4.933	−0.114	−5.291	−0.472
342	Printing & publishing	7.15	7.531	−0.192	−6.471	0.868
3522	Drugs & medicines	1.74	8.505	−0.821	−4.986	2.698
3529	Chemical products, nec	1.80	4.060	0.194	−3.115	1.139
355	Rubber products	1.47	4.041	−0.312	−4.745	−1.016
356	Plastic products	3.91	10.178	−0.250	−4.650	5.278
361	Pottery, china, etc.	1.23	5.377	−1.337	−3.107	0.933
362	Glass & products	0.99	5.845	−0.395	−3.460	1.990
369	Non-metallic products, nec	2.68	5.840	−0.511	−4.571	0.758
371	Iron & steel	2.18	1.893	0.169	−5.757	−3.695
372	Non-ferrous metals	0.99	3.360	−0.467	−5.036	−2.143
381	Metal products	7.69	5.361	−1.149	−3.804	0.408
3825	Office & computing machinery	1.27	11.094	1.273	−8.701	3.666
3829	Machinery & equipment, nec	14.33	5.462	−1.192	−5.949	−1.679
3832	Radio, TV & communication equipment	6.15	2.543	−0.158	−4.015	−1.630
3839	Electrical apparatus, nec	4.90	3.911	−0.310	−4.532	−0.931
3841	Shipbuilding and repairing	1.51	−0.399	−1.899	−3.406	−5.704
3842	Railroad equipment	0.44	1.883	−2.692	−9.608	−10.417
3843	Motor vehicles	6.10	8.965	−0.804	−9.292	−1.131
3844	Motorcycles & bicycles	0.08	8.228	−7.065	−9.786	−8.623
3845	Aircraft	3.91	7.615	1.198	−8.796	0.017
3849	Transport equipment, nec	0.08	4.153	−0.850	−2.980	0.323

Source: OECD Stan Database (1994)

this area. One obvious step is to relate employment directly to trade performance and to find how strong is the empirical relationship between unemployment and trade performance. For this limited purpose, the estimates of unemployment (ΔL_m), as in Table 5.3a, are regressed

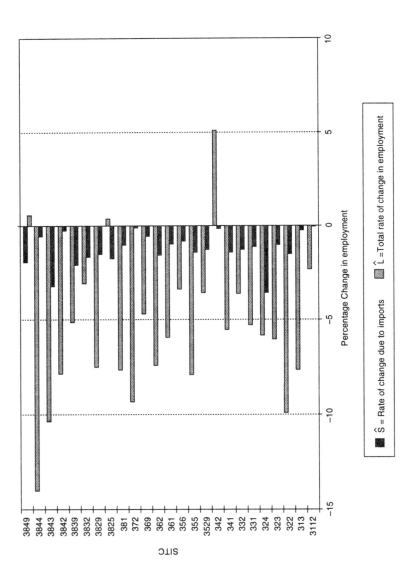

Figure 5.6 Relative importance of imports in employment change 1979–80 to 1984–85

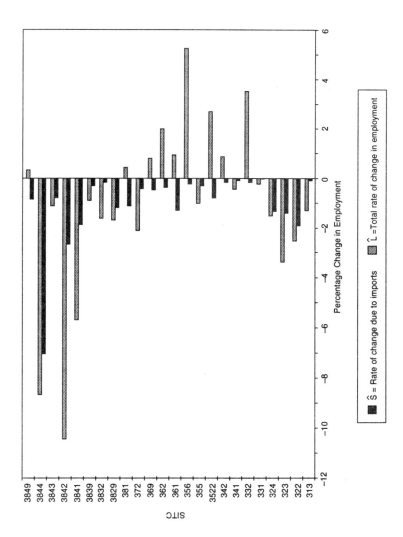

Figure 5.7 Relative importance of imports in employment change 1984–85 to 1989–90

Table 5.5

YEAR	Constant	Independent Variable $(X - M)$	R^2	F-ratio
1979–80	−4.2 (−1.27)	−0.01 (−1.47)	0.06	2.2
1984–85	−5.7 (−1.46)	0.02 (10.46)	0.76	109.4
1989–90	−11.1 (−1.61)	0.02 (9.49)	0.72	90.11

on trade balance for 32 sectors for 1979–80, 1984–5, and 1989–90. Table 5.5 presents these cross-section results. The estimated coefficient of trade balance for 1979–80 is negative but insignificant while the estimated coefficients for 1984–5 and 1989–90 are positive and highly significant, albeit small, noting that the figures in parentheses are the *t*-values. It is not clear how to interpret this result that trade balance is positively related to unemployment estimated on the basis of the *ceteris paribus* assumption. It is possible that an increase in trade balance is caused by an increase in labour productivity which, in turn, increases unemployment. However, regressing actual employment (L) on trade balance $(X - M)$ we did not get any significant results.

In order to be able to link changes in employment to international trade in a meaningful way, one requires not only a trade-theoretic framework but also a growth-theoretic framework. The hiatus here is to assert the straightforward implications of growth theory for employment. This is considered to be the most appropriate framework when unemployment is affected by massive deindustrialization and the economy is in transition from one equilibrium to another. We, therefore, do not use the labour-theoretic approach but concentrate on the growth-theoretic proposition that changes in employment are determined fundamentally by investment, that is, human and physical capital accumulation. Thus, for whatever reason, if disinvestment occurs, unemployment is likely to rise. It is new investment of physical capital which will lead to a fall in unemployment. This connects employment to human capital in the sense that acquirement of skill, in general, leads to employment. That is, a growing economy with new physical investment incorporating the latest vintage will require labour with appropriate skills so that growth of human capital is complementary to new investment which brings about economic growth. The first hypothesis that needs to be tested, therefore, is the following:

Table 5.6

Year	Constant	Independent Variable [K]	Independent Variable [H]	R^2	F-ratio
1980	−0.679 (−1.870)	0.223 (2.425)*	0.639 (6.024)**	0.86	115.32
1985	−0.918 (−2.169)	0.378 (3.963)**	0.431 (4.294)**	0.85	83.50
1990	−1.405 (−3.334)	0.262 (2.513)*	0.571 (4.696)**	0.87	104.18

**, * significant at 1% and 5% levels respectively

$$L_i = f(H_i, K_i), \text{ where } f_H > 0, f_k > 0 \tag{5}$$

In equation (5), L = employment, H = human capital, and K = physical capital. Assuming a log-linear relationship, L is regressed[9] on H and K (measurements of which are explained in note 10) for 3 different years, namely 1980, 1985 and 1990. Table 5.6 presents the results, which are surprisingly robust. The values of R^2 are high and all the estimated coefficients are significant, noting that the significance level of human capital is consistently higher. The coefficients of K and H are the elasticities of employment with respect to K and H, and all the elasticities are less than unity.

It now becomes clear that to link employment to international trade, a trade theoretic framework is required where trade performance is dependent on physical capital and human capital. We, therefore, turn to the neofactor proportions theory which, in its basic form, specifies trade performance as a function of K, H, and L. Trade performance or trade competitiveness is usually measured by $(X - M)$ where X and M are respectively sectoral exports and sectoral imports. We, therefore, have the following:

$$(X - M)_i = g(K_i, H_i, L_i), \text{ where } g_K > 0, g_H > 0, g_L < 0 \tag{6}$$

We now have a two-equation system given by equations (5) and (6). As explained earlier, employment is determined by K and H, while trade balance (TB) is determined jointly by K, H, and L. Thus, re-gressing L on TB directly will yield poors results, and this indeed is the case for 1980, 1985 and 1990 for the UK. Thus, a two-stage method becomes necessary since the the impact of trade on employment comes from the determinants of trade balance. The first step of the two-stage

Table 5.7

Year	Constant	Independent Variable [$\hat{TB}$]	R^2	F-ratio
1980	134.291 (4.041)	0.256 (3.374)**	0.27	11.38
1985	100.324 (4.147)	−0.208 (−3.646)**	0.30	13.29
1990	90.939 (3.655)	−0.089 (−3.373)**	0.27	11.38

**, * significant at 1% and 5% levels respectively

Table 5.8

Year	Constant	Independent Variable [$\hat{TB}$]	R^2	F-ratio
1980	90.185 (3.356)	0.363 (6.490)**	0.57	42.12
1985	115.604 (4.267)	−0.147 (−2.042)*	0.12	4.17
1990	108.270 (3.960)	−0.063 (−1.924)	0.11	3.69

**, * significant at 1% and 5% levels respectively

method is to estimate equation (6) by regressing TB on K, H, and L, to compute the predicted values of trade balance ($\hat{TB}$). The second step is to regress sectoral employment on $\hat{TB}$. In order to avoid obvious objections, we have two specifications of the trade balance regression equations, in one of which we drop L. The results, presented in Tables 5.7 and 5.8, are based on estimates of TB which respectively include and exclude L. The evidence is that estimated trade balance has small but significant negative impact on employment for the years 1985 and 1990 while the results for 1980 show positive and significant impact. This is not surprising for the UK where deindustrialization seriously occured at the beginning of the 1980s. This empirical finding does point to the conclusion that international trade had a negative impact on employment in the 1980s. Regressing unskilled labour only on the same two sets of predicted values of TB, we get similar results which

Table 5.9

Year	Constant	Independent Variable [$\hat{TB}$]	R^2	F-ratio
1980	70.982 (3.348)	0.225 (5.111)**	0.45	26.11
1985	76.081 (4.146)	−0.116 (−2.401)*	0.16	5.77
1990	68.732 (3.688)	−0.054 (−2.392)*	0.16	5.72

**, * significant at 1% and 5% levels respectively

Table 5.10

Year	Constant	Independent Variable [$\hat{TB}$]	R^2	F-ratio
1980	102.356 (4.129)	0.123 (2.459)*	0.16	6.04
1985	64.387 (4.101)	−0.163 (−4.408)**	0.39	19.43
1990	53.851 (3.397)	−0.757 (−4.511)**	0.39	20.34

**, * significant at 1% and 5% levels respectively

are presented in Tables 5.9 and 5.10 which respectively include and exclude L in estimating equation (6). It is interesting to note that the t-values and the values of R^2 have increased both for 1985 and 1990 when employment of unskilled labour is the dependent variable.

CONCLUSIONS

Deindustrialization in the UK during the 1980s was fairly deep. Both gross import penetration (GIP) and net import penetration (NIP) indicate the severity of that process. There seems to be a long-term (1975–90) decay in trade competitiveness in the manufacturing sector both in terms of the import penetration measures and measures of revealed comparative advantage. The impact of import penetration on UK manufacturing employment has been empirically assessed by using both the import-penetration method and the accounting-identity method. The impact appears to be fairly significant. Lastly, we have put forward a two-stage econometric approach in order to analyze the impact of trade on employment. The theoretical rationale of this approach is derived, on the one hand, from the growth theoretic proposition that disinvestment in the senescent industries reduces employment while new investment in the nascent industries (in the form of physical capital incorporating the latest vintage which requires human capital as a complementary factor) increases employment, and on the other hand, from the trade theoretic proposition that the net trade balance in the manufacturing products is determined by physical capital, human capital and labour. This two-stage approach essentially involves regressing employment on estimated values of trade balance when trade balance is estimated by using the neofactor proportions model. The cross-section results, using both total employment and employment of unskilled labour separately as dependent variables, show significantly that the trade balance has had a negative impact on UK manufacturing employment during the 1980s.

Notes

* This chapter has benefited from the comments of V. Balasubramanyam, John Black, Alec Chrystal and Adrian Wood. The author wishes to thank Andrew Ramsden for excellent research assistance.
 1. This study includes not only an analysis of closed plants and lost jobs but also an examination of the impact of private disinvestment on workers and their communities. A somewhat similar study has been carried out by Dore (1982) who analyses the decline of Blackburn, a Lancashire town in the UK.
 2. If both factors are sector-specific, the long-run production-possibility curve in Figure 5.1 need not necessarily be a smooth concave curve, as it essentially becomes the mapping of the production points like Q for various combinations of the sector-specific factors in the economy. It may easily be a wavy curve but it must always be negatively sloped, on the assumption that if investments falls in one industry, it increases in the other industry in the long run.
 3. This argument challenges the conventional wisdom. To quote Krugman and Lawrence (1993): 'The declining share of US employment in industry is often ascribed to a lack of manufacturing competitiveness, due to inadequate productivity growth. In fact, however, the shrinkage of that sector is largely due to its relatively *fast* productivity growth as compared with services' (pp. 7–8).
 4. The degree of openness is defined as $(X + M)/GDP$ where X = exports and M = imports.

5. The following respectively define gross and net import penetration:

$$M/(Q + M - X) \text{ and } (M - X)/(Q + M - X)$$

where Q = output, $(Q + M - X)$ = apparent consumption, and M and X are imports and exports respectively. We may also add here that revealed comparative advantage is measured by $(X - M)/(X + M)$.

6. This method estimates change in sectoral employment, ΔE_m, due solely to import penetration, say, between E_{1980} and E_{1985}, and then to find $\Delta E_m/\Delta E$ where ΔE is the actual change so that $\Delta E = E_{1985} - E_{1980}$.

The first step is to estimate E^*_{1985} in the following manner: $E^*_{1985} = \alpha E_{1985}$ where $\alpha = (1 - NIP_{1980})/(1 - NIP_{1985})$. Using the definition of NIP, α can also be expressed as:

$$\alpha = \left(\frac{Q}{Q + (M - X)}\right)_{1980} \div \left(\frac{Q}{Q + (M - X)}\right)_{1985}$$

where $Q/[Q + (M - X)] = S$ is the share of output in apparent consumption, so that $S = (1 - NIP)$. The second step is to estimate the change in sectoral employment, due only to an increase in import penetration, by using $\Delta E_m = E^*_{1985} - E_{1985}$ where E_{1985} is the actual sectoral employment. The third step is to find the actual change in employment ΔE, and then to find ΔE_m as a proportion of ΔE. This will estimate the contribution of import penetration to the change in employment. This third step has a clear meaning if actual unemployment is revealed.

7. Martin and Evans (1981) point out, for example, that the domestic producers may react to import competition and may endeavour to raise labour productivity. If this is the case, then a part of the employment loss due to productivity gains may be ascribed indirectly to import competition.

8. The formula used here is $A_t = A_0(1 + r)^n$ where A_0 is the initial value, A_t is the value at period t, and n is the difference between the initial period and period t, so that r is the average annual rate of growth.

9. The Goldfeld-Quandt tests on the three regressions show that heteroscedasticity does not exist.

10. Physical capital stock is measured by the sum of the sector's real investment of the preceeeding 10 years with radioactive depreciation of 10 per cent per annum. Human capital is measured by capitalizing the wage differential between skilled labour and unskilled labour at 10 per cent rate and then multiplying by the quantity of skilled labour.

References

Batra, R. N. and Pattanaik, P. K. (1971) 'Factor Market Imperfections and Gains from Trade', *Oxford Economic Papers*, pp. 182–188.

Bhagwati, J. N. (1982) 'Shifting Comparative Advantage, Protectionist Demands and Response', in J. N. Bhagwati (ed.), *Import Competition and Response* (Chicago: NBER, University of Chicago Press).

Bluestone, B. and Harrison, B. (1982) *The Deindustrialization of America* (New York: Basic Books).

Brecher, R. A. (1974a) 'Minimum Wage Rates and the Pure Theory of International Trade', Quarterly *Journal of Economics*, pp. 98–116.

Brecher, R. A. (1974b) 'Optimal Commercial Policy for a Minimum-wage Economy', *Journal of International Economics*, 4, pp. 139–149.

Cable, C. (1977) 'British Protectionism and Ldc Imports', *ODI Review*, 2, pp. 29–48.

Dore, R. P. (1982) 'Adjustment in Process: A Lancashire Town' in J. N. Bhagwati (ed.) *Import Competition and Response*, (Chicago: NBER, University of Chicago Press.

Frank, C. R. Jr. (1977) Foreign Trade and Domestic Aid, (Washington: Brookings Institution).

Grossman, G. M. (1982) 'Comment' in Chapter 13, in J. N. Bhagwati (ed.), *Import Competition and Response* (Chicago: NEBR, University of Chicago Press).

Grossman, G. M. (1986) 'Imports as a Cause of Injury: The Case of the US Steel Industry', *Journal of International Economics*, 20, pp. 201–223.

Kierzkowski, H. (1980) 'Displacement of labour by imports of manufacturers', *World Development*, pp. 753–762.

Kreuger, A. O. (1980a) 'Restructuring for Import Competition from Developing Countries, I: Labour Displacement and Economic Redeployment in the *United States'*, *Journal of Policy Modeling*, 2, pp. 165–184.

Kreuger, A. O. (1980b) 'Impact of Foreign Trade on Employment in United States' in J. Black and B. Hindley (eds), *Current Issues in Commercial Policy and Diplomacy* (London: Macmillan).

Krugman, P. and R. Z. Lawrence (1993) 'Trade, Jobs, and Wages', NEBR *Working Paper No. 4478.*

Lapan, H. (1976) 'International Trade, Factor-market Distortions, and the Optimal Dynamic Subsidy', *American Economic Review*, pp. 335–346.

Lawrence, R. Z. (1983) 'Is Trade Deindustrializing America? A medium term perspective', *Brookings Papers on Economic Activity*, pp. 129–171.

Lefeber, L. (1971) 'Trade and Minimum Wage rates' in J. N. Bhagwati *et al.*, (eds) *Trade, Balance of Payments, and Growth: Papers in Honour of Charles P. Kindleberger* North-Holland, Amsterdam.

Luttrell, C. B. (1978) 'Imports and Jobs: The Observe and the Unobserved', *Federal Reserve Bank of St Louis Review*, June, pp. 2–10.

Martin, J. P. and Evans, J. M. (1981) 'Notes on Measuring the Employment Displacement Effects of Trade by the Accounting Procedure', *Oxford Economic Papers*, 33, pp. 154–164.

Matusz, S. J. (1986) 'Implicit Contracts, Unemployment and International Trade', *Economic Journal*, pp.307–322.

Melvin, J. R. (1985) 'Unemployment, International Trade, and Welfare in a Fixed-coefficient Model', *The Manchester School of Economic and Social Studies*, pp. 149–155.

Mussa, M. (1982) 'Government policy and the adjustment process', in J. N. Bhagwati (ed), *Import Compitition and Response* (Chicago: NBER, University of Chicago Press).

Neary, J. P. (1982) 'International Capital Mobility, Wage Stickiness, and the

Case for Adjustment Assistance' in J. N. Bhagwati (ed), *Import Competition and Response* (Chicago: NBER University of Chicago Press).

Neary, J. P. (1985) 'Theory and Policy of Adjustment in an open Economy', in D. Greenaway (ed), *Current Issues in International Trade*, (London: Macmillan).

Srinivasan T. N. and Bhagwati, J. N. (1975) 'Alternative Policy Rankings in a Large, Open Economy with Sector-specific Minimum Wage', *Journal of Economy Theory*, 11, pp. 356–371.

Stern R. M. and Maskus, K. E. (1981) 'Determinants of the Structure of US Foriegn Trade, 1958–76', *Journal of International Economics*, 11, pp. 207–224.

Wolter, F. (1977) 'Adjusting to Imports from Developing Countries: the Evidence from a Human Capital Rich Natural Source Poor Country', in H. Guersch (ed) *Reshaping the World Economic Order,* (Tubingen: Mohr).

6 Trade and Manufacturing Employment in the United Kingdom

Robert C. Hine and Peter Wright

INTRODUCTION

One of the salient features of the UK economy over the last 15 years has been the large fall in manufacturing employment: from 7.3 million in 1979 the industial labour force fell to 5.5 million in 1983 and, more slowly but persistently, to 4.3 million in 1994. Only one year in the last 16 has seen an increase in manufacturing jobs, and within the total there has also been a shift from full-time to part-time work. From an employment perspective there has therefore been a substantial deindustrialization over recent years and this has been associated with a rise in the level of unemployment, which has persisted at a high level compared with that recorded in the 1950s and 1960s. Viewed more positively, since 1979 the UK has achieved a modest expansion in industrial production with a considerably reduced workforce. With employment falling by 40 per cent between 1979 and 1993, and output in real terms expanding 16 per cent, the rise in the output to labour ratio has been, if not miraculous, at least substantial.

In a market economy sectoral employment is the outcome of a combination of supply and demand factors which are themselves subject to a continuous process of change. Within this constellation of pressures, an important issue for economic policy is the role which trade factors play. It is evident that even a balanced expansion of imports and exports – a circumstance not often achieved in recent British experience – may not be neutral with respect to either the quantity or skill mix jobs in the national economy. What is particularly at issue is the quantitative significance of trade factors compared with other sources of labour market adjustment in the UK. This requires a consideration of both the impact effects of trade as well as the potentially more significant indirect effects through changes in productivity.

Table 6.1   Estimated direct labour content of UK trade 1979–91

Year	Tigers		Dragons		Japan		China	
	Exports	Imports	Exports	Imports	Exports	Imports	Exports	Imports
1979	43	89	14	7	22	72	5	9
1980	42	80	14	6	19	76	5	6
1981	42	89	12	7	17	81	5	4
1982	43	75	14	8	17	68	5	2
1983	40	84	12	8	17	86	5	3
1984	41	91	11	10	18	86	6	6
1985	39	78	11	12	18	84	6	7
1986	38	89	10	13	20	98	6	10
1987	41	107	10	15	23	99	9	7
1988	39	121	11	20	26	108	9	7
1989	41	124	12	25	28	106	10	6
1990	44	108	14	29	30	96	12	7
1991	44	110	14	33	27	95	15	4

Year	USA		EU		Total	
	Exports	Imports	Exports	Imports	Exports	Imports
1979	124	156	585	760	1 389	1 428
1980	113	159	572	667	1 367	1 281
1981	114	159	454	598	1 195	1 212
1982	109	151	444	650	1 141	1 226
1983	116	158	423	692	1 049	1 296
1984	139	169	438	717	1 065	1 349
1985	156	162	459	726	1 081	1 331
1986	146	137	488	783	1 081	1 402
1987	143	134	529	807	1 098	1 456
1988	134	149	535	833	1 071	1 566
1989	143	168	573	880	1 109	1 650
1990	137	159	634	864	1 172	1 541
1991	120	151	638	779	1 131	1 437

Figures are given in 1000s

Source: Own calculations based on data from HMSO Census of Manufacturing and OECD Foreign Trade Statistics

Attention has recently focused on trade with the East Asian countries as a source of adjustment pressures. Their dynamic growth performance and their determined effort – already realized in the case of Japan – to move upmarket, from simple labour-intensive manufactures to sophisticated advanced technology products, is seen as potentially disruptive for the European economies. Table 6.1 reports some calculations of the labour content of trade in manufactures with the East Asian countries[1] and the rest of the world using a simple methodology: the ratio of employment to gross output in each UK industry is applied to the value of trade in that industry. These are illustrated in Figure 6.1. Since 1979, the Asian countries' share of the labour content of UK imports is estimated by this method to have risen from 12 per cent to 17 per cent – they remain a relatively small source of imports but a rapidly growing one. While the labour content of UK imports as a whole was stable between 1979 and 1991 – and that of exports declined by 258 000 – the labour content of imports from the East Asian countries rose by 70 000. The export figure was unchanged. In the context of an overall decline in UK manufacturing employment of 3 million during the same period, it appears that the direct effect of trade changes, even with the East Asian countries, has been modest.

In this paper, which sets out some preliminary findings from a recently begun research project, we examine the issue of the role of trade in the changes in manufacturing employment in the UK in two steps which explore different methodological approaches but draw on the same disaggregated database. We pay particular attention to trade with the East Asian countries. The first approach attempts to isolate the salient features of employment change across UK manufacturing industry and to gauge the relative importance of trade and non-trade factors using a growth-accounting framework. A drawback of this approach is its failure to address properly the indirect effects of trade on productivity. The second part of the study thus develops an econometric model of industry level employment in the UK with particular emphasis on the role which trade factors play. Our final section draws some tentative conclusions.

THE IMPACT OF TRADE ON LABOUR MARKET OUTCOMES

There is some controversy concerning the likely impact of trade on the labour market. Trade in the Heckscher–Ohlin (H–O) model derives from differences in relative factor endowments between countries. Thus, since the UK is relatively richly endowed in capital and skilled labour, the H–O model predicts that the UK will specialize in capital and skill-intensive products, whereas less developed countries will specialize in low skill, labour-intensive goods. This pattern of specialization results in an increase in the demand, and hence the price, of both capital and skilled labour in the UK. The wage rates of unskilled labour decline. Within the H–O framework it is a standard assumption that factors of production are fully employed. Opening up to trade may lead to a reallocation of factors but not to unemployment.

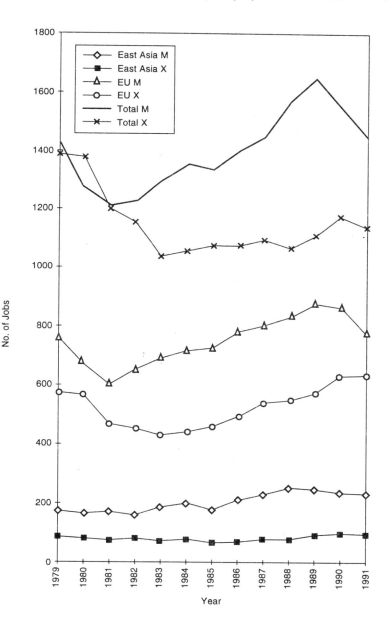

Figure 6.1 Estimated Direct Labour Content of UK Trade 1979–91

In contrast to the H–O view, in reality changing trade patterns may cause large adjustment problems. Workers with sector specific skills may find it hard to move from contracting to expanding industries as firms to adjust to changing competitive pressures. This problem will be exacerbated if there is hysteresis in labour or product markets, when even temporary external shocks may lead to permanently higher levels of employment.

More recently, 'new' theories of international trade have emphasized the role of product differentiation and economies of scale as motivations for trade. These considerations are important as the effects of inter- and intra-industry trade may be considerably different. Increased inter-industry trade may require workers to move from one industry to another, which may necessitate retraining, as the UK pattern of specialization changes. Intra-industry trade may however only require changes from one process to another within the same industry, with little re-skilling necessary.

In addition to the effects of trade on the labour market suggested above, trade may also have an indirect effect on employment via induced productivity growth. It is frequently argued, for example, that domestically concentrated industries use their resources in a relatively inefficient manner due to the lack of competitive pressure, that is, they are x-inefficient. Trade, especially that from low wage economies, increases the scope of competition and so forces firms to become relatively more efficient in their use of labour resources.

TRADE AND JOBS IN UK MANUFACTURING 1979–91: AN ACCOUNTING APPROACH

A number of studies have attempted to quantify the effect of trade, and especially the growth of imports, on employment. They have used various methodologies including factor content analysis and growth accounting (see Wood, 1994 for a survey and critique). The latter technique involves the use of a simple accounting procedure to decompose the contributions of domestic demand, imports, exports, and productivity change on employment growth. The objective is usually to quantify the relative impact of the changes on the evolution of manufacturing employment. The general conclusion is that trade has played a very small role in the loss of manufacturing jobs in the industrial countries. A UNIDO (1986) study, for example, that the loss of industrial jobs in six large developed countries between 1975 and 1980 accounted for by trade changes was only 1.5 per cent of that generated by productivity growth. Similarly, Cable (1983) found for the UK, in 1970–5, that productivity increase accounted for 30 times more job losses than increased imports from low wage economies.

As Martin and Evans (1981) point out, the growth accounting technique suffers from two serious deficiencies. First, there are a number of different formulations in use which reflect the somewhat arbitrary nature of the accounting identities and which may generate somewhat different results. Secondly, the accounting systems fails to address the interaction between the accounting components, and especially between changes in trade and changes in productivity. Whilst recognizing that these are substantial criticisms, we have applied the technique as a means of getting a first insight into what has been happening in the UK manufacturing sector, and in particular into the nexus of relationships between demand, trade, employment and productivity. Our intention is to focus on the short-run impact of trade on employment and productivity which we will then pursue through a more elaborate econometric model.

Studies which use the growth accounting approach attempt to relate changes in employment to changes in domestic demand (apparent consumption), exports and imports, and average labour productivity. In some cases (for example, UNIDO, 1986) a further elements is introduced to capture indirect effects on employment, based on input–output tables. As noted above, there are several versions of the growth accounting approach but all make use of two basic identities:

$$D_{it} = Q_{it} - X_{it} + M_{it} \tag{1}$$

$$P_{it} = Q_{it}/E_{it} \tag{2}$$

where D_{it} is domestic demand (apparent consumption) of the *i*th product in time period *t*; Q_{it} is domestic production; X_{it} are exports; M_{it} are imports; P_{it} is average labour productivity and E_{it} is employment (*D, Q, X and M* are measured in constant prices). Substituting equation (2) into equation (1) and then differentiating with respect to time gives an expression for the growth of employment as the sum of four decomposed elements. Neglecting a (second order) interaction term and weighting *D, X* and *M* by their respective shares in domestic output results in the following formula (see Frank, 1977):

$$r_E = r_D(D/Q) + r_X(X/q) - r_M(M/Q) - r_P \tag{3}$$

where r_E, r_D, r_X, r_M and r_P indicate rates of change of the respective variables. Equation (3) expresses the rate of growth of employment as the result of domestic factors $[r_D(D/Q) - r_P]$ and net foreign trade $[r_X(X/Q) - r_M(M/Q)]$.

In this paper, the growth accounting analysis is applied on to an integrated trade, employment and output database of UK manufacturing industry covering the years 1979 to 1991 and disaggregated at the four digit SIC level. There are approximately 185 industries for which full data are available, the precise number varying a little from year to year. Output and employment data are taken from the UK Census of Manufacturing; for trade, OECD data in $US have been converted at current exchange rates and reclassified from the SITC at the five digit level to the SIC. Data have been deflated using an index of manufacturing output prices. This database provides a very detailed picture of changes in the pattern of employment which have taken place in the United Kingdom over the 1980s and 1990s. However a number of caveats must be borne in mind regarding its use. Firstly, since it collected from the Census of Production it only refers to manufacturing industry and therefore to a minority of employment within the United Kingdom.[2] Developments of employment that have taken place within the service sector are therefore beyond the scope of this study. This is of potential importance since the 1980s have seen an increasing use of outsourcing of functions by manufacturing companies, with many activities previously done by direct employees now being done by external firms. If these secondary units are not included within the Census of Production sampling frame then a decline in employment will be registered even if no job losses have occurred. Another potential accounting problem is that the employment figures used in this study represent a head count of employees within the companies sampled. No attempt is made to assess whether the workers concerned are full-time or part-time and, to the extent that this ratio has changed, movements in the employment figures are potentially misleading. It should also be remembered that manufacturing itself consists of a diverse number of separate industries producing capital, intermediate and final products or outputs akin to services. These distinctions are however ignored for the sake of tractability. Finally, because the focus of this analysis is at the individual industry level, sectoral or economy wide influences which might affect an industry's employment are not analysed. Such factors might include the level of the exchange rate or the current state of expectations within the macro-economy.

The analysis can be used to address two related questions. First,

Table 6.2 Decomposition of employment change: median industry values for 1979–1991 and sub-periods.

	% *Change*		1979–83	1983–89	1989–91	1979–91	1979–91
D	Employment, actual		−27.26	−4.44	−8.76	−38.98	−38.38
	Apparent						
	consumption		−17.65	27.97	−13.57	−12.00	−8.35
X	Exports		−2.11	5.77	0.68	0.90	0.83
M	Imports		−0.30	−11.77	1.75	−7.55	
P	Productivity		−10.58	−25.48	2.58	−36.34	−38.10
D + X + M + P		total	−30.69	−5.74	−8.07	−53.76	−55.87
	Imports	East Asia					−1.24
		Other					−6.94
Number of			185	184	197	184	162
industries							

Figures are given in 1000s

what has been the relative importance of trade and other factors in the general evolution of UK manufacturing employment during the period 1979 to 1991 and sub-periods thereof? To consider this issue a means of representing the average outcomes is required since the analysis produces rates of change for each industry. Here the median values have been used. The second question which can be asked is – given that there has been a wide range of actual experience among UK industries – what distinguishes industries which have increasing employment from those where there is a decline, and to what extent in particular does their trade experience differ? For this purpose Spearman rank order correlation coefficients have been computed among the relevant variables, especially between actual employment change and the decomposed elements. A priori we expect increases in apparent consumption and exports to have a positive effect on income and increases in imports and productivity – at least in the short run – to have a negative effect.

Table 6.2 summarises the main results of the accounting analysis for UK manufacturing for 1979–91, and for selected sub-periods, as reflected in the median industry value. For the period as a whole, the sum of the accounting components substantially overstates the actual change, whether measured using medians or means, but as can be seen from Table 6.2 this discrepancy largely disappears if more homogeneous periods in relation to the growth of the UK economy are used. The results for the period as a whole are in line with those of previous studies of this kind: productivity growth appears to be the main factor 'accounting for' the loss of labour in UK industry over this period. That is, the growth in home demand and exports was not sufficient to offset the reduced labour requirements from rising productivity. According to this analysis, trade factors played only a secondary role in job losses in the sense that the direct displacement effect of rising imports was small relative to the productivity effect. What the analysis does not, and cannot, show is how far the productivity effect was itself the outcome of growing trade pressure. Table 6.2 shows that the median exposure to trade through both exports and imports increased substantially during the 1980s and this must have increased pressure on industry to raise efficiency in labour use in order to remain viable.

A different perspective is given by conducting the analysis on an annual basis (Table 6.3). The match between actual and estimated changes in employment is close, with employment dropping sharply at the beginning and end of the period and showing some recovery, or at least a less steep decline, during the second half of the 1980s. The productivity component appears less important in the annual changes than for the period as a whole. Part of the explanation is that whereas the productivity component had a negative effect on employment in all except the two end years, the apparent consumption component was more variable: negative in five cases and positive in the remaining seven. Thus over the period as a whole gains and losses associated with changes in apparent consumption were largely offsetting, in contrast to the productivity effect which was largely cumulative. On a year-to-year basis it appears that changes in apparent consumption are the biggest single component in eight out of 12 cases, changes in productivity in three (1981–2, 1982–3 and 1984–5), and changes in trade in just one (1985–6).

The annual data show a pronounced cyclical pattern in apparent consumption with peaks in 1983–4 and 1987–8. Imports, as a component in domestic demand, move broadly in line with apparent consumption. The pace of productivity growth appears also to be linked to the rate of change in domestic demand, rising fastest in periods of strong domestic demand (and import growth). The export component exhibits a more complex pattern of change reflecting developments in both domestic and international markets. If the analysis is extended to changes over successive three year periods the export component displays shows a simpler pattern, showing an upward trend but also reflecting the cyclical movement in the domestic economy. For imports, apparent consumption and productivity, the three year pattern follows very closely the annual one. Taking a growth in imports as having a negative effect on jobs and a growth in exports a positive one, the sum

Table 6.3 Decomposition of employment change: annual median industry values for 1979–1991

ONE YEAR

	1979–80	1980–81	1981–82	1982–83	1983–84	1984–85	1985–86	1986–87	1987–88	1988–89	1989–90	1990–91
Change in Apparent consumption	-10.68	-7.92	-1.07	5.31	5.72	1.45	0.19	6.82	8.16	3.05	-4.71	-10.11
Exports	-0.46	-1.77	0.01	0.01	0.96	1.06	-0.08	1	0.23	0.93	1.29	-0.31
Imports	1.73	-0.07	-1.08	-2.22	-2.3	-0.55	-0.75	-0.147	-0.191	-1.58	0.33	1.6
Productivity	3.12	-1.02	-5.88	-6.15	-5.26	-4.34	-0.8	-4.87	-4.31	-2.46	-0.55	2.54
Total above	-5.29	-11.15	-8.32	-4.88	-2.17	-1.15	-1.22	-0.99	0.77	0.43	-2.38	-6.42
Employment actual	-5.83	-10.96	-7.59	-4.67	-2.3	-1.37	-1.26	-0.86	-0.1	0	-2.51	-6.91

THREE YEAR (MIDPOINT)

	1980–81	1981–82	1982–83	1983–84	1984–85	1985–86	1986–87	1987–88	1988–89	1989–90
Change in Apparent consumption	-20.84	-0.38	10.27	14.4	6.25	6.82	13.39	20	6.57	-11.13
Exports	-2.36	-1.88	0.68	1.5	1.41	1	1.3	2.51	3.07	1.38
Imports	-0.75	2.78	6.58	5.35	3.16	1.47	5.64	6.14	3.56	-0.47
Productivity	4.46	14.62	18.86	17.28	10.94	4.87	9.91	13.7	7.38	1.21
Total above	-24.54	-26.38	-15.88	-9.69	-4.97	-0.99	-0.48	1.6	-1.84	-7.61
Employment actual	-23.58	-22.22	-13.64	-8.7	-4.65	-0.86	-1.05	0	-1.97	-8.33

Figures are given in 1000s

Note: Growth in imports and in productivity are recorded as having a negative effect on employment

of the trade effects was negative for jobs in eight out of the 12 cases in the annual analysis. The positive cases occurred only when the UK economy was stationary or declining. The peak loss was in 1982–3 when exports were stable but the growth in imports was estimated to displace over 2 per cent of manufacturing jobs. Changes in trade appear to have a rather consistent negative direct impact on the number of jobs in manufacturing. However, the timing of the losses has been mildly counter-cyclical with imports in particular falling back in periods of slack domestic demand and thereby cushioning the effect of the business cycle on jobs.

In summary, the accounting analysis suggests that over the long term rising labour productivity not accompanied by a similarly buoyant growth in domestic demand has resulted in large scale job losses. In a shorter term view, fluctuations in domestic demand have more prominent effects. In both contexts, fluctuations in trade have played a secondary and generally negative role.

Turning to the second part of the accounting analysis it is clear that the average results for UK industry as reflected in the median values are the result of a wide diversity of individual industry outcomes. About 10 per cent of the industries gained jobs between 1979 and 1991, but in over 25 per cent of cases employment fell by more than a half. What understanding can the accounting approach give of this diverse pattern? As indicated earlier the correlation between actual employment change and the components resulting from the accounting analysis will be examined. With 185 industries a correlation coefficient of ±0.15 or greater can be regarded as significantly different from zero at the 95 per cent level, and a coefficient of ±0.19 at the 99 per cent level.

Applying this procedure to the results for the period 1979–91 as a whole, the strongest correlation with actual employment change is with changes in apparent consumption: the correlation is close to +0.8 (Table 6.4). For shorter periods the correlation is less strong but still high – even on an annual basis it is typically around +0.5 (Table 6.5). The primary factor distinguishing growing from declining industries in employment terms seems to be therefore the behaviour of the domestic demand facing that industry. The growth of exports also, as expected, has a positive correlation with the growth of economic at the industry level. For the period as a whole the correlation coefficient is +0.34 (Table 6.4). On an annual basis, the correlation was positive in 11 out of 12 cases, and in nine instances the coefficient was significant at the 95 per cent level. However, there appears to be a progressive

Table 6.4 Decomposition of employment change: Spearman rank order correlation coefficients for 1979–1991 and sub-periods.

Correlation		1979–83	1983–89	1989–91	1979–91	1979–91
Change in	*Change in*					
Employment	Apparent consumption	0.696	0.68	0.415	0.794	0.79
Employment	Exports	0.528	0.167	*0.104*	0.345	0.355
Employment	Imports	0.286	0.227	*0.081*	0.289	
Employment	Productivity	*−0.111*	−0.146	−0.186	*−0.098*	*−0.056*
Employment	Total above	0.964	0.886	0.928	0.892	0.843
Employment	Imports from East Asia					0.084
Employment	Imports other					0.308
Exports	Imports	0.358	0.51	0.25	0.506	
Exports	Imports from East Asia					0.286
Exports	Imports other					0.532
Productivity	Exports	0.173	0.195	0.36	0.198	0.248
Productivity	Imports	0.182	0.243	0.326	0.225	
Productivity	Imports from East Asia					*0.119*
Productivity	Imports other					0.158

Note: Coefficients in italics not significantly different from zero at the 95% level

weakening of the link between export and employment changes during the 1980s, as export growth became more pronounced: the three non-significant coefficients all occur during the last four years.

Productivity growth is a two-edged sword as far as employment is concerned. In the short term, other things being equal, productivity growth reduces employment. In the longer term productivity growth enables firms to compete more effectively in foreign and domestic markets. These counter-posed factors are reflected in the correlation results. On an annual basis, the correlation between employment and productivity changes is negative in 11 out of 12 cases; in six cases the coefficient is significantly different from zero. But for the period as a whole, the coefficient while negative is not significant at the 95 per cent level. There is some empirical support therefore for the view that while productivity growth is likely to have a negative effect on employment in the short run, its long term implications are less clear.

The growth of imports, like that of productivity, should reduce jobs in an industry, other things being equal. However, the annual analysis suggests that import growth is *positively* associated with employment growth in all but three years, though only one of the coefficients is statistically significant. Taking the whole period, the positive correlation is almost as strong as for exports. Interestingly, when imports are split between those from East Asia and those from elsewhere, only the latter have a significantly positive correlation with employment change

Table 6.5   Decomposition of employment change: Spearman rank order correlation coefficients values for annual changes 1979–1991.

ONE YEAR

Correlation	*Change in*	*Change in*	1979–80	1980–81	1981–82	1982–83	1983–84	1984–85	1985–86	1986–87	1987–88	1988–89	1989–90	1990–91
	Employment	Apparent consumption	0.521	0.332	0.479	0.516	0.652	0.451	0.44	0.524	0.552	0.482	0.459	0.5
	Employment	Exports	0.312	0.433	0.29	0.145	0.158	0.165	0.167	0.157	-0.034	0.043	0.174	0.135
	Employment	Imports	0.115	0.089	-0.061	0.003	0.172	-0.015	0.062	0.013	0.067	0.068	-0.01	0.098
	Employment	Productivity	0.12	-0.227	-0.137	-0.197	-0.163	-0.163	-0.083	-0.117	-0.179	-0.09	-0.242	-0.064
	Employment	Total above	0.977	0.974	0.98	0.99	0.992	0.981	0.98	0.995	0.871	0.948	0.992	0.954
	Exports	Imports	0.032	0.038	0.101	0.271	0.479	0.426	0.229	0.281	0.467	0.204	0.138	0.273
	Productivity	Exports	0.282	0.141	0.14	0.317	0.16	0.146	0.229	0.281	0.467	0.204	0.138	0.273
	Productivity	Imports	0.231	0.187	0.112	0.196	0.195	0.19	0.265	0.111	0.312	0.319	0.313	0.247

THREE YEAR (MIDPOINT)

	Change in	*Change in*	1979–80	1980–81	1981–82	1982–83	1983–84	1984–85	1985–86	1986–87	1987–88	1988–89	1989–90	1990–91
	Employment	Apparent consumption	0.676	0.519	0.601	0.627	0.591	0.524	0.596	0.586	0.573	0.489		
	Employment	Exports	0.498	0.476	0.188	0.255	0.215	0.157	0.096	0.032	0.121	0.068		
	Employment	Imports	0.226	0.199	0.101	0.169	0.098	0.013	0.167	0.102	0.111	0.116		
	Employment	Productivity	-0.051	-0.201	-0.258	-0.185	-0.146	-0.117	-0.107	-0.087	-0.199	-0.191		
	Employment	Total above	0.950	0.969	0.955	0.0988	0.98	0.995	0.89	0.861	0.932	0.923		
	Exports	Imports	0.391	0.181	0.312	0.432	0.328	0.281	0.431	0.415	0.37	0.226		
	Productivity	Exports	0.238	0.183	0.124	0.196	0.186	0.065	0.16	0.22	0.243	0.187		
	Productivity	Imports	0.226	0.183	0.229	0.137	0.316	0.111	0.214	0.272	0.216	0.37		

Note: Coefficients in italics not significantly different from zero at the 95% level

(Table 6.4). Clearly for imports the assumption of 'other things being equal' does not hold and in particular imports appear to have grown fastest in industries with a strong expansion in domestic demand. Furthermore, import and export growth rates are strongly positively correlated reflecting the phenomenon of (marginal) intra-industry trade: in this scenario jobs lost to increased imports will be offset by jobs created in the same industries by rising exports. In general, the results suggest that the connection between changes in imports and changes in employment is not a simple one, and it is clearly incorrect to suppose that the industries which have the fastest growth of imports will also be those which suffer the sharpest decline in jobs. Trade policy may of course have played a role in this, to the extent that protection is heaviest in the older, declining industries.

This analysis has supported the view that the direct impact of trade on changes in manufacturing employment is generally secondary compared with the evolution of domestic demand and productivity. The key issue then is how much of the productivity growth results from increasing exposure to trade. In part, this will be a long-term phenomenon as industries reorganize to meet foreign competition. The growth accounting method has nothing to contribute on this. In part, however, there may be an immediate impact on productivity from trade expansion. As imports increase, the displacement effect is likely to force the closure of the least efficient firms; those are likely to be the more labour-intensive producers. By similar reasoning, a growth of exports will result from the expansion of the more efficient firms in the industry. Thus we expect a growth in imports and a growth in exports both to the positively correlated with productivity growth at the industry level. We find empirical support for this both in the results for the period as a whole and in the annual observations. For 1979–91 the correlation coefficients with employment are +0.23 for exports and +0.20 for imports: growth in productivity is associated with growth in trade (Table 6.4). From the annual results all the correlations are positive; for imports 10, and for exports eight, of the 12 cases have significant coefficients at the 95 per cent level (Table 6.5). These links between trade growth and productivity are interesting – even in the short-run the impact of trade on jobs may be greater than the simple displacement/creation scenario suggests. To explore them further requires a more powerful analytical technique, and the next section outlines an econometric methodology.

AN ECONOMETRIC ANALYSIS OF THE EFFECTS OF TRADE ON EMPLOYMENT

As described earlier, two main approaches have previously been used to investigate the employment effects of changing trade patterns; the factor content of trade and the accounting decomposition methods. More recently a number of studies have used regression techniques to examine the determinants of revealed comparative advantage. Of the existing econometric studies which have directly examined the impact of trade on labour market outcomes, the majority are based on North American data. Revenga (1992) uses a price measure to study the impact of trade on wages and employment in US manufacturing. She concludes that the import price elasticity of employment ranges between 0.24 and 0.39 and for wages between 0.06 and 0.09. Thus, most of the adjustment in the labour market in response to a trade shock occurs via employment. This result is in contrast to the findings of Grossman (1982), though Revenga attributes this to Grossman's use of ordinary least squares, as opposed to two-stage least squares, which biases the employment elasticity downwards.[3]

The econometric analysis of employment within this paper is conducted within the framework of a fairly simple static profit-maximizing model of firm behaviour. We begin by assuming a Cobb–Douglas production function of the form:

$$Q = A^\gamma K^\alpha L^\beta \tag{4}$$

where:
Q = real output of industry
K = capital stock
L = units of labour utilized

and where α, β represent the factor share coefficients and γ allows for factors changing the efficiency of the production process. A profit maximizing firm will employ labour and capital at such levels that the marginal product of labour equals the wage and the marginal product of capital equals the user cost. Thus, solving this system simultaneously to eliminate capital from the expression for firm output allows us to obtain the following expression:

$$Q = A^\gamma \left(\frac{\alpha L}{\beta} \cdot \frac{w}{c} \right)^\alpha L^\beta \tag{5}$$

Taking natural logarithms and rearranging equation (5) allows us to derive an expression for the firm's, and therefore the industry's, derived demand for labour of the form:

$$\ln L = \beta_0 + \beta_1 \ln(^w/_c) + \beta_2 \ln Q \tag{6}$$

This equation will form the basis of estimations conducted later in this paper.

The effect of trade on sectoral employment is investigated by modifying the production function by the introduction of import and export intensity terms.

MSH = import intensity = (imports/net home demand)

XSH = export intensity = (exports/output)

These two variables may exert two distinct influences on labour utilization. Firstly, the level of import and export intensity should reflect the differences in labour intensity associated with relative comparative advantage. Since the UK's comparative advantage has generally been in goods intensive in capital, the sign on import intensity should therefore be positive and on export intensity negative. Secondly, changes in the UK's competitive position may act as an incentive to rationalize on the use of resources. Thus increased import penetration would be expected to cause a decrease in labour usage. Similarly, it might be thought that the UK may need to become more efficient if it is to capture additional overseas markets. Hence, the signs on both changes in import penetration and changes in export penetration would be expected to be negative.

As is described in the previous section, the dataset which is used in this study has been assembled using a diversity of sources in order to allow the construction of an integrated database of industrial, labour market and trade statistics. Thus we have a panel of 160 manufacturing industries (corresponding to approximately four-digit SIC level of aggregation) from 1979 to 1991.[4] Since we have information both cross-sectionally and through time, within the above methodological framework the estimating equation for the panel of industries in our study is of the form:

$$\ln L_{it} = \Sigma \; \alpha_{ij}X_{jit} + \beta_1 \; \ln(w/c)_{it} + \beta_2 \; \ln Q_{it} + \varepsilon_{it} \quad t = 1 \ldots T_i \; (7)$$
$$i = 1 \ldots N$$

$$E(\varepsilon_{it}) = 0$$

$$Var(\varepsilon_{it}) = \sigma_\varepsilon^2$$

where:

L_{it} = total employment in industry i
$(w/c)_i$ = ratio of average real wage to user cost of capital in industry i
Q_i = real output in industry i
X_j = variables which affect the efficiency of the production function.

The estimation techniques which are used for analysis of the data are standard two factor fixed effects linear models for panel data. Whereas simple pooling of the data would result in a common intercept for all industries, the fixed effects model assumes that systematic differences across industries are captured by industry specific constant terms for each term. Thus the X matrix contains $N - 1$ group-specific constants. The model also allows for time-specific fixed effects by the introduction of year dummies. An advantage of using such a simple econometric framework is that it is trying to measure the immediate impact of trade on employment, and therefore remains close in spirit to the accounting approach of the previous section.

The estimation results of the panel data estimation for 1981–91 are given in Table 6.6. Column 1 shows the basic derived labour demand equations without modification to allow for trade effects, with the other columns allowing for a variety of augmentations. The basic equation produces results much as would be expected. Increases in industry output increase the demand for labour, whereas increases in the ratio of wages to the cost of capital cause labour demand to fall.

The degree of concentration is allowed to affect the demand for labour for a number of reasons. Firstly, the industrial economics literature emphasises that capital intensity and other features of technology which give rise to extensive economies of scale are associated with concentration. Derived labour demand would therefore be expected to be inversely related to concentration. In contrast, it is often argued that oligopolistic industries may be inefficient in their use of resources due to the lack of competitive pressures, suggesting that relatively more labour resources will be demanded in concentrated industries. As can be seen, the regression results indicate that concentrated industries

Table 6.6 The influence of trade on employment

	1	2	3	4	5	6	7
constant	−0.88(−2.164)	−0.70(−1.762)	−0.89(−2.273)	−0.89(−2.288)	−0.89(−2.296)	−0.89(−2.277)	−0.90(−2.296)
$\ln Q$	−0.57(31.627)	0.55(30.419)	0.62(34.513)	0.62(34.522)	0.62(34.504)	0.62(34.504)	0.62(34.308)
$\ln(w/c)$	−0.34(−5.965)	−0.33(−5.980)	−0.33(−6.027)	−0.33(−6.044)	−0.33(−6.047)	−0.33(−6.037)	−0.33(−6.053)
Concentration (5-firm)	−0.46e−2(−5.540)	−0.35e−2(−4.144)	−0.28e−2(−3.432)	−0.29e−2(−3.489)	−0.29e−2(−3.485)	−0.30e−2(−3.632)	−0.29e−2(−3.494)
concentration* $\ln Q$	0.38e−2(11.536)	0.34e−2(10.224)	0.29e−2(8.803)	0.29e−2(8.847)	0.29e−2(8.845)	0.30e−2(8.969)	0.29e−2(8.843)
MSH_{it}		−0.23(−3.567)					
XSH_{it}		−0.12(−2.261)					
ΔXSH			−0.27(−3.605)	−0.28(−3.784)	−0.28(−3.784)	−0.30(−3.978)	−0.29(−3.831)
ΔMSH			−0.33(−4.028)				
ΔMSH oecd				−0.29(−3.161)			
ΔMSH ec12					−0.27(−2.535)	−0.24(−2.240)	−0.26(−2.391)
ΔMSH otheroecd					−0.31(−2.165)	−0.30(−2.089)	−0.31(−2.149)
ΔMSH non-oecd				−0.47(−3.403)	−0.47(−3.396)		
ΔMSH E and SE Asia						−0.74(−4.217)	
ΔMSH Singapore							1.15(0.637)
ΔMSH South Korea							−0.26(−0.451)
ΔMSH Hong Kong							−0.70(−2.115)
ΔMSH Taiwan							−1.13(−1.984)
ΔMSH Other							−0.38(−2.036)
log-likelihood	1732.62	1770.60	1802.70	1804.67	1804.70	1808.16	1808.37
n	1726	1726	1726	1726	1726	1726	1726
period	1981–1991	1981–1991	1981–1991	1981–1991	1981–1991	1981–1991	1981–1991

Table 6.7 Test statistics for model one

	Likelihood-ratio	Sum of squares
constant term only	−2573.43	1993.47
group effects only	768.65	41.47
x variables only	−939.06	300.01
x and group effects	1464.26	18.52
x and industry and time effects	1732.06	13.58

generally employ less labour than non-concentrated industries, though the sensitivity of the level of employment to output falls as the degree of concentration rises. Note that the coefficients on the ratio of wages to the user cost of capital, concentration and of output appear to be stable across specifications.

It is also important to notice the important part that industry-specific fixed effects play in determining employment. Table 6.7 gives the log-likelihoods and sum of squares for a number of alternative models. A likelihood ratio test strongly rejects the simple pooled regression model in favour of the two way fixed effects model.

Column 2 (Table 6.6) shows the results of adding the import and export penetration variables to the derived labour demand equations. The export intensity variable takes a negative sign as would be expected, since the revealed comparative advantage and the induced efficiency effects work in the same direction. The sign on the import intensity is also negative which suggests that the revealed comparative advantage element is outweighed by the efficiency effect.

As is apparent from the above discussion, the import and export penetration variables compound two effects – that arising from the UK's comparative advantage position and that arising from induced efficiency effects. In order to assess the induced efficiency effects of changing trade patterns more directly, the import and export intensity terms are replaced in Column 3 (Table 6.6) by the year-on-year change in imports and the year-on-year change in exports. Since these reflect the impact of changing current trade patterns on labour usage rather than that of a historically inherited position, both of these variables would be expected to have a negative sign. As can be seen from Column 3 the signs of these variables meets the above priors, with both variables being statistically significant at the 95 per cent level and of the expected sign.

The effect of trade on employment is enriched somewhat in the subsequent columns. Clearly the countries with which the United Kingdom trades are not a homogeneous grouping. OECD countries are similar to the United Kingdom in terms of their factor endowments and compete in capital intensive sectors. Trade with other developed countries also tends to be more intra-industry in form than trade with non-OECD countries. It might therefore be surmised that the incentive to economize on labour use in response to increased imports from these countries is somewhat less than that from less developed, low wage economies. This point is investigated in Column 4 (Table 6.6) where changing import penetration is broken down into that part deriving from the OECD and that deriving from other countries. The relative size of the coefficients is much as would be expected from the preceding argument. The splitting of import penetration in this way is also statistically significant on the basis of a likelihood ratio test ($\chi_1^2 = 3.94$).

The OECD and non-OECD sub-divisions may be further subdivided into their components. Column 5 (Table 6.6) divides the OECD category into European Community and non-EC countries. As can be seen, the coefficient associated with trade from within the EC is less than that from OECD countries outside the EC and less still than non-OECD countries. This again conforms with the argument that the largely intra-industry nature of inter-Community trade ameliorates the incentive to economize on labour inputs.

In a similar way, non-OECD trade may be broken down into its constituent elements. Column 6 (Table 6.6) decomposes non-OECD trade into that deriving from East and Southeast Asia (excluding Japan) from that originating from elsewhere. As might be expected from the earlier discussion, trade from East and Southeast Asia appears to have a large disciplinary effect on employment in the United Kingdom. However, the pattern is not quite so straightforward as might at first be thought as the trade effects from this region are far from homogeneous. Column 7 shows that Singapore and South Korea exert a statistically insignificant effect on labour usage in the UK, though the effect from Hong Kong and Taiwan is much stronger.

In this section we have used a relatively simple panel data model to estimate the impact effects of trade on sectoral employment levels in the UK. This model was adopted since it is similar in spirit to the accounting decomposition approach, though it allows the disciplinary effect of trade on productivity to be measured. This analysis has demonstrated that strong trade effects exist, but that the impact of trade on the UK labour market depends on which country the United Kingdom is trading with. This is consistent with the differing factor endowments of the United Kingdom's trading partners.

CONCLUSIONS

This paper has been concerned with the impact of trade on employment in UK manufacturing. Empirical analysis has been based on disaggregated output, employment and trade database for the period 1979–91. Two forms of analysis have been used, a growth accounting technique and an econometric model of labour demand. The accounting approach supports the view that the large loss of manufacturing jobs in the UK since 1979 is the outcome of a cumulatively large growth in labour productivity accompanied by a relatively slow growth in domestic demand. Within the manufacturing sector there has been a wide diversity of experience, industries with rising employment generally experiencing more buoyant domestic and export demand. Differences in productivity growth do not appear to explain much of the observed difference in employment growth since the effect of growing productivity is ambivalent, cutting jobs in the short-term but making them more secure in the longer term. This exposes a general weakness of the accounting approach, in that it is not able to isolate the effect of a single variable. Thus a faster growth in imports in an industry is found to be associated with the preservation of more, not fewer, jobs in that industry. This is, however, a useful reminder of the complexity of the import effect. Imports grow faster in industries where domestic, and indeed export, demand is most buoyant.

Both the accounting and the econometric methods suggest that trade has a stimulating effect on labour productivity. The econometric study takes this further by disaggregating imports among sources and shows that it is competition from low wage economies, especially in Asia, which exerts the biggest pressure towards capital–labour substitution in UK industry. Our main conclusion is therefore that although the displacement effect of trade on employment in manufacturing may in general be modest, trade has a potentially very important effect on productivity growth which has been the principal source of labour displacement.

Notes

*   These authors gratefully acknowledge the financial support of the ESRC under the Asia-Pacific programme (Grant No. L324253045). The usual disclaimers apply. Thanks go also to Amanda Greenwood for excellent research assistance.
1. In particular Japan, the four Tigers (Hong Kong, Taiwan, Singapore and South Korea), the three Dragons (Indonesia, Malaysia and Thailand) and China.

2. Ranging from about 30 per cent in 1980 to 22.5 per cent in 1990.
3. Other papers which examine the impact of import competition on collectively bargained wage and employment outcomes include Abowd (1987) for the US, with Abowd and Lemieux (1990) and Caves (1990) providing a comparison with Canada. Vroman and Abowd (1988), Mishel (1986) and McPherson and Stewart (1990) examine the impact of imports on wages for the US inter alia.
4. Details of the data sources used are available from the authors on request.

References

Abowd, J. M. (1987) 'The Effects of International Competition on Collective Bargaining Agreements in the United States', Princeton University, unpublished.

Abowd, J. M. and Lemieux, T. (1990) 'The Effects of International Competition on Collective Bargaining Outcomes: A Comparison of the United States and Canada' NBER Working Paper 3352.

Cable, C. (1983) *Protectionism and Industrial Decline*, (London: Hodder and Stoughton).

Caves, R. E. (1990) *Adjustment to International Competition: Short Run Relations of Prices, Trade Flows and Inputs in Canadian Manufacturing Industry*. Economic Council of Canada.

Denny, K. and Machin, S. (1991) 'The Effects of Import Competition on Wages and Employment', Mimeo, Institute for Fiscal Studies.

Frank, C. R. Jr. (1977) *Foreign Trade and Domestic Aid*, (Washington: Brookings Institution).

Grossman, G. M. (1986) 'Imports as a cause of injury: the case of the US steel industry' *Journal of International Economics*, 20 (2), pp. 201–223.

Grossman, G. M. (1982) 'The Employment and Wage Effects of Import Competition in the United States' NBER Working Paper 1041. Reprinted in *Journal of International Economic Integration*, 1987, 2, pp. 1–23.

Martin, J. P. and Evans, J. M. (1981) 'Notes on Measuring the Employment Displacement Effects of Trade by the Accounting Procedure', *Oxford Economic Papers* 33(1) pp. 154–164.

McPherson, D. A. and Stewart, J. B. (1990) 'The Effect of International Competition on Union and Non-union Wages' *Industrial and Labor Relations Review* (43), pp. 434–446.

Mishel, L. (1986) 'The Structural Determinants of Union Bargaining Power' *Industrial and Labor Relations Review* (40), pp. 90–115.

Revenga, A. L. (1992) 'Exporting Jobs? The Impact of Import Competition on Employment and Wages in US Manufacturing' *Quarterly Journal of Economics*, 107(1), pp. 255–284.

UNIDO (1986) 'Industry and Development Global Report', (Vienna: UNIDO).

Vroman, W. and Abowd, J. (1988) 'Dis-aggregated wage developments' *Brookings Papers on Economic Activity* (14), pp. 313–346.

Wood, A. (1994) *North–South Trade, Employment and Inequality* (Oxford: Clarendon Press).

7 How Trade Hurt Unskilled Workers

Adrian Wood*

INTRODUCTION

This paper will argue for what is still a minority view among economists: that the main cause of the deteriorating situation of unskilled workers in developed countries has been expansion of trade with developing countries.[1] This view was advanced in Wood (1991a, b), and later developed into a book (Wood, 1994), but much the same line is taken by Batra (1993) and by Leamer (1993, 1994). It has been strongly attacked, however, by economists who think the effects of trade have been small – notably Lawrence and Slaughter (1993) and Krugman and Lawrence (1994). By way of a counterattack, this paper will outline the evidence which suggests that trade is the main cause of the problems of unskilled workers, respond to some criticisms of this evidence, and challenge the evidence for the alternative view that these problems are caused mainly by new technology. At the end, it will consider some of the implications of this debate for public policy.

COMMON GROUND

Before entering disputed territory, it is worth listing five points of fact on which most participants in the debate agree, and which will therefore be taken for granted here.

First, the demand for unskilled labour (defined as workers with no more than a basic education) has fallen substantially over the past couple of decades, relative to the demand for skilled labour, in most developed countries. This shift in demand has increased wage inequality, or, where labour market institutions have propped up unskilled wages, as in Europe, raised unemployment among the unskilled (Freeman, 1994, 1995).

Second, over the same period in these countries, employment in manufacturing, as a share of total employment, has fallen much faster than would have been predicted from its earlier trend (Sachs and Shatz, 1994, pp. 6–7; Wood, 1994, pp. 201–3).

Third, the timing of these changes in labour markets has coincided with rapid growth of imports of low-skill-intensive manufactures from developing countries (Sachs and Shatz, 1994, p. 34; Wood, 1994, pp. 257–60).

Fourth, these changes in labour markets have also coincided with the rapid diffusion of computers in the workplace, and hence the most plausible alternative explanation of the declining demand for unskilled workers is an autonomous surge of technical progress biased against them.

Fifth, most empirical studies find that trade has made some contribution to these changes in developed-country labour markets, but only a *small* contribution, and so conclude by default that the main causal force must have been new technology. Recent examples are Borjas *et al.* (1992) and Sachs and Shatz (1994), but many earlier studies (reviewed in Wood, 1994, chs. 3 and 7) arrived at much the same conclusion.

It is this common conclusion about the size of the effects of trade that is the main target of this article. The methods used in most studies underestimate the impact of trade on labour markets. Modified methods that avoid their downward biases suggest a far larger impact.

THEORETICAL FRAMEWORK

Before examining the evidence more closely, it is also worth looking at the theory, not least in order to explain what exactly might be meant by trade − an obviously endogenous variable − 'causing' changes in labour markets. The main theory involved is Heckscher–Ohlin (H–O), whose central insight is that countries export goods which use intensively the factors of production with which they are relatively abundantly endowed, and import goods which use intensively factors which are relatively scarce at home. A side-effect of this sort of trade, not surprisingly, is to alter the wages or earnings which different factors can command in the domestic economy.

To explain the effect on wages more precisely, consider a simple H–O model with two countries (developed and developing), two factors (skilled and unskilled labour), two traded manufactures (skill-intensive machinery and labour-intensive apparel), and an even more labour-intensive non-traded service.[2] The developed country has a relatively large endowment of skilled labour, which gives it a comparative advantage in machinery, while the developing country has a relatively large endowment of unskilled labour and so a comparative advantage in apparel. The wage story is then a matter of one link, two forces, and three cases.

One link

In H–O theory, trade and wages are linked simply and solely through changes in product prices. For example, an externally-induced fall in the domestic producer price of apparel, relative to the price of machinery, reduces the wages of unskilled, relative to skilled, workers. This linkage, known as the Stolper–Samuelson theorem, exists because H–O theory assumes technology (that is, the production function for each type of goods) to be given. In other words, it assumes a fixed functional relationship between outputs of goods and inputs of factors, which (with no excess profits) implies a similarly fixed relationship between the prices of goods and the wages of factors.

Two forces

What exactly are the 'external' forces which might change domestic producer prices? In H–O theory, with given technology (and tastes), there are two possibilities. One is reduction of barriers to trade. Transport costs and tariffs, for example, drive wedges between the prices of goods in the two countries (and may even result in no trade – or 'autarky'). In particular, they keep the price of apparel lower in the developing country than in the developed country, and vice versa for machinery. A reduction in barriers, and the resulting expansion of trade, would thus lower the relative price of apparel in the developed country.

The second force is alterations in relative world supplies of skilled and unskilled labour. For instance, population growth or expansion of basic education in the developing country, by increasing its supply of unskilled manufacturing workers, would raise its output and exports of apparel. This in turn could drive down the relative price of apparel on world markets, and hence in the developed country.

Three cases

The effects of externally induced price changes on wages vary, depending on the situation of the country, as can be shown by comparison of three cases, using a type of supply-and-demand-curve diagram

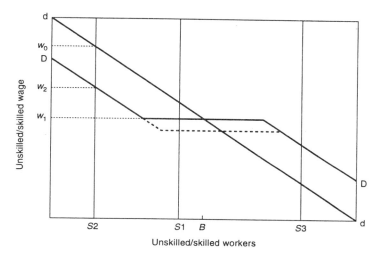

Figure 7.1 Effects of trade on wages

invented by Leamer (1995). In Figure 7.1, the vertical axis measures the unskilled wage, relative to the skilled wage, while the horizontal axis measures the number of unskilled workers, relative to the number of skilled workers.

(1) Autarky. The downward-sloping line, dd, is the demand curve for unskilled labour in a country where high barriers prevent trade. Wages are determined by the intersection of this demand curve with a supply curve (assumed for simplicity to be completely inelastic), whose position depends on the country's endowments of skilled and unskilled labour. For example, with supply S2, as in a country with few unskilled workers, the relative wage of unskilled labour would be at the high level, w_0.

(2) Diversified trade. The demand curve in a country completely open to trade is the line DD, which has two downward-sloping segments separated by a flat segment in the middle.[3] This flat (infinitely elastic) segment covers the range of factor endowments in which a trading country would be 'diversified', in the sense of producing both of the two traded goods. In this range, for example in a country with labour supply S1, relative wages are set purely by relative world prices, at the level w_1. Thus changes in domestic labour supply, unless they are big enough to affect world prices, do not change wages – they alter only the composition of output and trade. However, if a change

in world labour supplies or a fall in trade barriers abroad were to lower the import price of apparel, the flat segment of the demand curve would shift down, as shown by the dashed line in the figure, reducing the relative wage of unskilled workers.

(3) *Specialized trade.* A trading country with few unskilled workers, as at S2, will produce no apparel, and specialize in machinery plus the non-traded service (a country with many unskilled workers, as at S3, would correspondingly specialize in apparel). This puts it on a downward-sloping segment of the demand curve DD, where changes in domestic labour supply do affect relative wages. For instance, an increase in the relative number of skilled workers would raise the relative wage of unskilled labour (it could do this also by moving the country from the flat to the sloping segment of the curve – from S1 to S2). By contrast, a fall in the world price of imported apparel would not affect the relative wage, w_2: it would benefit both skilled and unskilled workers in their role as consumers, but would not affect them as producers, since apparel is not produced domestically.[4]

To summarize, in a developed country, with relatively few unskilled workers by world standards (that is, to the left of point B in the figure), trade with developing countries (to the right of point B) causes the relative wage of unskilled workers to be lower than it would be without trade, whether the outcome is diversified or specialized. In both cases, this happens because of a fall in the relative domestic price of apparel, which in both cases is reflected in a shift of the demand curve against unskilled labour. The two cases differ, though, as regards the effects on wages of subsequent changes in world prices and domestic labour supplies.

Falling barriers and specialization

In discussing the evidence below, particular emphasis will be placed on the comparison between autarky and specialized trade, because it encapsulates most of what I believe to have happened in reality over the past couple of decades. More specifically, I argue in Wood (1994) that reduction of trade barriers has shifted developed countries from 'manufacturing autarky', in which they produced all the manufactures they consumed (skill-intensive and labour-intensive), to specialization in the production of skill-intensive manufactures and reliance on imports from developing countries to supply their needs for labour-intensive manufactures.[5]

Barriers to developed-developing country trade in manufactures have fallen over the past couple of decades partly because international transport and telecommunications have become much cheaper, quicker and of better quality, and partly because of changes in trade policies, particularly in developing countries, more and more of which have switched to export-oriented trade regimes. These barrier reductions have done more than simply ease the flow of goods from developing to developed countries. Just as vital has been easier movement of inputs in the other direction – components, machinery, finance and information, including visits by technical and marketing experts. More generally, developed-country companies have learned how to manage globally dispersed production and procurement activities.

That these reductions in trade barriers have occurred seems beyond dispute. More open to argument is whether they were the main cause of the growth of manufactured exports from developing countries, and whether they were truly exogenous – independent, in particular, of other demand and supply shifts in developed-country labour markets. Neither question has a simple answer, but the evidence suggests 'yes, as a first approximation' to both of them (Wood, 1994, pp. 171–82). Particularly supportive is the coincidence of widening wage gaps within developed countries, implying that the imports of labour-intensive goods were not sucked in by shortages of unskilled labour, and narrowing wage gaps within the main East Asian exporters, which makes falling barriers to trade more plausible than rising internal surpluses of unskilled labour as the cause of their growing exports.

My barrier reduction theory is clearly partly a story about new technology, which contributed to the improvements in transport and communications. But this is by no means the only way in which trade and technology explanations of changing relative wages might be combined. H–O theory takes technology as given, which leaves room to introduce autonomous technical change as an additional influence on wages and on trade (Leamer, 1994, 1995; Richardson, 1995. Conversely, the pace and direction of technical change may be influenced by trade, as will be argued below. So, however one looks at it, trade and new technology are intertwined: no story that excludes one or the other of them is likely to be the whole story.

CROSS-COUNTRY VARIATION

Since most of the evidence on trade and labour markets refers to the United States, it is interesting to start in a broader perspective, by

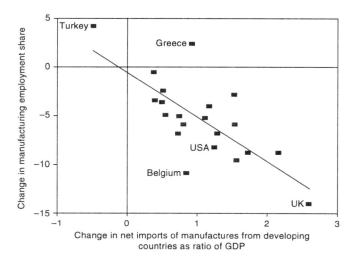

Figure 7.2   Deindustrialization and developing-country import penetration (OECD countries: percentage point changes from 1970 to 1990)

Source: Saeger (1995). The regression line shown was fitted by OLS. To avoid cluttering the graph, only the USA and a few outliers are labelled.

examining differences among developed countries. All these countries increased their trade in manufactures with developing countries, but the extent of the increase varied, because of differences in their own barriers to trade and in geographical proximity. Thus, if this trade were really the main cause of the problems of their unskilled workers, one would expect to find some cross-country association between these variations in the rise in trade and variations in relevant labour market indicators – and indeed one does.

Figure 7.2, a scatter plot from Saeger (1995), refers to all OECD countries with the necessary data. Its horizontal axis shows the 1970–90 change in net imports of manufactures from developing countries, measured as a percentage share of GDP. In the United States, for example, these imports (minus exports) rose from −0.6 per cent of GDP in 1970 to +0.6 per cent in 1990, which puts the US at 1.2 on the horizontal axis. The vertical axis shows the percentage point change in the share of manufacturing in total employment over the same period. There is a clear inverse association: countries with larger increases in import penetration experienced larger falls in manufacturing employment. Saeger finds a similar correlation with the change in the gross (rather than the net) import penetration ratio.

In principle, the correlation in Figure 7.2 might not reflect causality, but rather some common influence on both import penetration and manufacturing employment. It is not easy, however, to find plausible candidates for this excluded variable (Wood, 1994, pp. 203–9). One possibility is shortages of unskilled labour, which might have forced labour-intensive manufacturing to contract and imports to be substituted. But this would imply a negative cross-country correlation between import penetration and deterioration of the relative wage and unemployment position of unskilled workers, whereas the actual correlation is strongly positive – unskilled workers did worst where import penetration rose most (Wood, 1994, pp. 265–9). There is also a positive cross-country correlation between changes in import penetration and in the overall unemployment rate, when allowance is made for differences in wage flexibility (Wood, 1994, pp. 309–21).

It is striking that such simple cross-country tests suggest so strongly the influence of increased trade with developing countries. Their results make it hard to believe that trade had only small effects, for if this were so, the association would surely be disguised by other influences.

It is also striking how tiny the numbers on the horizontal axis of Figure 7.2 are. The largest rise in developing-country net import penetration during 1970–90 was not much over 2 per cent of GDP, and the average only about 1 per cent. Even taking the level of gross import penetration (rather than the change in net import penetration), manufactured imports from developing countries were under 3 per cent of GDP in the US in 1990. Numbers such as this are emphasized by economists who dismiss the influence of trade. 'How on earth', they ask, 'could such a small tail wag the large dog of developed-country labour markets?'

There are three answers to this question. Two of them point to ways in which trade can hurt unskilled labour even where it does not raise import penetration: one is by depressing the prices of labour-intensive goods, the other by forcing firms to find ways of using less unskillled labour to stay competitive. The third is that these imports from developing countries are highly labour-intensive goods, and thus displace more domestic workers than might be supposed by simply comparing their dollar value to that of the US GDP. But how many more? That question leads us into the next section.

FACTOR CONTENT OF TRADE

The most commonly used method of estimating the effects of trade on labour markets is to calculate its *factor content*. This involves figuring out how much skilled and unskilled labour is used in producing a country's exports, and how much would have been used to produce its imports. The differences between exports and imports are then interpreted as the impact of trade on the demand for skilled and unskilled workers – by comparison with what it would have been in the absence of trade (or if trade had remained at some earlier lower level).

For example, Sachs and Shatz (1994) use factor content methods to estimate the impact of the 1978–90 change in trade on the employment of skilled and unskilled (or, more precisely, non-production and production) workers in US manufacturing. For each of 51 manufacturing sectors, they calculate the effect of the increase or decrease in net exports (exports minus imports) on the level of output. They then assume both skilled and unskilled employment in each sector changed in the same proportion as its output. Summed across sectors, their results show that trade with developing countries reduced manufacturing employment, particularly of unskilled workers, since output declines were concentrated on sectors with relatively few skilled workers.

Non-competing imports

These (and most other) factor content calculations are biased downwards because of the way in which they calculate the labour content of imports. The numbers of skilled and unskilled workers displaced by a dollar of imports in each sector are taken to be the same as the numbers needed to produce a dollar of exports, and both are estimated simply from the numbers used to produce a dollar of domestic output. The implicit assumption is that the imports in each statistical category, say 'electrical machinery', are goods of the same types, and in particular of the same skill intensity, as the goods produced in the corresponding domestic sector.

This assumption is unreasonable for manufactured imports from developing countries, which consist mostly of items of low skill intensity that are no longer produced on any significant scale in developed countries. This is true both of finished goods – especially when finely distinguished by type and quality – and of intermediate goods and stages of production, of which the most labour-intensive (like assembly of electrical consumer goods) have been delegated to low-wage countries. In theoretical terms, as explained earlier, developed countries have become specialized producers of skill-intensive manufactures, and imports of labour-intensive manufactures are now 'non-competing' with domestic production.

In this situation, by using domestic labour coefficients which refer to the production of different and more skill-intensive goods, the usual method of calculation for imports inevitably underestimates their unskilled labour content. To put it another way, conventional factor content calculations understate the number of workers, particularly unskilled workers, who would be needed, in the absence of trade, to meet the demand for the goods that are now imported. Conventional factor content results thus understate the extent to which trade shifts relative demand against unskilled workers.

To obtain more accurate results, one must start by measuring the amounts of labour used to produce these imports in developing-country trading partners (since goods of this sort are not produced at home). These actual inputs of labour must then be adjusted to allow for the much higher level of wages in developed countries, which would cause more skill- and capital-intensive techniques to be used if these goods were produced domestically rather than imported. It is also vital to adjust for the fact that these goods would cost more if they were produced domestically, and hence that people would buy fewer of them. After these two adjustments, the estimated displacement of unskilled labour by the imports is much smaller than the actual amount of labour embodied in them – but much larger than suggested by conventional factor content calculations.[6]

Table 7.1 compares the conventional factor content results of Sachs and Shatz with results obtained by this alternative method (Wood, 1994, ch. 4). Part of the difference between them arises from the coverage and definitions of the data, but most is due to the methods used. Each number in the table is an estimated percentage change in demand for labour in manufacturing caused by trade. In the first row, both numbers are negative, implying agreement that trade with developing countries reduced the demand for manufacturing workers in general. (The fundamental reason for this outcome is that the goods imported by developed countries are more labour-intensive than those they export: it would occur even if trade were balanced, and thus does not depend on the existence of a trade deficit, which is often portrayed as the culprit in the US – see, for example, Borjas and Ramey, 1994.) However, the estimated reduction in demand is about twice as large in the alternative calculations as in the conventional ones.

Table 7.1   Factor content estimates of impact of trade with developing countries on demand for labour in manufacturing in 1990 (percentage difference from counterfactual situation without trade)

	Sachs and Shatz (United States only)	Wood (All developed countries)
All workers	−5.7	−10.8
Skilled workers	−4.3	0.3
Unskilled workers	−6.2	−21.5
Unskilled minus skilled	−1.9	−21.8

Note: As well as the differences in method of calculation and geographical coverage of the estimates, there are differences in: (1) the definition of skilled workers (Sachs and Shatz = non-production workers, Wood = workers with post-basic education or training); (2) the definition of manufactured exports (Sachs and Shatz include, Wood excludes, goods with a high natural resource content); and (3) the counterfactual (Sachs and Shatz assume no change from the 1978 net export/output ratio in each sector, Wood assumes no manufactured imports from developing countries and a corresponding reduction in exports).

Sources: Sachs and Shatz (1994, Table 13), Wood (1994, Table 4.9 and p. 151, note 45, but recalculated as a percentage of without-trade, rather than actual,. employment).

The second and third rows show the effects on skilled and unskilled workers separately. Again, there is agreement between the two sets of calculations that the unskilled are hit harder than the skilled, but a big difference in the estimated magnitudes. Sachs and Shatz conclude that trade reduced the demand for skilled workers nearly as much as for unskilled workers: thus, as shown in the last row, the *relative* demand for unskilled labour declined by only 2 per cent (similar to the results of earlier studies using the same method – Wood, 1994, Table 3.10). By contrast, the alternative calculation suggests that trade slightly increased the demand for skilled labour (due to greater production of skill-intensive exports), and that the entire net reduction in demand was concentrated on the unskilled. The relative demand for unskilled labour is thus estimated to have been reduced by 22 per cent – roughly ten times more than in the conventional calculation.

Two further sources of understatement

Even the modified calculations, though, underestimate the effects of trade on labour demand, for two reasons (Wood, 1994, pp. 158–65).

The first is that they, like other factor content estimates, ignore the contribution of trade to technical progress. This is misleading, because a common reaction of developed-country firms to low-wage competition has been to look for new methods of production that economize on unskilled labour. (Their incentive to do so is being reduced somewhat by falling unskilled wages in developed countries, but the *level* of unskilled wages remains far higher than in most developing countries.) In some cases, this innovative effort has failed, and domestic production has been extinguished by imports. In other cases, however, 'defensive innovation' has enabled firms to fight off the imports – but has still reduced their demand for unskilled labour.

At first sight, the idea of defensive innovation may seem inconsistent with economic theory: if labour-saving cost-reducing technologies existed, why weren't profit-maximizing firms already using them? But, in practice, firms do not have complete knowledge of all technical possibilities, and to learn about new possibilities they must incur search costs – R&D expenditure, for example, and managerial time and effort. Their decisions about where and how to search depend on the likely benefits, which in turn depend on market conditions. And, for many firms, the emergence of low-wage competitors was a drastic change in market conditions – a matter not of marginal shifts in profits, but of survival – which radically altered their search priorities.

Whatever may be the most appealing theoretical rationalization of defensive innovation, its empirical existence is apparent in a lot of case-study and anecdotal evidence. It gets some statistical support from Sachs and Shatz (1994, p. 33), who find acceleration of total factor productivity growth during the 1980s in low-skill-intensive manufacturing sectors, relative to high-skill sectors. Faster productivity growth in low-skill than in high-skill sectors is also documented by Lawrence and Slaughter (1993, Figure 10) and Leamer (1994, Tables 3 and 4).

There is no acceptably accurate way, as yet, of quantifying the impact of defensive innovation on labour demand. However, the case study evidence suggests that its effects have been at least as large as the relocation and reallocation effects measured by factor content estimates (Wood, 1994, p. 161). This assessment receives some support from calculations of the recent rise in the proportion of skilled workers in developed-country manufacturing, relative to non-traded sectors (Wood, 1994, App. A2). The tentative conclusion is thus that allowance for defensive innovation would require something like a doubling of the modified factor content estimates.

The second source of understatement is that the factor content estimates are confined to manufacturing. Expansion of trade in services has added to the labour market impact, with developing countries emerging as substantial exporters in low-skill-intensive sectors such as shipping, tourism and key-punching, and as purchasers of more skill-intensive services from developed countries. In addition, there is an impact on the demand for skilled and unskilled labour in the non-traded sectors which sell intermediate inputs to producers of manufactures and traded services.

Although these effects in the service sectors seem too big to ignore, there is, again, no accurate way to measure them at present (Wood, 1994, pp. 162–5). However, we know that the service exports of developing countries are about 50 per cent as large as their exports of manufactures. We also know that the value added to manufactured exports in the non-traded sectors which supply intermediate inputs is about 40 per cent as large as the value added within manufacturing. So, as a first approximation, the estimated impact of trade on labour demand in manufacturing might be raised first by 50 per cent, and then by another 40 per cent, which would roughly double it.

To summarize, what does all this suggest about the general magnitude of the labour market effects of trade with developing countries? As of 1990, in round numbers, the modified factor content estimates in Table 7.1 imply a 10 per cent cut in the overall demand for labour in developed-country manufacturing. Double this figure to 20 per cent to allow for defensive innovation. Manufacturing is now about one-fifth of total employment: without the 20 per cent cut, it would have been one-quarter, so that trade has reduced the share of manufacturing by about 5 percentage points. Virtually all the reduction in demand, Table 7.1 also implies, was concentrated on unskilled workers. Taking such workers to be half of the labour force, the 5 point cut in manufacturing employment reduced the economy-wide demand for their labour by about 10 per cent – relative to skilled workers, for whom demand hardly altered. Doubling this last figure to allow for the impact on services leads to the conclusion that trade lowered the economy-wide relative demand for unskilled labour by about 20 per cent.

CRITICISM OF THE ESTIMATE

This number, obviously, is a rough estimate. Also, it is for developed countries as a group, not for any particular country. Many specific doubts about the data and assumptions used in the modified factor content calculations, and some sensitivity analysis of the results in Table 7.1, are discussed in Wood (1994, pp. 152–8). But there is no point in debating here whether the estimate should be a bit bigger or a bit smaller: the real issue is whether it is an order of magnitude too large, or deeply flawed in its method, or misleading in some other way. Four criticism merit special attention.

Sectoral skill intensities moved the wrong way

The modified factor content calculations assume that imports from developing countries are concentrated on goods which are much less skill-intensive than the average in each sector. Sachs and Shatz (1994, p. 32) test this claim by comparing, across different manufacturing sectors, the rise in skill intensity during the 1980s with the initial level of skill intensity. They expected to find a negative correlation: sectors which were of low skill intensity to begin with, because they contained a high proportion of labour-intensive activities, should have experienced a bigger rise in skill intensity when competition from developing countries forced labour-intensive activities to contract (or to become more skill-intensive by defensive innovation). In fact, the correlation is slightly positive: sectors which were initially less skill-intensive experienced, if anything, a *smaller* rise in skill intensity.

This is a surprising result. One can construct examples where the relative sizes and growth of non-labour-intensive activities within sectors are such that trade causes skill intensity to increase more in an initially more skill-intensive sector than in an initially less skill-intensive one, but it takes some ingenuity. It is possible that the results are distorted by the coarseness of the measure of skill intensity used by Sachs and Shatz. They use the relative numbers of non-production and production workers, but much of the change in the skill mix of employment has occurred *within* these categories – expansion of professional relative to clerical non-production jobs, and of skilled relative to semi-skilled production jobs (Berman *et al.*, 1994, Table 1; Machin, 1994, p. 8). However, this and other possible reconciliations are as yet unexplored.

Further investigation of this cross-sectoral relationship would thus be of considerable interest. It should be recognized, though, that it is at best an indirect test of the argument that imports from developing countries are much less skill-intensive than developed-country production in the 'same' sectors. The case-study and anecdotal evidence in support of this argument seems so strong that only a direct negative test could overturn it.

The assumed elasticities are too low

Calculating the labour content of non-competing imports, as outlined above, involves two downward adjustments – to allow for higher wages in developed countries, and for lower demand if the goods were produced domestically at a higher price. In making these adjustments, assumptions are needed about elasticities of substitution in production and consumption. The larger are these elasticities, the smaller are the labour market effects of trade. For example, if the higher price of domestically produced substitutes would deter most buyers, then the absence of imports would not much increase the demand for unskilled labour.

The results in Table 7.1 are based on elasticities of 0.5 both in production (between unskilled labour and a combined input of capital and skill) and in consumption (the price elasticity of demand for labour-intensive goods).

Values of up to 0.9 were tried in the sensitivity analysis without greatly altering the results. However, further increases in the assumed values of these elasticities cause the labour market effects of trade to melt away quite rapidly. This may arouse concern, since econometrically estimated elasticities are often well above the range used in these calculations.

The values used are defended, and related to the empirical literature, in Wood (1994, pp. 131–3, 143–4), but it is worth mentioning two general reasons why the elasticities used in the factor content calculations should be on the low side. One is that most econometric estimates of substitution in production are based on quite coarsely aggregated sectoral data, and so pick up factor-price-induced differences in product mix and quality, as well as in the choice of technique for producing specific goods. They thus overstate the scope for substitution of techniques, which is what matters here. A second reason is that much of the trade in manufacturers between developed and developing countries involves intermediate goods or stages of production, between which there is probably little substitutability.

The magnitudes are still not big enough

Although my estimate of the impact of trade is much larger than those of other economists, it is arguably not large enough to explain the observed changes in labour markets. There is no difficulty with the falling share of employment in manufacturing: its recent acceleration is fully accounted for by the estimated trade-induced reduction of 5 percentage points (Wood, 1994, pp. 201–3). The issue, rather, is whether a 20 per cent fall in the relative demand for unskilled labour is sufficient to explain the marked widening of skill differentials in wages and unemployment rates, since there have also been shifts in relative supply. In particular, taking the 1970s and 1980s together, the relative supply of skilled labour may well have risen by more than 20 per cent, suggesting that the net effect should have been to narrow, rather than widen, skill differentials.[7]

One possible response would be to argue that trade has made the demand for labour so elastic that shifts in supply have little effect on wages – that, in terms of Figure 7.1, supply in developed countries is in the region of S2, putting them on the flat segment of the demand curve DD. This, however, is not a good defense of my particular position, since I maintain that supply in developed countries is actually in the region of S2, putting them on a downward-sloping segment of the demand curve, where supply shifts do affect wages. It is clear from Figure 7.1 that the coincidence of a demand shift from dd to DD and a leftward shift of S2 (a rise in the relative supply of skilled labour) could increase the relative wage of unskilled workers.

For me, a better defense is to argue that trade accelerated a pre-existing downward trend in the relative demand for unskilled labour (which had been shifting dd and DD to the left). Large increases in the relative supply of skilled labour over the past century have been absorbed with little narrowing of skill differentials in wages, except when supply shifts have been unusually fast, which suggests that the relative demand for skilled labour has also risen, and to much the same extent as supply (for some recent evidence, see Katz and Murphy, 1992, pp. 37, 54).

This secular demand shift might be attributed to exogenous technological progress, but its similarity to the supply shift suggests a more specific hypothesis, namely that it is a lagged function of the supply shift. The causal mechanism could be that employment of skilled workers creates needs and opportunities to employ other skilled workers (through externalities of some sort). But whatever the cause of the secular demand shift, it has been amplified by recent changes in trade: thus an *additional* 20 per cent shift in relative demand could have markedly widened skill differentials, despite opposing shifts in supply.

Factor content calculations are misguided

The most fundamental criticism of my estimates of the impact of trade has been made, ironically, by another proponent of the view that this impact is large. Leamer (1994) rejects factor content calculations – my basic method – as 'measurement without theory'. His criticism is aimed at people who have used such calculations to argue that the effects of trade are small, but sauce for the goose is sauce for the gander! Let me lay out his three specific charges, and to each of them offer a response.

First, factor content calculations are *unnecessary*. In H–O theory, trade changes wages only if it changes product prices, so why do more than look at prices? My response: suitable price data may not be available (as will be explained in the next section).

Second, factor content calculations are *insufficient*. Externally induced changes in prices cause changes in trade flows (for example, if a country's terms of trade improve, it usually trades more), so in principle one can work out from changes in the factor content of trade what happened to wages. But this requires data on domestic labour demand and supply elasticities (in order to move from trade-induced shifts in numbers of workers demanded to changes in their wages), if not proper general equilibrium calculations, way beyond standard factor content estimates. My response: at least it can be done, as an extension of factor content calculations. There are data on elasticities (which I use), and the error caused by neglect of second-round general equilibrium effects is likely to be small.

Third, factor content calculations are *inaccurate*, for two reasons. One is that the factor content of a country's trade is altered over time no only by external forces, such as changes in world prices, but also by internal forces, such as shifts in tastes, technology and factor supplies. Factor content calculations usually fail to control for shifts in internal forces, and hence mismeasure the effects of external forces. My response: I argue, with some evidence, that the whole of the rise of manufactured imports from developing countries was due to forces external to developed countries, and in particular to reduction of barriers to trade.

The second reason for inaccuracy arises where a country is specialized, and does not produce some types of goods that it imports. If it never produced these goods, then the imports cannot have affected the domestic demand for labour. Even if it did formerly produce them, the impact on the domestic demand for labour cannot be accurately measured by standard factor content calculations. My response: because I assume that developed countries are specialized, I do my factor content calculations in a non-standard way (as explained earlier).

EVIDENCE ON PRICES

Although factor content calculations can be defended, it remains important to look at product price movements. For if it is true that H–O forces have reduced the relative wages of unskilled workers, then there must have been accompanying reductions in the relative prices of labour-intensive goods. Have such price movements been observed?

Lawrence and Slaughter (1993) and Lawrence (1994) conclude that the answer is 'not'. They calculate two averages of price movements during the 1980s across manufacturing sectors, one weighted by each sector's share of all skilled (non-production) employment, the other by its share of unskilled (production) employment. If relative prices were falling in less skill-intensive sectors, the production-weighted average should rise less rapidly than the non-production-weighted average. But this was not the case for import prices in the United States, Japan or Germany.

Sachs and Shatz (1994, pp. 34–40), re-analyse the US price data, and arrive at different conclusions. After eliminating series that do not cover the whole period, and excluding computers, whose massive fall in price distorts the overall pattern, they find that import prices have in fact risen less rapidly for low-skill-intensive goods. They also examine movements in *domestic* producer prices for a much larger sample of sectors, and find a similar but statistically more significant trend: during 1978–89, prices in the least skill-intensive decile of sectors fell by about 9 per cent relative to the most skill-intensive.

Sachs and Shatz suggest that this change in relative prices, though in the right direction, is too small to explain the observed change in relative wages. This assessment appears to be incorrect. Logically, proportional changes in relative prices must be smaller than the associated changes in relative wages, since all goods are produced by mixtures of skilled and unskilled workers, as well as other factors.[8] But over this period, their measure of the skill differential in wages – the gap between non-production and production workers – widened by only 8 per cent (Sachs and Shatz, 1994, Table 2), which is far less, rather than more, than one would expect from a 9 per cent change in relative prices.

In Japan and Germany, relative prices (of both imports and domestic output) rose faster during the 1980s in more skill-intensive sectors, even when computers are excluded (Lawrence, 1994). However, this is much less of a paradox, since the changes in relative wages in these two countries have been far smaller than in the United States. In Germany, wage rigidity has caused much of the shift in relative demand to emerge as changes in relative unemployment and vacancy rates (Wood, 1994, pp. 431–47), and in Japan there has been little widening of skill differentials in either wages or unemployment.

Feenstra and Hanson (1995) point out another feature of the Lawrence and Slaughter results for the United States, Japan and Germany, namely the consistent difference between domestic and import price changes. In all three countries, and for both the weighted sectoral averages, import prices rise more slowly – or, in Japan, fall faster – than domestic prices. (Sarker and Singer, 1989, likewise find a trend deterioration in developing countries' terms of trade in manufactures with developed countries.) Feenstra and Hanson interpret this as evidence that, within each sector, imports consist of a less skill-intensive mix of goods than domestic output – which is what I assume in my factor content calculations.

This heterogeneity of goods within statistically defined sectors is a major limitation of all the price data, and one which has become worse over time.

Manufactured imports from developing countries used to be concentrated on a few sectors, such as apparel and footwear, but are now spread across many sectors, partly because, for a wide range of goods, the production process has been split up, with the labour-intensive stages performed in developing countries, the skill-intensive ones at home.[9] This is probably why Leamer (1993, 1995) finds a large fall in the relative prices of labour-intensive two-digit sectors during the 1970s, but no clear pattern during the 1980s, even in more disaggregated sectoral data – which is in line with the mixed 1980s results of Lawrence and Slaughter (1993), Sachs and Shatz (1994), and Richardson (1995).

So the price evidence turns out to be rather disappointing. In theory, it ought to settle the dispute over whether or not trade is the main cause of the widening wage gap between skilled and unskilled workers. In practice, however, it fails to deliver a clear verdict, one way or the other.

RISING INTRA-SECTORAL SKILL INTENSITY

A different sort of evidence, which Lawrence and Slaughter (1993), Berman *et al.* (1994) and Machin (1994) argue decisively favours the technology explanation over the trade explanation, is the rising proportion of skilled workers *within* most sectors – despite the rise in their relative wage, which should tend to cause fewer of them to be employed.

The critics emphasise that the H–O story is about *inter-sectoral* shifts in the structure of employment: for example, lower trade barriers cause skill-intensive sectors to expand and labour-intensive sectors to contract. The associated decline in the relative wage of unskilled workers, by contrast, should give firms in all sectors an incentive to adopt less skill-intensive techniques. The fact that the ratio of skilled to unskilled workers has *risen* within most sectors thus suggests (a) that technical progress must be biased against unskilled workers, and hence (b) that it is this bias in new technology, rather than trade, that is widening wage differentials.

One possible response, made by Leamer (1994, 1995), is to accept conclusion (a), but to stress that conclusion (b) does not necessarily follow from it. In a country whose trade was diversified, where domestic prices and wages were set by world prices, unskilled-labour-saving technical progress in all sectors could have no effect on relative wages. In terms of Figure 7.1, such a country would be on the flat segment of the demand curve DD, and thus the relative wage would not be affected by a leftward shift of the curve. All that would change is the composition of output and trade: excess supply of unskilled workers would increase the output of labour-intensive sectors and reduce net imports of labour-intensive goods.

Sectoral versus factoral biases

What *would* alter relative wages in such a country, other than changes in world prices, as Leamer explains, is different rates of technical progress in different sectors. In other words, what matters is the sectoral, not the factoral, bias of technical progress. In particular, if product prices were fixed, the gap between skilled and unskilled wages would be widened by technical progress that was slower in labour-intensive than in skill-intensive sectors (essentially because labour-intensive sectors would need to offset their growing technical disadvantage by restraining the wages of the majority of their workers). However, as mentioned earlier, the recent pattern of sectoral bias seems to have been in the other direction – faster in labour-intensive than in skill-intensive sectors – and thus cannot help to explain why the relative wages of unskilled workers have been falling.[10]

The response to the critics is less simple if trade is specialized. For in this case (which I believe is more relevant to developed countries today), wages could be affected also by factorally biased technical progress. In Figure 7.1, a specialized country would be on a downward-sloping segment of the demand curve DD, so that a leftward shift of the curve would lower its intersection with S2. Excess supply of unskilled workers, caused by their displacement from both the machinery sector and non-traded services, has to be absorbed by a rise in consumption and output of the labour-intensive non-traded service, which requires a fall in its relative price, and hence in the relative wage of unskilled workers (which also induces firms in both sectors to switch to more labour-intensive techniques, thought not by enough to offset the technological trend towards greater skill intensity).

I also believe, as discussed earlier, that there has been a secular decline in the relative demand for unskilled labour, possibly as a lagged response to a rising skill supply, which long pre-dates the recent changes in trade. This trend is likely to have been spread widely across sectors, and thus to have emerged in the form suggested by the critics: technological progress that is neutral across sectors but biased against unskilled workers. But, precisely because this is a trend of long standing, the critics must argue, in order to explain the sudden widening of skill differentials, that it has recently accelerated – and for reasons unconnected with trade. This is not implausible, in light of the rapid diffusion of computers over the past two decades, but at present the supporting evidence is distinctly thin.

Intra-sectoral effects of trade

The critics assume that rising intra-sectoral skill intensity is due to new technology and thus independent of trade. This assumption is unreasonable, especially in manufacturing, to which most of their studies refer. Even at the four digit level of the Standard Industrial Classification, each sector contains hundreds of goods and processes, of varying skill intensity. Moreover, the cross-sectoral effects of trade with developing countries are replicated within each sector: exports expand the more skill-intensive activities, while imports shrink the less skill-intensive ones. This would cause the ratio of skilled to unskilled workers to rise in every traded sector, even if there were no technical progress. This intra-sectoral effect of trade is clear from case-study and anecdotal evidence. It also emerges from an econometric attempt to explain changes in the skill intensity of some 400 US manufacturing sectors by Feenstra and Hanson (1995). They follow Berman *et al.* (1994) in most respects, but introduce, as an additional independent variable, the rise in import penetration in each sector. Its coefficient is highly significant, and large enough to account for up to one third of the increase in the average skill intensity of manufacturing during 1979–87.

Similarly, Bernard and Jensen (1994) find that exporting explains a lot of the rise in the skill intensity of US manufacturing. Using a panel data set of more than 50 000 plants, they show that one third of the increase in the average employment share of non-production workers during 1980–7 was due to more rapid growth of exporting plants than of non-exporting plants (since exporting plants employ more non-production workers), and that this occurred mainly within, rather than between, industries. Another third of the increase was due to rising skill intensity of employment *within* exporting plants. Bernard and Jensen also find that almost all the widening of the average difference in wages between non-production and production workers was due to faster growth of exporting plants, which not only employ more non-production workers, but also pay them relatively more.

Correlation with technology indicators

Trade pressures surely do not explain all the rise in skill intensity even in traded sectors, let alone in those service sectors which are not exposed to trade, either directly or as suppliers of intermediate inputs to traded sectors. Moreover, various studies have found rises in the skill intensity of employment in particular industries or firms to be correlated with rises in 'technology indicators', meaning measures of capital stock, computer use, R&D expenditure, and so on. Mishel and Bernstein (1994) survey many of these studies, but see also Berman *et al.* (1994), Bernard and Jensen (1994), Feenstra and Hanson (1995), and Machin (1994). Some of their authors have taken this association to be strong evidence against the trade explanation of the recent widening of skill differentials in wages.

Like other correlations, however, this one is neutral on causation. There is a lot of econometric evidence that skill and capital are complementary, and it is no surprise to find that many skilled workers now use computers. Thus, for example, in a sector where trade was pushing up the proportion of skilled workers, either through changes in activity mix or through defensive innovation, one would also expect to see a rise in the amount of capital and the number of computers per worker. (if you hire more skilled workers, you'd better buy them something to work with!) But it would be the trade-induced rise in the skill intensity of employment that was causing the rise in technology indicators, not the other way round. The autonomous effects of new technology are hard to isolate, especially when innovation is partly induced by trade.

More plausible as evidence for the new technology explanation of widening wage differentials are studies which find an association between wages and use of computers, while controlling for education and other skill-related worker characteristics (Krueger, 1993; Van Reenen, 1994). One can then argue, as Krueger does, that the increased use of computers during the 1980s, being concentrated on more skilled workers, must have contributed to the rise in wage inequality. Mishel and Bernstein (1994), too, find that changes in technology affect the wage structure, but not much difference in this regard between the 1970s and the 1980s. So they reject the hypothesis that new technology caused the rise in wage inequality in the latter decade (and attach more importance to the erosion of unions and of minimum wages).

Where does all this leave the 'trade versus technology' debate? It seems certain that new technology contributed to the recent deterioration in the relative economic position of unskilled workers – as a background trend, as a cause of lower trade barriers, and as a response to foreign competition. The key question, though, is whether spontaneous diffusion of computers and new management methods would have reduced unskilled workers to anything like their current plight if developed countries had remained industrially self-sufficient, and developing countries simply suppliers of a few primary products. The answer to this question, on the basis of the evidence now available, appears to me to be 'probably not'.

PROSPECTS AND POLICIES

The debate concerns the causes of past events, but what about the future? It is striking that even some of the people who argue that trade has so far had only minor effects go on to predict that it will have major effects in the future (for example, Sachs and Shatz, 1994, pp. 51–7; Slaughter 1994). They argue that the emergence as exporters of labour-intensive manufactures of such vast countries as China and India will greatly expand the effective world supply of unskilled labour, to the serious detriment of the unskilled in developed countries. The dispute is thus sometimes portrayed as being over whether the effects of trade that I describe have already occurred, or are just about to occur (Woodall, 1994, p. 22).

Actually, there is disagreement about the future, too! In particular, I do not expect unskilled workers in developed countries to be much hurt by even major new entry into the world market for low-skill-intensive manufactures, simply because these goods are no longer produced in developed countries. The entry of China and India, pushing down the world prices of these goods, will benefit developed-country workers, skilled and unskilled alike.

Relatively unskilled workers in developed countries do, however, have two other things to fear from trade in the future.[11] One is stiffer competition in the world market for middling-skill-intensive manufactures, partly through developing nations such as Korea accumulating skills, and partly from the countries of eastern Europe and the former Soviet Union, whose labour forces are already well-educated. The second worry is increased tradeability of services, due to changes in technology and trade rules, which will expose the unskilled to foreign competition in previously sheltered sectors. And it is clearly just a small step from discussing trade in services to the even more thorny issue of unskilled immigration.

What should be the policy response? Even economists who argue that trade has a large impact on labour markets usually also argue that raising trade barriers is the wrong solution. Batra (1993) is an exception. But is our work, as some suggest, unwittingly giving ammunition to protectionists? That is certainly a risk, but one to which those who argue against us are just as exposed, since a guaranteed way to lose a public debate with a protectionist is to assert that imports are a minor influence on the labour market – something which few audiences of non-economists are likely to believe. It is much more persuasive to emphasise that economic analysis confirms that there are losers as well as gainers from trade, but shows that protection is inferior to other ways of helping the losers.

What are these other, better ways? A familiar one is to try to offset the reduction in demand for unskilled workers by a parallel reduction in their supply. To some extent, this will happen automatically, since the widening economic gap between the skilled and the unskilled sharpens the incentive to acquire skills. But this supply response can probably be amplified and accelerated by government action to improve education and training. Even at best, though, this strategy will yield results only slowly: it may be a couple of decades before the relative supply of unskilled workers is cut by enough to raise their relative wage substantially.

In the meantime, we need other measures, and in particular subsidies to the unskilled. In America, where wages are flexible, the need is for subsidies to boost the living standards of workers who take low-paying jobs, in the form of tax cuts, cash supplements to wages, and better public services. In Europe, where an institutionally determined floor to the unskilled wage has to be accepted as a political constraint, the need is for subsidies to employers, to encourage them to hire more unskilled workers, especially in non-traded services. A more thorough discussion of these policy options is offered in Wood (1994, ch. 10).

Since (once protection is ruled out) the appropriate policy responses to a falling demand for unskilled labour are the same, whether it is caused by trade or new technology, the opponents in the debate over causation often agree on solutions. But economists can always find something to disagree about: in this case, some argue that subsidies, by easing the plight of the unskilled, will slow the supply response, and thus protract the problem. However, low wages and unemployment are an obstacle as well as an incentive to skill acquisition: the net effect of the subsidies, particularly on the education of the children of the unskilled, is quite likely to be positive. A more serious risk is political: it is the reluctance among the skilled to pay the taxes needed to finance the subsidies to the unskilled.

Notes

* This paper first appeared in the *Journal of Economic Perspectives* (Summer, 1995). It is reproduced here with the kind permission of the American Economic Association. The paper owes much to the reactions of participants in seminars on Wood (1994) at many American and British universities, to the work and advice of Edward Leamer, and to comments from Alan Auerbach, Gene Grossman, Lawrence Mishel, Carl Shapiro, Howard Shatz and Timothy Taylor. I am grateful for financial support from the UK Overseas Development Administration through its research programme at IDS.

1. The impact of trade on labour markets in *developing* countries is just as important and controversial an issue, but lies beyond the scope of this

paper. See, for example, Wood (1994, ch. 6), Robbins (1994), Feenstra and Hanson (1995) and Revenga and Montenegro (1995).

2. The exposition can be elaborated with more goods, factors and countries, without changing its essence (see Wood, 1994, chs. 2 and 9; Leamer, 1995).

3. Point B, where dd and DD cross, is the endowment ratio at which even an open country would not trade: countries to the left of B are net exporters of machinery, and those to right are net exporters of apparel.

4. With more than two traded goods, DD would look rather different: instead of a single flat segment in the middle, it would have alternate flat and downward-sloping segments. On each flat, a country produces two traded goods (adjacent in skill intensity), and on each downward-sloping segment only one. All countries are specialized, since none of them produces all of the traded goods. The simple two-good story about specialization thus requires only minor modifications. It remains true (a) that labour supply changes can alter wages (by movement along a downward-sloping segment or from one segment to another), and (b) that relative wages are not affected by changes in the world prices of goods which the country does not produce. However, if a country is on a flat, and there is a change in the relative world price of the two goods it produces, then relative wages do alter.

5. Rowthorn (1994) provides a general equilibrium simulation which nearly illustrates and extends the argument in Wood (1994).

6. A possible third adjustment, further reducing the estimated displacement of labour, would be for lower efficiency in developing countries (due to inferior technology or poor infrastructure). However, despite inefficiency in much of developing-country manufacturing, the particular countries and firms which manufacture for export to developed countries do not in general have either backward technology or low labour productivity (for references to case-study evidence on this point, see Wood, 1994, p. 134).

7. This specific point was put to me by Kevin Murphy in a seminar, but much the same concern has been expressed by other labour economists (for example, Bound and Johnson, 1992). It would be hard to find data on relative supply and wages that were strictly comparable with my estimate of the trade-induced demand shift, which refers to two coarse skill categories in all developed countries (for a partial attempt, see Wood, 1994, pp. 260–65, 433–4, 447–53). However, a rough indication of the size of the supply shift can be obtained from education statistics for the US and other countries.

8. This is known as a magnification effect. As a simple numerical example, consider two goods, the total cost of each of which consists half of wages (skilled and unskilled) and half of payments to capital and other inputs. The ratio of skilled to unskilled workers is 70/30 for one good and 30/70 for the other, and the skilled wage is initially twice the unskilled wage (so that skilled wages are 41 per cent of total costs for one good and 23 per cent for the other). To cause a 1 per cent rise in the relative price of the skill-intensive good requires more than a 5 per cent rise in the relative wage of skilled workers.

9. There is disagreement about this. Berman, Bound and Griliches (1994),

and Lawrence (1994), present evidence that "outsourcing" by U.S. firms is small, but Feenstra and Hanson (1995) criticise them for using too narrow a definition of outsourcing (namely importing intermediate inputs). There is no reason why the splitting up of production should leave the final stage in the U.S.: if anything, it seems more likely that final assembly, usually a labour-intensive operation, would be undertaken abroad, and that the U.S. would supply skill-intensive intermediate components and services.

10. Note, though, that insofar as the faster technical progress in labour-intensive sectors is a defensive response to low-wage competition, it must be associated with falling prices in these sectors, which makes its effects on wages less straightforward than when prices are assumed to be fixed.

11. By focusing on the *relative* position of skilled and unskilled workers, this article avoids a second debate about trade with developing countries, namely whether it has reduced (or will reduce) the average real wage of all workers in developed countries. On the past, Lawrence and Slaughter (1993, pp. 166–79) show that it has not. On the future, there must be more doubt: the main risk is probably not a massive outflow of capital (which has been mobile for decades), but that the high earnings of skilled workers in rich countries are a scarcity rent that wider diffusion of knowledge will erode, rather than an enduring return to investment in human capital.

References

Batra, R. (1993) *The Myth of Free Trade* (New York: Charles Scribner's Sons).

Berman, E., Bound, J. and Griliches, Z. (1994) 'Changes in the Demand for Skilled Labor within U.S. Manufacturing: Evidence from the Annual Survey of Manufactures', *Quarterly Journal of Economics*, May, *CIX*, pp. 367–97.

Bernard, A. B. and Bradford Jensen, J. (1994) 'Exporters, Skill Upgrading and the Wage Gap', Research Paper 94–13, Center for Economic Studies, Bureau of the Census, Washington, DC.

Borjas, G., Freeman, R. and Katz, L. (1992) 'On the Labor Market Effects of Immigration and Trade', in George Borjas and Richard Freeman (eds.), *Immigration and the Work Force* (Chicago: University of Chicago Press and NBER) pp. 213–44.

Borjas, G. and Ramey, V. (1994) 'Time Series Evidence on the Sources of Trends in Wage Inequality', *American Economic Review*, May, 84, pp. 10–16.

Bound, J. and Johnson, G. (1992) 'Changes in the Structure of Wages in the 1980s: An Evaluation of Alternative Explanations', *American Economic Review*, June, 82, pp. 371–92.

Feenstra, R. C. and Hanson, G. (1995) 'Foreign Investment, Outsourcing and Relative Wages', mimeo, University of California at Davis and University of Texas at Austin, March [forthcoming in *Political Economy of Trade Policy: Essays in Honor of Jagdish Bhagwati* (Cambridge: MIT Press)].

Freeman, R. B. (1994) *Working Under Different Rules* (New York: Russell Sage Foundation).

Freeman, R. B. (1995) 'Are your Wages Set in Beijing?', *The Journal of Economic Perspectives*, 9, pp. 15–32.

Katz, L. F. and Murphy, K. M. (1992) 'Changes in Relative Wages 1963–1987: Supply and Demand Factors', *Quarterly Journal of Economics*, February, CVII, pp. 35–78.

Krueger, A. B. (1993) 'How Computers Have Changed the Wage Structure: Evidence from Microdata 1984–89', *Quarterly Journal of Economics*, February, CVIII, pp. 33–60.

Krugman, P. and Lawrence, R. Z. (1994) 'Trade, Jobs, and Wages', *Scientific American*, April, pp. 44–9.

Lawrence, R. Z. (1994) 'Trade, Multinationals, and Labor', Working Paper No. 4836, National Bureau of Economic Research, Cambridge.

Lawrence, R. Z. and Slaughter, M. J. (1993) 'International Trade and American Wages in the 1980s: Giant Sucking Sound or Small Hiccup', *Brookings Papers on Economic Activity*, 2, pp. 161–226.

Leamer, E. E. (1993) 'Wage Effects of a U.S.–Mexican Free Trade Agreement' in Peter M. Garber (ed.), *The Mexico–U.S. Free Trade Agreement* (Cambridge, Mass: MIT Press) pp. 57–125.

Leamer, E. E. (1994) 'Trade, Wages and Revolving-Door Ideas', Working Paper No. 4716, National Bureau of Economic Research, Cambridge.

Leamer, E. E. (1995) 'A Trade Economist's View of U.S. Wages and "Globalisation"', paper prepared for a Brookings Institution conference on Imports, Exports and the American Worker, mimeo, Anderson Graduate School of Management, University of California at Los Angeles, February.

Machin, S. (1994) 'Changes in the Relative Demand for Skills in the UK Labour Market', Discussion Paper No. 952, Centre for Economic Policy Research, London.

Mishel, L. and Bernstein, J. (1994) 'Is the Technology Black Box Empty? An Empirical Investigation of the Impact of Technology on Wage Inequality and the Employment Structure', mimeo, Economic Policy Institute, Washington DC, April.

Revenga, A. L. and Montenegro, C. (1995) 'North American Integration and Factor Price Equalisation: Is there Evidence of Wage Convergence between Mexico and the United States?', paper prepared for a Brookings Institution conference on Imports, Exports and the American Worker, mimeo, The World Bank, January.

Richardson, J. D. (1995) 'Income Inequality and Trade: How to Think, What to Conclude', *The Journal of Economic Perspectives*, 9, pp. 33–56.

Robbins, D. J. (1996) 'Earnings Dispersion in Chile after Trade Liberalisation', mimeo, Harvard University, July.

Rowthorn, R. (1996) 'Unemployment, Trade and Capital Formation in the OECD', mimeo, Faculty of Economics, Cambridge University, October.

Sachs, J. D. and Shatz, H. J. (1994) 'Trade and Jobs in U.S. Manufacturing', *Brookings Papers on Economic Activity*, 1, pp. 1–84.

Saeger, S. S. (1995) 'Trade, Industrial Structure and Employment: Evidence from the OECD', mimeo, Harvard University, March.

Sarkar, P. and Singer, H. (1995) 'Manufactured Exports and Terms of Trade Movements of Less Developed Countries in Recent Years', Discussion Paper No. 270, Institute of Development Studies, University of Sussex.

Slaughter, M. J. (1994) 'The Impact of Internationalisation on U.S. Income Distribution', in Richard O'Brien (ed.), *Finance and the International Economy*, 8 (The Amex Bank Review Prize Essays) (London: Oxford University Press for American Express Bank Ltd.).

Van Reenen, J. (1994) 'Getting a Fair Share of the Plunder? Technology, Skill and Wages in British Establishments', Discussion Paper No. 881, Centre for Economic Policy Research, London.

Wood, A. (1991a) 'How Much Does Trade with the South Affect Workers in the North', *World Bank Research Observer*, January, 6, pp. 19–36.

Wood, A. (1991b) 'The Factor Content of North-South Trade in Manufactures Reconsidered', *Weltwirtschaftliches Archiv*, December, 127, pp. 719–743.

Wood, A. (1994) *North-South Trade, Employment and Inequality: Changing Fortunes in a Skill-Driven World* (Oxford: Clarendon Press).

Woodall, P. (1994) 'War of the Worlds', *The Economist*, 1 October.

8 Occupational Employment and Wage Changes in the UK: Trade and Technology Effects

Anthony Courakis, Keith E. Maskus and Allan Webster*

INTRODUCTION

Recent studies, most notably of US labour markets, have identified a growing trend of inequality in both wages and employment opportunities. Less skilled, lower wage workers have experienced a decline in their relative wages at the same time that their share in total employment has also declined. More skilled, more highly paid workers have experienced more rapid growth in real wages accompanied by an increasing share of total employment. Evidence of a similar pattern of change also exists for the UK.

The main controversy has concerned whether trade (more properly globalization) or technology has been primarily responsible for these changes. Work by Revenga (1992), Leamer (1993 and 1995), Sachs and Shatz (1994) and Wood (1994) has emphasized the role of globalization in US labour markets. Other authors, including Bound and Johnson (1992), Katz and Murphy (1992), Lawrence and Slaughter (1993) and Berman et al. (1994), have found a dominant role for technological change in influencing US labour markets. Katz and Murphy (1992) also find a subsidiary role for changes in labour supplies. To date there have been relatively few studies of the UK although work by Greenhalgh et al. (1989) has provided some insight into these issues.

In this paper we argue that the basis of most of the findings that technology rather than globalization is the cause of the widening inequality of wages and employment opportunities is inconsistent with trade theory. Specifically, following Leamer (1993 and 1995) we argue that trade theory predicts that tradeables are characterized by perfectly

169

elastic factor demands. In consequence, employment in tradeables production can only respond to changes in factor supplies, in factor demands by non-tradeables and in technology. As a residual employer the volume of tradeables output is, therefore, incapable of being the cause of aggregate employment changes in a trade theoretic framework.

This implies that those who argue that technology rather than trade is responsible for employment changes are addressing an issue that is redundant in terms of trade theory. It also implies that authors who argue trade (as opposed to globalization) is responsible are arguing from a position that is not consistent with trade theory. Instead we argue that authors such as Leamer (1993 and 1995) who assign a role to globalization do so from a perspective that is consistent with the theory of trade.

Globalization in this context means the determination of the prices of tradeable goods in world markets. This includes technological effects because changes in world technology, like changes in world factor prices, change these product prices. These changes determine the prices faced by domestic producers and for any given, linearly homogeneous technology, determine domestic wage changes in competitive markets. That is, domestic factor price changes diverge from world factor price changes only by the extent that domestic technological progress diverges from that of the world. The key link in this process is world tradeables prices. It also follows that, if world product prices and domestic technology change wages by shifting the perfectly elastic factor demand curves of the tradeables sector, they also affect employment.

Moreover, we contend that, in a trade theoretical framework, the argument that domestic technological change reduces employment is misplaced. Specifically, we argue that domestic technological progress in an open economy facing given world prices will increase rather than reduce wages and employment. Technological progress in the world, however, has the reverse effect.

We start our analysis by developing the conceptual basis of these arguments. We then consider changes in occupational employment in tradeables in the UK as a response to the stimuli of various changes rather than as an exercise in allocating blame between trade and technology. That is, we treat changes in tradeables employment as a passive response rather than as an active cause of change and offer evidence of the magnitude of these changes.

Finally we consider globalization effects in the form of linkages between product prices, domestic technology and wages. We provide evidence, in the form of econometric estimates, that provide some support for the existence of such linkages. This, then, provides an explanation of globalization and technological change which does not rely on trade and technology as competing explanations. Rather we argue that globalization and technological change are largely inseparable processes in terms of their effects on factor employment.

CONCEPTUAL ISSUES

The implications of trade theory

The Heckscher–Ohlin (H–O) model of international trade is well known so we confine ourselves to summarizing only the predictions of relevance to this paper. Readers requiring a fuller summary of the model's predictions are referred to Leamer (1995). There are three predictions of relevance to this paper:

Prediction 1 (Heckscher–Ohlin) : countries will tend to export goods intensive in their abundant factors of production and to import goods intensive in their scarce factors.

Prediction 2 (Rybczynski theorem) : for an open economy facing given world product prices, changes in the endowments of factors affect outputs but not factor prices.

Prediction 3 (factor price insensitivity) : for an open economy facing given world prices the derived factor demands are perfectly elastic.

Prediction 3 can be shown to be a corollary of prediction 2. Note that factor price insensitivity is a property distinct from factor price equalization, which requires stronger assumptions.

The three predictions given above require assumptions of competitive factor and product markets, internationally immobile but intersectorally mobile factors, common world product prices and identical homothetic preferences. In the standard exposition internationally invariant technology is also assumed.

To examine the implications of these predictions for employment and wages we start with the simplest case where all goods are tradeable. Figures 8.1a and 8.1b, which we attribute to Leamer, provide a representation of the factor price insensitivity property. Figure 8.1a is drawn for a scarce factor of production and Figure 8.1b for an abundant factor of production.

In both figures, S_d is the domestic supply of labour and S_w the perfectly elastic world supply of labour. This means that the demand for domestic labour is, in effect, perfectly elastic for all levels of factor employment to the right of the intersection of S_d and S_w. D is the derived demand for domestic and foreign factor services. If factor prices are equalized D is the actual demand for both domestic and foreign labour. If factor prices are not equalized it is a hypothetical demand – that is, it is the quantity of domestic factors that would be needed to produce total consumption at fixed input–output coefficients.

Assume that, in both figures, world factor supply is initially given by S_{w0} such that wages are w_0. Domestic employment is at E_0 and the demand for total (domestic and foreign) labour services is given by F_0. Net exports of factor services are the difference between these two points ($E_0 - F_0$). Suppose now that world product prices change such that the world factor supply curve is shifted down in Figure 8.1a and shifted up in Figure 8.1b. In both cases these changes in product prices change both the net exports of factor services and employment.

There are two implications of this analysis that are worth emphasizing. Firstly, factor prices do not respond to supply changes, only to shifts in perfectly elastic demand. Secondly, it is mistaken to assume, as a number of previous authors such as Katz and Murphy (1992) have done, that changes in the factor content of trade are a direct loss (gain) to domestic employment. For example, the net imports of factor services in Figure 8.1a are increased by ($F_1 - E_1$) less ($F_0 - E_0$) but the loss in employment is only ($E_0 - E_1$). This means that any proper assessment of employment effects requires knowledge of movements in both S and S_w and these cannot be deduced from changes in the factor content of trade alone.

Consider now the case where some products are non-tradeables. As authors such as Lebow (1993) have noted, changes in the non-tradeables sector interact with changes in tradeables. This gives rise to a need to explain how factors are allocated between tradeables and non-tradeables. For a given set of factor prices and given technology we can draw the type of diagram (Figure 8.2) more normally associated with the specific factors model. The distance $O_{nt}O_t$ represents the total domestic supply of a particular factor at the given factor price. Employment in the production of non-tradeables is measured from left to right and employment in tradeables production from right to left. Wages (w_0)

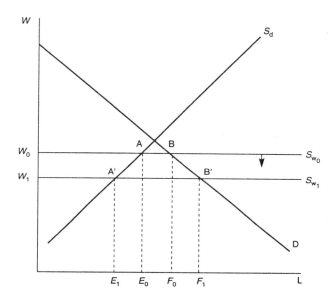

Figure 8.1a

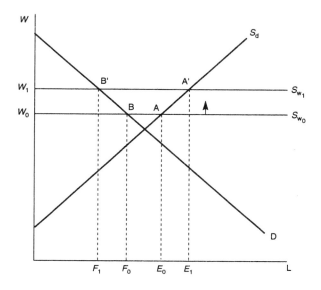

Figure 8.1b

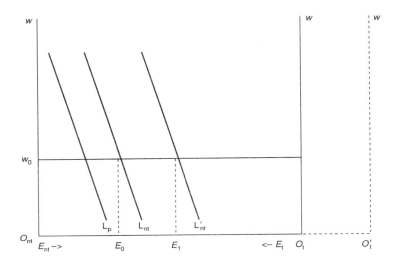

Figure 8.2

are given by the perfectly elastic demand for the particular factor by
the tradeables sector.

With given factor prices and given linearly homogeneous technology, the cost minimizing techniques employed in the non-tradeables
sector do not vary. This means that the demand for the factor by the
private non-tradeables sector (L_p) is given by the output demand. Thus,
the output, product prices and employment of private non-tradeables
are given by the intersection of L_p and w_0. Public goods are almost
invariably non-tradeables but do not normally have prices. Employment in public goods is, therefore, a parallel addition to the demand
by private sector non-tradeables. The total demand for any factor by
the non-tradeables sector is given by the addition of public goods
employment to the demand by private non-tradeables (curve L_{nt}).

This representation of the inter-sectoral allocation of labour gives
rise to three propositions.

Proposition 1: an increase (decrease) in the total supply $(O_t$ to $O_t')$ of
a domestic factor at given factor prices and technology is wholly absorbed by employment in the tradeables sector. That is, only tradeables
are subject to Rybczynski effects.

Proposition 2: any change in the demand for private non-tradeables or

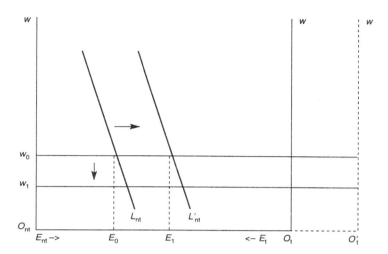

Figure 8.3

in the demand for labour by the production of public goods (L_{nt} to L_{nt}') at given factor prices and technology is wholly absorbed by employment in the tradeables sector. From the point of view of the tradeables sector such changes are equivalent to a change in the overall factor supply. Such changes, therefore, also have Rybczynski effects on the tradeables sector.

Consider now the effects of a shift in w_0, for example as the result of a change in world prices of tradeables. Figure 8.3 shows a downward movement in w_0. This downward movement has two main effects. Firstly, with an upward sloping domestic supply curve for the factor the total supply is moved inward from O_t' to O_t. This affects only the tradeables sector. Secondly, the downward shift in the perfectly elastic demand by tradeables is a movement down the nontradeables demand curve. That is:

Proposition 3: shifts in the perfectly elastic demand for labour by tradeables cause the switching of employment between tradeables and non-tradeables.

As Figure 8.1 showed, it is too simplistic to use only changes in the factor content of trade to measure the effects of trade on employment. Issues of factor allocation between the production of tradeables and non-tradeables further undermine such an approach. The output and employment of the tradeables sector can rise or fall independently of any changes in the external environment if, for example, public goods employment is changed.

Externally originated changes in the perfectly elastic factor demands of the tradeables sector also cause employment switching between tradeables and non-tradeables. In effect, the employment of the domestic tradeables sector is the residual after changes in factor supply and the demand by non-tradeables have been taken into account. This means that any proper assessment of the sources of employment changes in the tradeables sector must not only consider movements in (a) factor supply and (b) movements in the perfectly elastic factor demand by tradeables but must also (c) examine changes in the demand by non-tradeables. Note, however, that whilst trade theory suggests that the tradeables sector is a passive respondent in terms of employment, wages are determined by the interaction of domestic and world conditions in the markets for tradeable products.

Trade and technology

The preceding discussion showed that the effects of trade on employment are not as readily measurable as some have previously supposed, even without the inclusion of technological change. In this section we will argue that (a) trade and technology effects are much less readily separable than many authors have presumed and (b) the effects of domestic technological progress will, contrary to many previous authors, raise and not lower employment in a trade theoretic model.

The intuition of this point is simple. The argument that technology reduces the demand for labour is essentially one that asserts that technological progress means that the same output can be produced with fewer inputs. This is true but there is no reason why an open economy facing perfectly elastic demand should face fixed output levels. The alternative representation – that a greater output can be produced with the same inputs – is much nearer to an accurate representation.

The simplest approach to trade and technology is that taken by studies such as that by Berman *et al.* (1994). They assign inter-industry employment changes to a number of factors, including trade and within-industry changes to technology. From the preceding discussion it should be obvious that this is not consistent with trade theory. For example, changes in relative product prices change relative factor prices and, thus, factor proportions. Within-industry employment changes can result with no change in technology.

The approach of other authors, such as Lawrence and Slaughter (1993), who focus on trade and technology as competing explanations of changes in trade and employment is less obviously inconsistent with trade theory. We would, however, take issue with the basis of their findings that technology rather than trade has been mainly responsible for employment and wage changes in the US. Firstly we will argue that technology affects trade as well as employment. It is not, therefore, apparent how the employment effects of one are separable from the other. Secondly, we argue that, in an open economy purely domestic technological progress increases rather than reduces wages and employment.

Consider the first argument, that technology also determines trade. Jones (1965) recognized that, in a trade model, technological progress has effects which closely resemble those of an increase in factor endowments. This can readily be shown in the context of the Heckscher–Ohlin–Vanek (HOV) model. The model is given for k factors and n goods as:

$$AT = V - sV_w \tag{1}$$

where A is the $(k \times n)$ matrix of factor requirements, T the $(n \times 1)$ vector of net exports of goods, V the $(k \times 1)$ vector of domestic factor endowments, V_w the $(k \times 1)$ vector of world factor endowments and s is the share of the domestic country in world consumption, (that is, $C = sC_w$), where C is the domestic consumption vector and C_w is the world consumption vector. All are presumed measured at time t.

To take the simplest possible representation of technological change, assume that all factors and industries are subject to a single uniform Hicks-neutral technological change, given by the parameter $\pi \geq 1$. The implication of this for domestic factor market equilibrium in terms of efficiency units is that:

$$\pi AQ = \pi AT + \pi AC = \pi V \tag{2}$$

where T is the $(n \times 1)$ vector of net exports and C the $(n \times 1)$ vector of consumption of goods. Note that the effect of the uniform Hicks neutral change is to increase by π the endowment of each factor in terms of efficiency units.

The unchanged equilibrium in world factor markets is given as:

$$AQ_w = AC_w = V_w \tag{3}$$

where subscript w denotes world.

The relationship between domestic and world consumption after domestic technological change is:

$$\pi C = (s\pi)C_w \qquad (4)$$

Note that one effect of the uniform domestic Hicks-neutral change is to increase the share of the domestic country in world consumption from s to $(s\pi)$. Taking the difference between the domestic and scaled world employment vectors gives:

$$\pi A T = \pi(V - sV_w) \qquad (5)$$

This simple model makes two clear predictions about the effects of domestic technological change. Firstly, equation (5) predicts that technological progress will increase the exports of goods intensive in abundant factors and the imports of goods intensive in scarce factors. That is, domestic technical progress may itself be the cause of increased trade. There is a body of empirical evidence which supports the influence of technology upon trade – see Bowen *et al.* (1987), Trefler (1993 and 1994) and Maskus and Webster (1995). Secondly, it also increases domestic consumption for any given level of world income. Moreover, the same predictions can be derived with more general representations of technological change (see Courakis *et al.*, 1995). It is, therefore, clear that the separate effects of technology and trade on employment are not readily identified.

An obvious limitation of this line of reasoning is that technology changes in the rest of the world as well as in the domestic economy. To consider the interaction of domestic and world technological change we start with the linkages between prices and wages. Ethier (1984) derives the following relationship between changes in prices and wages:

$$dP = dW \cdot A \qquad (6)$$

where dP is a $(k \times 1)$ vector of price changes, dW is a $(k \times 1)$ vector of wage changes and A is a $(k \times k)$ matrix of factor requirements. Note that this requires that the number of factors and the number of goods be the same. However, Ethier also shows that, if there are more goods (n) than factors the relationship holds for any subset of goods $k < n$.

In effect equation (6) stacks k equations of the form:

$$dP_i = \Sigma_j(dW_j \cdot a_{ij}) \tag{7}$$

where subscript i denotes industry i, subscript j factor j and where a_{ij} is given as the quantity of factor j used to produce one unit of good i (L_{ij}/Q_i).

Each of these equations can be expressed in terms of proportionate changes:

$$p_i = \Sigma_j(w_j \cdot \theta_{ij}) \tag{8}$$

where lower case letters denote proportionate changes and where the values of θ_{ij} are the shares of each factor in the total output value. This equation is simply an extension of the well known relationship derived in Jones (1965) to more than two factors.

Jones also shows that this relationship can be extended to include changes in the values of a_{ij} such that:

$$p_i = \Sigma_j(w_j \cdot \theta_{ij}) + \Sigma_j(a^*_{ij} \cdot \theta_{ij}) \tag{9}$$

where a^*_{ij} is the proportionate change in a_{ij}.

The proportionate changes given by a^*_{ij} can be de-composed into two components. These are:

$$a^*_{ij} = c_{ij} - b_{ij} \tag{10}$$

where c_{ij} is the proportionate change in each a_{ij} caused by a change in factor prices at given technology and b_{ij} is the change attributable to technological change. This is defined as:

$$b_{ij} = -(1/a_{ij}) \cdot (da_{ij}/dt) \tag{11}$$

Note that, as Jones (1965) shows, c_{ij} has the following property:

$$\Sigma_j(\theta_{ij}c_{ij}) = 0 \tag{12}$$

That is, the weighted sum of the values of c_{ij} (using shares in total output values as weights) is zero.

Equation (9) can now be rewritten as:

$$p_i = \Sigma_j[\theta_{ij}(w_j - b_{ij}), \text{ or equivalently} \tag{13a}$$

$$p_i + \Sigma_j(\theta_{ij} \cdot b_{ij}) = \Sigma_j(\theta_{ij} w_j) \tag{13b}$$

Equations (13a) and (13b) are the basis of key predictions concerning international technological linkages. Both equations state that, given linearly homogeneous production and competitive markets, proportionate changes in wages can only diverge from the change given by changes in product prices if there is technological progress. Note also that both equations imply that the perfectly elastic demand curve for labour in Figures 8.1 will shift upward if there is domestic technological progress at given factor prices. From Figure 8.1 it should be obvious that this upward shift would increase rather than reduce employment in tradeables.

From the point of view of the domestic economy the values of p_i are given world prices but how are these determined? By exactly the same procedure changes in world prices can be written as:

$$p_i = \Sigma_j[\theta_{ijw}(w_{jw} - b_{ijw}) \tag{14}$$

where w_{jw} and b_{ijw} are given by changes in world factor endowments and world technology.

Since the domestic economy must face exactly the same set of changes in world prices it follows that:

$$\Sigma_j[\theta_{ij}(w_j - b_{ij}) = \Sigma_j[\theta_{ijw}(w_{jw} - b_{ijw}), \text{ or} \tag{15a}$$

$$\Sigma_j(\theta_{ij} w_j) - \Sigma_j(\theta_{ijw} w_{ijw}) = \Sigma_j(\theta_{ij} b_j) - \Sigma_j(\theta_{ijw} b_{ijw}) \tag{15b}$$

These equations link proportionate changes in domestic wages and technology with proportionate changes in world wages and technology. Product prices are the key transmission mechanism by which change in world conditions are transmitted to domestic labour markets. Equation (15b) argues that, for each good, the difference between domestic and world weighted averages of proportionate wage changes depends on differences in technological change.

Finally, equations (15a) and (15b) can be expressed in terms of the familiar concept of total factor productivity. Total factor productivity (tp) changes are given as:

$$tp_i = q_i - \Sigma_j(\theta_{ij} \cdot l_{ij}) \tag{16}$$

where q_i is the proportionate change in output of good i and the l_{ij} is the proportionate change in each factor of production employed in industry i.

Since $\Sigma_j \theta_{ij} = 1$ by construction it follows that:

$$tp_i = \Sigma_j [\theta_{ij}(q_i - l_{ij}) = -\Sigma_j (\theta_{ij} a_{ij}^*) = \Sigma_j (\theta_{ij} b_{ij}) \tag{17}$$

This means that equation (15b) can be re-stated as:

$$\Sigma_j [\theta_{ij} w_j) - \Sigma_j (\theta_{ij} w_{ijw}) = tp_i - tp_{iw} \tag{18}$$

That is, the difference in the (weighted) average proportionate wage changes is given by the differences between domestic and world changes in total factor productivity. Note that, again, equation (18) predicts that, all other things being equal, domestic technological change will tend to raise not lower wages. Consequentially (see Figure 8.1) it will tend to raise and not lower employment.

DECOMPOSITIONS OF EMPLOYMENT CHANGES

Methodology

In the preceding section we argued that an implication of previous work, for example by Leamer (1993), is that the causes of changes in employment cannot be identified without also identifying shifts in (a) factor supply functions and (b) perfectly elastic factor demands by the tradeables sector. However, we also showed that knowledge of changes in the employment by the tradeables sector is also necessary since the tradeables sector determines wages but is a residual employer at these wages.

We, therefore, start by decomposing the occupational employment of the tradeables and non-tradeables sectors. Consider how the factor market equilibrium relationship given by equation (2) changes over a discrete period of time. Thus, the change in total employment of factors is given by:

$$V_{t_2} - V_{t_1} = A_{t_2} Q_{t_2} - A_{t_1} Q_{t_1} = A_{t_2} T_{t_2} - A_{t_1} T_{t_1} + A_{t_2} C_{t_2} - A_{t_1} C_{t_1} \tag{19}$$

where V is the $(k \times 1)$ vector of factor supplies and where subscripts refer to time t_2 and t_1.

Let the change in the A matrix between time t_1 and t_2 be given as a matrix D where:

$$D = (A_{t_2} - A_{t_1}) \tag{20}$$

This means that equation (19) can be rewritten as:

$$V_{t_2} - V_{t_1} = DQ_{t_2} + A_{t_1}(T_{t_2} - T_{t_1}) + A_{t_1}(C_{t_2} - C_{t_1}) \tag{21a}$$

That is, the change in total factor demands can be decomposed into three main components. These are:

(a) the difference (DQ_{t_2}) in the actual factor requirements of current period output and the requirements needed to produce current outputs using base period values of a_{ij}.
(b) the change in net exports evaluated at base period factor requirements (a_{ij}).
(c) the change in consumption vectors evaluated at base period factor requirements.

There are two qualifications that need to be made to this relationship. Firstly, the $(k \times 1)$ vector DQ_{t_2} is not a measure of technological change alone because it includes changes in factor requirements due to factor price changes. However, from equation (17), the sum of the elements of this vector are a measure of total factor productivity change. Secondly, evaluation of the change in employment associated with changes in net exports does not imply causality. Indeed our earlier analysis would suggest that equation (21a) should be more properly written as:

$$(V_{t_2} - V_{t_1}) - DQ_{t_2} - A_{t_1}(C_{t_2} - C_{t_1}) = A_{t_1}(T_{t_2} - T_{t_1}) \tag{21b}$$

This, more appropriately, represents the change in factor employment in the tradeables sector as the residual change after changes in factor supplies, the values of a_{ij} and the consumption vector.

The right hand side of equation (12a) can be further decomposed into changes for three sectors: $x = 1 \ldots nx$ tradeable goods (x), $y = 1 \ldots ny$ private non-tradeables (y) and public goods (z). Thus:

$$(V_{t_2} - V_{t_1}) = (V_{t_2}^z - V_{t_1}^z) + D^x Q_{t_2}^x + D^y Q_{t_2}^y + A_{t_1}^x(T_{t_2} - T_{t_1}) +$$
$$A_{t_1}^x(C_{t_2}^x - C_{t_1}^x) + A_{t_1}^y(Q_{t_2}^y - Q_{t_1}^y) \tag{22}$$

where the terms are defined as:

$(V_{t_2}^z - V_{t_1}^z) =$ the $(k \times 1)$ vector of changes in public goods employment
$D^x =$ the $(k \times nx)$ matrix of changes in a_{ij}'s in tradeables production
$Q^x =$ the $(nx \times 1)$ vector of tradeable outputs
$D^y =$ the $(k \times ny)$ matrix of changes in a_{ij} in the production of non-tradeables
$Q^y =$ the $(ny \times 1)$ vector of non-tradeable outputs
$A^x =$ the $(k \times nx)$ matrix of values of a_{ij} in tradeables production
$C^x =$ the $(nx \times 1)$ vector of consumption of tradeables
$A^y =$ the $(k \times ny)$ matrix of values of a_{ij} in non-tradeables production

Changes in public goods are defined in terms of employment only because the absence of prices makes output immeasurable. Changes in the consumption of private non-tradeables are identical to output changes since, by definition, there are no net exports.

UK data

Because of the property that the sum of the elements of DQ_{t_2} are a measure of total factor productivity, estimation of equation (22) for all factors of production would have the advantage of providing some evidence on technological change. However, we were unable to find sufficient data to calculate estimates of the capital stock for every economic activity in the UK. Our estimates are only for changes in the employment of 12 different occupational categories of labour. These were:

1. Scientific, engineering and technology professionals
2. Other professionals
3. Managers
4. Clerical and related occupations
5. Sales occupations
6. Service occupations
7. Farming, fishing and related occupations (skilled and part-skilled manual)
8. Materials processing and repairing (largely skilled manual)
9. Painting, repetitive assembling, packaging and so on (largely part-skilled manual)
10. Construction and mining occupations (skilled and part-skilled manual)
11. Transport and storage occupations (skilled and part-skilled)
12. Labourers and other unskilled workers.

For consistency with published input–output tables we chose two periods: 1984 to 1989 and 1989 to 1991. Data on employment by industry and by occupation were taken from the Labour Force Surveys for 1984, 1989 and 1991. These are, however, samples. To scale these samples to population estimates we used data on employment by industry for production industries from the Census of Production (HMSO) for each year. For agriculture and service activities (including public goods) we used employment data from the Employment Gazette (Department of Employment).

Data on output and net exports by economic activity were taken from the UK input–output tables for 1984, 1989, 1991 (HMSO). Consumption data were calculated as apparent consumption (that is, output less net exports). For 1989 these data were deflated to 1984 prices for comparison with 1984 and inflated to 1991 prices for comparison with 1991. For agriculture, construction and production industries producer price indices taken from the Annual Abstract of Statistics (HMSO, various years) were used for this purpose. For services, gas and electricity consumer price indices were used, taken from the Employment Gazette (Department of Employment, various years).

For the purposes of classification we considered government (national and local), justice, police, fire, defence, education, health and other public services to be public goods. We defined private non-tradeables to be any activity in which exports accounted for less than 5 per cent of total output *and* imports accounted for less than 5 per cent of total apparent consumption. This comprised electricity, gas supply, water supply, textile finishing, construction and distribution and repairs.

Estimates for the UK 1984–9 and 1989–91

Table 8.1 reports changes in total labour employment for 1984–9 and 1989–91 for each of the economic activities given by the UK input–output classification. Total labour employment increased by 8.7 per cent between 1984 and 1989 and decreased by 2.2 per cent between 1989 and 1991. Employment in non-tradeables increased by proportionately more than in tradeables between 1984–9 and fell by proportionately less. The evidence, then, is of a consistent rise in the relative size of non-tradeables in employment.

It is also clear from Table 8.1 that there are considerable inter-industry variations within each of these two sectors. The period 1984–9 saw substantial proportionate reductions in total labour employed in agriculture, extraction of mineral fuels, fertilizers, agricultural machinery,

Table 8.1 Changes in UK employment, by economic activity

Economic activity	1984–9 1000s	%	1989–91 1000s	%
A. TRADEABLES				
Agriculture	−48.7	−15.4	−24.6	−9.2
Forestry & fishing	−2.0	−10.4	1.1	6.4
Coal, oil, gas extraction	−139.3	−50.1	−6.9	−5.0
Extraction of metal ores, etc.	−1.3	−23.2	−0.5	−11.6
Iron and steel	−16.6	−14.5	−14.2	−14.5
Aluminium, etc.	0.3	1.7	−1.0	−5.6
Other non-ferrous metals	−5.5	−17.9	−2.2	−8.7
Extraction of stone, etc.	2.4	34.3	−4.6	−48.9
Clay products	0.4	2.0	−4.2	−20.9
Cement, etc.	−1.6	−15.2	−1.1	−12.4
Concrete, etc.	5.3	6.2	−13.2	−14.6
Glass	4.5	11.2	−3.4	−7.6
Refractory and ceramic goods	4.8	9.5	−7.4	−13.3
Inorganic chemicals	−0.3	−2.0	−2.0	−13.5
Organic chemicals	2.3	7.0	−3.7	−10.5
Fertilizers	−6.0	−43.8	−3.0	−39.0
Synthetic resins, etc.	1.5	7.7	−1.1	−5.3
Paints, dyes, etc.	1.2	2.9	−2.6	−6.1
Special chemicals	−3.1	−6.0	4.6	9.5
Pharmaceuticals	8.7	12.9	2.0	2.6
Soap and toiletries	4.4	13.9	−0.9	−2.5
Chemical products, nes	−1.2	−7.8	−2.4	−16.9
Man-made fibres	−1.7	−14.8	−0.8	−8.2
Metal castings, etc.	−4.3	−3.0	−13.0	−9.4
Metal doors, windows, etc.	−1.9	−9.4	−0.8	−4.3
Metal packaging products	−6.3	−20.3	−0.8	−3.2
Metal goods, nes	8.7	6.0	−12.0	−7.8
Industrial plant and steelwork	−17.0	−18.2	3.1	4.1
Agricultural machinery, etc.	−7.1	−30.1	−1.3	−7.9
Machine tools	1.0	3.8	−4.0	−14.7
Engineering small tools	−1.6	−4.7	−2.5	−7.7
Textile etc machinery	−1.3	−3.2	−7.3	−18.6
Processing machinery, etc.	−8.8	−16.5	−3.9	−8.8
Mining, etc. equipment	−4.6	−5.4	−7.6	−9.5
Mech power transmission equipment	−4.8	−10.6	−6.5	−16.0
Other machinery, etc.	−3.0	−1.4	−9.9	−4.6
Ordnance, etc.	−9.6	−36.0	−2.7	−15.8
Office machinery, computers, etc.	11.9	27.1	8.6	15.4
Insulated wires and cables	1.7	5.4	−7.4	−22.3
Basic electrical equipment	−10.0	−9.2	−11.9	−12.1

continued on page 186

Table 8.1 continued

Economic activity	1984–9 1000s	%	1989–91 1000s	%
Industrial electrical equipment	−1.9	−3.3	−2.4	−4.3
Telecommunication, etc. equipment	−19.0	−10.4	−21.2	−12.9
Electronic components	−2.4	−2.7	−10.5	−12.1
Electronic consumers goods, etc.	0.4	1.7	1.0	4.1
Domestic electric appliances	2.0	5.3	−5.7	−14.3
Electric lighting equipment	3.1	11.2	−6.6	−21.4
Motor vehicles and parts	−21.5	−7.5	−20.9	−7.8
Shipbuilding and repairing	−23.8	−26.0	−9.1	−13.5
Aerospace, etc.	−1.7	−1.0	−1.2	−0.7
Other vehicles	−16.7	−39.5	−0.3	−1.2
Instrument engineering	7.9	9.9	−9.4	−10.7
Oils and fats	−0.6	−9.0	−0.9	−14.8
Slaughtering & meat processing	9.7	9.0	−0.7	−0.6
Milk and milk products	−1.1	−2.6	−1.6	−3.9
Fruit, vegetable and fish processing	2.4	5.3	−8.0	−16.7
Grain milling and starch	1.2	18.5	−0.5	−6.5
Bread, biscuits, etc.	5.1	3.4	−5.3	−3.4
Sugar	−1.5	−18.3	−1.5	−22.4
Confectionery	−7.0	−13.0	4.0	8.6
Animal feeding stuffs	−2.4	−10.6	−0.1	−0.5
Miscellaneous foods	−2.5	−4.0	0.4	0.7
Alcoholic drink	−9.7	−16.2	−2.5	−5.0
Soft drinks	4.1	21.4	−2.4	−10.3
Tobacco	−12.4	−46.4	−2.2	−15.4
Woollens and worsted	−4.9	−11.7	−8.0	−21.6
Cotton, etc. spinning & weaving	−4.4	−11.7	−5.8	−17.5
Hosiery and other knitted goods	−12.3	−13.7	−14.0	−18.0
Carpets, etc.	1.6	8.2	−1.2	−5.7
Jute, etc.	−0.3	−1.2	−3.1	−12.8
Leather and leather goods	−2.5	−11.6	−2.7	−14.2
Footwear	−1.5	−2.9	−5.7	−11.5
Clothing and furs	−11.2	−4.8	−38.1	−17.3
Household and other textiles	2.4	8.1	−3.6	−11.2
Timber and wood products	−0.7	−0.8	−14.3	−15.7
Wood furniture	22.6	22.4	−11.4	−9.2
Pulp, paper and board	0.1	0.3	−1.2	−3.7
Paper and board products	−3.2	−2.5	−11.7	−9.5
Printing and publishing	14.0	4.7	−14.1	−4.5
Rubber products	−4.6	−6.7	−6.2	−9.6
Processing of plastic	38.0	28.3	−7.1	−4.1
Other manufacturing	11.7	14.5	−15.5	−16.8
Hotels, catering, etc.	133.2	14.7	125.2	12.0
Railways	−24.2	−15.5	−4.6	−3.5
Road transport, etc.	−1.3	−0.3	30.2	7.9

Table 8.1 continued

Sea transport	−8.0	−18.5	−3.9	−11.0
Air transport	25.9	61.1	−6.9	−10.1
Transport services	32.2	13.5	4.1	1.5
Postal services	4.1	2.1	6.2	3.1
Telecommunications	15.6	7.0	−33.2	−13.9
Banking and finance	138.0	27.4	−26.7	−4.2
Insurance	31.6	13.6	5.0	1.9
Business services, etc.	669.6	65.4	47.8	2.8
Other services	−124.5	−13.7	−45.0	−5.7%
B. NON-TRADEABLES				
Electricity & nuclear power	−7.3	−4.3	−22.2	−13.8
Gas supply	−14.1	−15.2	−3.1	−3.9
Water supply	−8.6	−19.0	1.1	3.0
Textile finishing	−0.7	−3.1	−1.6	−7.2
Construction	58.7	6.1	−37.0	−3.6
Distribution & repairs	189.8	5.9	−46.3	−1.4
National government	70.9	14.4	−39.6	−7.0
Local government	−38.4	−6.4	7.4	1.3
Justice, police, fire	26.8	8.9	−9.4	−2.9
Defence	−0.3	−0.2	−13.2	−10.4
Education	205.3	13.3	−13.9	−0.8
Health	133.6	10.3	−4.4	−0.3
Other public services	247.1	40.8	35.7	4.2
C. TOTALS				
All tradeables	1069.8	7.7	−377.1	−2.5
All non-tradeables	673.0	10.7	−100.2	−1.4
Total	1742.8	8.7	−477.3	−2.2

Sources: Census of Production, PA 1002 (production activities), Employment Gazette (other activities)

ordnance, shipbuilding, vehicles (other than motor, aerospace or ships and boats) and tobacco. Substantial proportionate increases in labour employment were in stone extraction, office machinery and computers, soft drinks, wooden furniture, plastic processing, air transport, banking and finance, business services and other public services. In 1989–91 the largest proportionate reductions in labour employment were in stone extraction, fertilizers, insulated wires and cables and sugar. The largest proportionate increases were in special chemicals, office machinery and computers, confectionery and hotels and catering.

Whilst the significant variations in employment changes by economic activity suggest that an important role was played by product markets they do little to provide any evidence on more systematic changes. Table 8.2 therefore, sets out the decomposition of changes in occupational employment given by equation (22).

The first feature of note from Table 8.2 is the pattern of changing occupational employment. Estimates of the total numbers of employees in farming/fishing, transport and unskilled occupations show declines in employment for both 1984–9 and 1989–91. In each of these cases the number of workers declined by more than 25 per cent between 1984 and 1991. On the other hand employment of both categories of professional labour and managerial labour was estimated to have increased in both 1984–9 and 1989–91. Taken overall the data suggest a broad positive correlation between levels of skill and the proportionate change in employment. That is, the data provide evidence of an increase in the share of more highly skilled and educated labour in the workforce.

Turning to the decomposition of employment changes, consider firstly the changes in public goods employment. For a number of categories (principally the professional and clerical categories) employment in public goods provision was increased in both 1984–9 and 1989–91. For most others numbers were increased in one period but reduced in the other. Taken over both periods, however, the net effect was for public goods employment to mainly increase in the more highly skilled categories and to reduce in the less skilled categories. This implies that with all other influences removed (labour supply, changes in a_{ij}, changes in non-tradeable outputs) these changes would have required reductions in highly skilled but increases in low skilled employment in tradeables.

Between 1984 and 1989 there were only modest net increases in employment of most types of labour in private non-tradeables. For all categories except farming/fishing and construction/mining occupations changes in requirements (a_{ij}) represented hypothetical employment losses which were more than offset by increases in output (consumption). For only two categories was the net effect more than marginally negative – transport and unskilled occupations. Again, with all other influences removed, this would have implied a fairly modest drain of more highly skilled labour from the tradeables sector and the need for the tradeables sector to absorb some less skilled labour.

The picture for 1989–91 is somewhat different. Changes in factor requirements per unit actually tended to increase employment in private non-tradeables for a number of labour categories but, in several cases, these were more than offset by falls in output (consumption). Taken overall the net effect of changes in both requirements (a_{ij}) and in output imply modest reductions in private non-tradeables employment of most labour categories. The exceptions were science professionals and transport occupations (modest increases in employment) and sales occupations (substantial reductions).

Note that, in the trade theoretic framework, changes in the labour supply (that is, total employment) of each category and changes in the labour demands by both public and private non-tradeables are sufficient to determine changes in tradeables employment for any given technology. In other words, the perfectly elastic factor demands mean that tradeables absorb all residual labour. Labour-saving changes in requirements, either from changing factor prices or changing technology or both, imply that output growth must be correspondingly larger.

For all categories of labour, for both 1984–9 and for 1989–91, the estimated change in the requirements matrix $((D^x Q^x_{t_2})$ for tradeables would have led to significant reductions in employment had all other effects been absent. The change in any individual category cannot be attributed to technology alone because the effects of factor price changes have not been excluded. However, because changes are negative for every type of labour we can also reject the hypothesis that these are explained solely by the substitution of one type of labour for another at unchanged technology. This means that at least one of two possible explanations must also apply: (a) technological progress and (b) changes in capital per worker.

Consider now the effects of changes in the consumption of tradeables. By virtue of our earlier discussion, changes in tradeables consumption have no effect on domestic employment in a trade-theoretic view. They do, however, affect the factor content of net exports. For the period 1984–9, there are substantial estimated changes in the consumption of labour services which are partially offset by much smaller reductions in net exports for all but two categories (which showed increases in net exports of factor services). This means that changes in the output of tradeables between 1984 and 1989 were such that substantial employment increases would have been needed were techniques of production (a_{ij}) to have remained constant. Note also that the net effect of changes in techniques and of output changes for tradeables would be to increase employment of the more highly skilled occupations but to reduce employment of the least highly skilled.

To summarize, it is a conceptual impossibility in a trade theoretic framework for employment changes in tradeables to cause any overall

Table 8.2 Estimated changes in UK employment, by occupational category and source of change

ESTIMATED EMPLOYMENT CHANGE (1000s):

	TOTAL (1000s)	%	ATTRIBUTABLE TO CHANGE IN: Tradeables			Non-tradeables		Public sector
			Reqmts.	Consmp.	Net export	Reqmts.	Consmp.	
A. 1984-9								
Science & technology professionals	65.1	6.4	−198.6	243.6	−2.3	−2.1	20.7	3.8
Other professionals	588.2	17.1	−142.8	447.7	−26.5	−57.5	91.9	275.3
Managerial	138.9	6.6	−109.6	267.3	−20.4	−319.5	354.1	−32.9
Clerical & related	569.6	15.6	−452.8	862.5	−20.1	−194.8	258.2	116.6
Sales occupations	220.5	14.9	−50.2	123.6	−5.2	−362.6	515.0	−0.2
Service occupations	437.7	15.3	−55.0	136.9	−49.2	−10.3	39.4	375.9
Farming & fishing occupations	−20.4	−6.9	−52.8	24.1	−3.4	7.3	2.8	1.6
Processing & making occupations	22.1	1.0	−765.5	872.5	−86.3	−245.7	240.5	6.8
Repetitive assemblers, packers, etc.	78.9	9.9	−81.6	162.2	−18.0	−30.4	45.3	1.6
Construction & mining occupations	94.0	15.0	−64.8	70.9	4.4	35.0	58.9	−10.4
Transport occupations	−329.5	–	−372.9	329.1	7.6	−390.0	175.2	−78.5
Labourers & other unskilled workers	−122.4	–	−173.7	85.1	−5.7	−28.6	15.1	−14.5
B. 1989–91								
Science & technology professionals	67.5	7.2	−30.0	21.1	12.8	−0.2	10.3	53.4

Table 8.2 continued

Other professionals	320.8	8.3	−54.8	146.7	16.1	60.8	−16.1	168.1
Managerial	44.4	2.1	−56.5	30.1	22.7	24.5	−67.4	90.9
Clerical & related	−171.9	−4.4	−458.1	121.1	22.0	29.7	−37.2	150.6
Sales occupations	−176.8	–	−37.3	11.0	4.8	−42.2	−127.4	14.2
Service occupations	−289.8	−9.0	−63.9	322.2	30.9	−9.8	−8.6	−560.6
Farming & fishing occupations	−47.3	–	−105.2	41.2	4.9	−4.6	−1.3	17.6
Processing & making occupations	−219.1	−6.6	−219.0	−221.4	87.1	82.5	19.2	32.5
Repetitive assemblers, packers, etc.	−50.8	−6.7	−17.7	−56.9	25.3	5.1	3.6	−10.1
Construction & mining occupations	−48.7	−9.4	−18.6	2.9	1.4	−69.7	32.1	3.2
Transport occupations	−11.4	−1.0	−86.1	40.0	22.1	34.2	−20.4	−1.2
Labourers & other unskilled workers	−13.8	−8.1	−15.1	−0.1	3.3	−6.4	0.4	4.0

Sources: see text

changes in employment. This is because the perfectly elastic factor demands mean that employment in tradeables is a response to changes in factor supplies and changes in factor demands by non-tradeables. Our evidence does not, therefore, constitute a plea of 'not guilty' for trade because we have already claimed an alibi of absence from the scene of the crime in the form of the theoretical factor price insensitivity prediction. What it does is to provide a coherent and theoretically consistent way of establishing how technology, factor supplies and the demand of non-tradeables interact in the markets for labour.

WAGES, PRICES AND TECHNOLOGY

Methodology

The argument that changes in factor employment in the tradeables sector respond to, rather than cause, other changes in employment is only part of the picture. Earlier we argued that the tradeables sector, by virtue of the factor price insensitivity property, responds to employment changes but determines wage changes. That is, product prices for tradeables are determined by world markets in a way that links domestic and foreign wages and technology (equations 15a, 15b and 18).

One estimable equation linking price and wage changes in the absence of technological change is equation (8) above (from Jones, 1965). Baldwin and Cain (1995) estimate a version of this equation. Their cross-sectional regressions use changes in industry prices as the dependent variable and the shares of capital/land and skilled and unskilled labour as regressors. The resulting coefficient estimates are the theoretically predicted proportionate changes in factor prices which can then be compared with actual changes.

Substituting equation (17) into equation (13b) extends this equation to include technological change in the form of total factor productivity such that:

$$p_i = \Sigma_j(\theta_{ij}w_j) - tp_i \tag{23}$$

The basis of our approach is to follow Baldwin and Cain in estimating theoretically predicted parameters using changes in product prices and factor shares in total output values. Instead of estimating implied wage changes we use actual wage changes to infer implied technological change. However, one further modification is needed.

Total factor productivity indices, as used by equation (23), imply industry-specific disembodied technological progress that is invariant by factor of production. This is not necessary because total factor productivity indices can be written as a composite of factor specific embodied changes and industry specific disembodied changes. Suppose that, for each factor of production (L) there is embodied technological progress of the form:

$$L^*_{jt_2} = e^{(1+\alpha j)}L_{jt_1} \tag{24}$$

where L_{jt_1} represents one unit of factor j at time t_1, $L^*_{jt_2}$ is the number of efficiency units of one unit of factor j at time t_2 and α_j is a parameter varying by factor but not by industry. Thus, equation (24) provides a representation of technological progress that is embodied in factors themselves.

Technological progress of this type can occur at the same time as industry specific disembodied changes. Let such disembodied changes by represented by $(l + \delta_i)$ where δ_i varies by industry but not by factor. Note that the proportionate change (l^*_j) in the number of efficiency units of each factor is given by:

$$l^*_{ij} = (1 + \alpha_j) + l_{ij} \tag{25}$$

where l is the proportionate change in the physical quantity of factor j employed in industry i.

Next define $(1 + \alpha_i)$ to be the change in total factor productivity not attributable to changes in the number of efficiency units embodied in each factor. That is:

$$(1 + \delta_i) = q_i - \Sigma_j[\theta_{ij}(1 + \alpha_j)] - \Sigma_j(\theta_{ij}l_j), \text{ or} \tag{26}$$

$$(1 + \delta_i) = tp_i - \Sigma_j[\theta_{ij}(1 + \alpha_j)] \tag{27}$$

The proportionate change in wages per efficiency unit of each factor is, therefore, given by:

$$p_i + (1 + \delta_i) = \Sigma_j(\theta_{ij}w^*_j) \tag{28}$$

where w^*_j is the wage per efficiency unit of factor j.

Each factor now embodies more efficiency units per physical unit. That is the proportionate change in efficiency units is given by $(1 + \alpha_j)$

such that the proportionate change in wages per physical unit is:

$$w_j = w_j^* + (1 + \alpha_j) \tag{29}$$

Rewriting equation (28) in terms of physical units gives:

$$p_i + (1 + \delta_i) = \Sigma_j\{\theta_{ij}[w_j^* + (1 + \alpha_j)]\} \tag{30}$$

This is not estimable because $(1 + \delta_i)$ is not directly measurable. The change in total factor productivity tp_i is, however, measurable. Substituting from equation (27) gives:

$$p_i + tp_i - \Sigma_j[\theta_{ij}(1 + \alpha_j)] = \Sigma_j(\theta_{ij}w_j), \text{ or} \tag{31}$$

$$p_i + tp_i = \Sigma_j\{\theta_{ij}[w_j + (1 + \alpha_j)]\} = \Sigma_j\{\theta_{ij}[w_j^* + 2(1 + \alpha_j)]\} \tag{32}$$

Equation (32) shows that, in the presence of technological progress embodied in factors, using total factor productivity changes involves double counting of the values of $(1 + \alpha_j)$. It is, however, an estimable equation and, if the values of w_j are known, each coefficient estimate (β_j) could, in principle, be used to provide an estimate of embodied technological progress. Thus:

$$(1 + \alpha_j) = \beta_j - w_j \tag{33}$$

This, then, provides a basis to estimate linkages between prices, technological change and wages. In practice, we estimate a normalized form of equation (32). Dividing both sides of this equation by θ_k where subscript k denotes capital gives:

$$(p_i + tp_i)/\theta_k = \beta_k + \Sigma_{j-1}(\theta'_{ij}\beta_j) \tag{34}$$

where the values of θ'_{ij} are the shares of factors in total output relative to that of capital.

Data

Calculation of total factor productivity indices requires estimates of the capital stock. The approach used by previous authors (see Leamer, 1984, or Oulton and O'Mahony, 1994) is to estimate the capital stock at time t (K_t) by the following procedure:

$$K_t = \Sigma(1 - d)^{t-w}(I_w/P_w) \qquad (34)$$

for $w = 0 \ldots t$, where t is the presumed end of the asset's life, d is the discount rate, I_w investment at time w and P_w the appropriate deflator.

Data on fixed investment on three types of asset – buildings, machinery and vehicles – were available from the Census of Production (HMSO). These we depreciated over 5 years for vehicles, 10 years for machinery and 12 years for buildings. However, these data did not provide a full coverage by economic activity. Firstly, the data set includes only production industries. We could not, therefore, include services. Secondly, for some industries a full time series was unavailable. These we also excluded. Finally, for theoretical reasons we excluded activities which we earlier classified as non-tradeables. This left a sample of some 66 manufacturing industries. Note that, as we discussed earlier, Ethier (1984) shows that price–wage relationships remain theoretically valid even with the exclusion of a number of goods.

Calculation of factor shares, including that of intermediates, was performed using the data set described earlier. In calculating the total value of intermediates at constant prices we used the input–output tables to deflate each input by its own price index. Outputs did not require deflation since the term $(p_i + tp_i)$ can be directly measured by calculating a normal total factor productivity index without deflating outputs. Thus, following Diewert (1976) these terms were calculated as:

$$p_i + tp_i = q'_i - \Sigma_j(\theta^*_{ij} \, l_{ij}) \qquad (35)$$

where q'_i is the proportionate change in the nominal value of the output of industry i and θ^*_{ij} is the average of the base and current period values of θ_{ij}. Intermediates were included in these calculations. Note also that, as Diewert (1976) shows, this requires an assumption of a translog production function.

Wage data for each of the occupational categories were taken from the New Earnings Survey (Department of Employment) for each of the relevant years.

Estimates

Since regression estimates of equation (32) do not separately identify estimated changes in total factor productivity we start by reporting these in Table 8.3 Note that these were calculated by subtracting the proportionate change in output prices from $(p_i + tp_i)$.

Table 8.3   Total factor productivity indices

	1984–9 TP (nominal) (%)	Prices (%)	TP Deflated (%)	1984–9 TP (nominal) (%)	Prices (%)	TP Deflated (%)
Mineral oil processing	4.9	−11.3	16.1	23.5	17.5	6.1
Extraction of metal ores, etc.	18.6	32.4	−13.8	13.2	3.0	10.2
Iron and steel	43.8	20.9	22.9	−7.2	3.7	−10.9
Non-ferrous metals	35.0	17.4	17.6	−9.1	3.0	−12.0
Extraction of stone, etc.	54.5	34.1	20.4	4.5	1.9	2.6
Clay products	37.5	45.9	−8.4	−12.0	3.6	−15.6
Concrete, etc.	36.8	27.1	9.7	−0.7	10.0	−10.7
Glass	45.7	16.6	29.1	3.6	13.3	−9.7
Refractory and ceramic goods	51.8	32.0	19.8	9.7	16.2	−6.5
Basic chemicals	27.8	18.4	9.5	−2.6	1.3	−3.9
Paints, dyes, etc.	52.6	42.3	10.3	7.1	12.7	−5.6
Special chemicals	36.2	14.7	21.6	2.7	21.6	−18.8
Pharmaceuticals	65.5	25.0	40.5	14.8	4.0	10.9
Soap and toiletries	36.7	38.3	−1.6	13.7	23.2	−9.5
Chemical products, nes	44.0	29.8	14.2	4.3	16.8	−12.6
Metal castings, etc.	43.5	28.0	15.5	3.0	9.6	−6.5
Metal doors, windows, etc.	44.5	38.6	5.9	0.2	10.7	−10.5
Metal goods, nes	50.9	29.1	21.8	8.6	14.8	−6.1
Industrial plant and steelwork	32.0	25.3	6.7	13.5	0.5	13.0
Agricultural machinery, etc.	7.0	25.8	−18.7	3.1	9.7	−6.6
Machine tools & small tools	49.8	32.6	17.1	8.3	13.2	−4.9
Textile, etc. machinery	26.9	33.2	−6.3	6.9	16.2	−9.3
Processing machinery, etc.	47.6	27.1	20.5	13.3	12.2	1.0
Mining, etc. equipment	50.1	20.2	30.0	4.3	11.9	−7.6
Mech power transmission equipment	34.1	31.3	2.7	2.0	17.2	−15.3
Other machinery, etc.	52.0	27.4	24.6	6.0	15.8	−9.9
Ordnance, etc.	12.0	29.2	−17.1	11.0	14.3	−3.4
Office machinery, computers, etc.	60.1	18.6	41.5	11.6	14.6	−3.1
Insulated wires and cables	20.8	15.4	5.5	2.8	7.6	−4.8
Basic electrical equipment	39.2	35.2	4.0	16.2	17.3	−1.1
Industrial electrical equipment	46.7	38.9	7.9	6.1	16.7	−10.6
Telecoms eqpt. & electronic components	29.7	25.3	4.4	8.8	11.0	−2.2
Domestic electric appliances	31.6	18.2	13.5	11.1	5.0	6.1
Electric lighting equipment	9.7	25.4	−15.7	6.9	17.2	−10.4
Motor vehicles and parts	67.1	41.2	25.9	0.1	13.9	−13.8
Aerospace, etc.	53.6	24.7	28.9	16.0	7.4	8.6
Other vehicles	34.2	20.1	14.1	11.3	6.2	5.2
Instrument engineering	20.2	26.8	−6.6	15.9	13.8	2.1
Oils and fats	−7.9	−27.6	19.7	6.1	2.3	3.8
Slaughtering & meat processing	12.3	14.0	−1.7	6.0	1.8	4.2
Milk and milk products	23.5	22.8	0.8	7.6	5.5	2.1
Fruit, vegetable and fish processing	42.4	16.4	26.0	9.7	19.5	−9.8

Table 8.3 continued

Grain milling and starch	14.2	14.7	−0.5	3.3	4.8	−1.4
Bread, biscuits, etc.	29.6	29.0	0.6	12.9	14.0	−1.1
Sugar	40.9	17.7	23.1	9.5	15.0	−5.5
Confectionery	29.5	15.7	13.8	15.3	9.8	5.5
Animal feeding stuffs	21.7	4.0	17.7	3.7	3.9	−0.3
Miscellaneous foods	32.1	20.5	11.6	10.8	14.5	−3.7
Alcoholic drink	73.5	29.6	43.9	6.8	18.4	−11.6
Soft drink	37.3	30.2	7.1	7.8	14.0	−6.1
Woollens and worsted	24.4	28.9	−4.5	3.2	−3.4	6.6
Cotton, etc. spinning & weaving	17.3	12.9	4.4	6.8	7.4	−0.7
Hosiery and other knitted goods	40.4	33.5	6.9	9.8	14.6	−4.9
Carpets, etc.	43.7	32.7	11.0	2.6	9.5	−7.0
Jute, etc.	40.4	32.5	7.9	10.3	11.6	−1.2
Leather and leather goods	26.5	22.5	4.0	−1.5	−43.0	41.5
Footwear	26.6	28.2	−1.6	−2.2	10.2	−12.4
Clothing and furs	31.9	20.9	10.9	7.8	9.1	−1.3
Timber and wood products	50.8	29.4	21.4	7.1	9.3	−2.2
Wood furniture	45.9	31.2	14.7	9.2	13.2	−4.0
Pulp, paper and board	24.0	30.5	−6.5	6.8	0.4	6.3
Paper and board products	47.2	33.9	13.3	9.8	10.4	−0.6
Printing and publishing	45.9	38.5	7.3	6.9	20.6	−13.7
Rubber products	50.5	23.5	27.0	7.9	8.7	−0.8
Processing of plastic	42.3	25.5	16.8	5.6	12.1	−6.5
Other manufacturing	34.6	40.4	−5.9	7.5	12.3	−4.8

The results for 1984–9 suggest considerable variation in the total factor productivity indices (deflated) by industry. This does not necessarily imply considerable variation in industry-specific technology because, as we have shown, the indices could equally capture factor specific changes which would cause tp_i to vary by industry according to factor proportions. What the results do imply is that the variation in total factor productivity is such that its effects cannot be ignored in a priori specifications of wage changes.

The results for 1989–91 are more problematic because tp indices are negative for a large number of industries. That the effects of macro-economic fluctuations can exert an influence is a well known problem with such measures. We, therefore, suspect that the choice of a two year period (as opposed to 5 years for 1984–9) has meant that we have been unable to even out such fluctuations over the macro-economic cycle. Nonetheless, for 1989–91 as for the earlier period, there is evidence of sufficient variation by industry to justify a priori inclusion of the effects on wages.

For the regression analysis we estimated equation (34) for both 1984–9 and 1989–91 on two different bases. Since prices in this context should be relative prices and changes in wages should be real changes it was necessary to deflate the dependent variable by some numeraire. For each period we used (a) the producer price index for all manufactures and (b) the consumer price index (all items) as numeraires. Since the share of a number of labour categories (sales, service, farming, construction and transport occupations) we also aggregated these into a single 'labour not elsewhere specified' category. The results are reported in Table 8.4.

In Table 8.4 each regression equation is identified by the dependent variable. Thus, TPP/KS is nominal total factor productivity (TPP) relative to the share of capital (KS), using aggregate producer prices as the numeraire. Similarly, TPC/KS is the same measure but using aggregate consumer prices as the numeraire. Labour categories are as listed above and 'inputs' lists the coefficient estimates for intermediates. In each equation there were one or two outlying observations and the coefficients for the appropriate dummy variables are also reported.

For each regression equation a series of specification tests are also reported. These are the standard F test of the overall significance of the regression, the well known Jarque–Bera test for normality, Koenker's (1981) test for heteroskedasticity and an F test of the deletion of a labour share variables.

The first feature of these results is that only one labour share coefficient in one regression is statistically significantly different from zero at 95 per cent confidence levels. On the other hand, we tested for the joint exclusion of the labour share coefficients for each regression and were not able to accept the null hypothesis at 95 per cent confidence levels in any of the four cases. Since no coefficient is individually significant but labour share coefficients are jointly significant we suspect multicollinearity. There are a number of reasons why labour share may be multicollinear. Firstly, their construction (shares of all factors must sum to unity) suggests this. Secondly, factors will normally be substitutes or complements to each other and this, too, suggests a degree of collinearity.

Our conclusion, therefore, is that the confidence intervals associated with each coefficient are too wide to allow any meaningful interpretation of individual coefficients. Nonetheless, all four regressions do provide evidence which supports an overall relationship consistent with the theoretical prediction. In particular, all four regressions provide a high degree of explanation of the total variation in prices and total factor productivity. That is, the evidence suggests that inter-industry variations in price and total factor productivity changes do vary systematically according to factor shares. Thus, the evidence does support the

Table 8.4 OLS regression results

DEPENDENT REGRESSION COEFFICIENTS

VARIABLE	CONST.	LAB. 1	LAB. 2	LAB. 3	LAB. 4	LAB. 8	LAB. 9	LAB. 12	LAB	NESINPUTS	DUMMY	DUMMY	R SQ./ R SQ. (adj)
1984-9													
TPP/KS:													
coefficient	2.093	-0.279	2.273	-2.129	-0.157	1.188	0.125	0.609	0.789	-0.380	2.731	4.324	0.654
std error	0.504	1.380	3.114	4.129	5.192	0.648	1.811	6.156	2.138	0.059	0.873	1.217	0.584
TPC/KS:													
coefficient	2.028	-0.428	2.066	-2.256	-0.174	1.099	0.077	0.756	0.724	-0.477	2.678	4.370	0.718
std error	0.511	1.397	3.157	4.187	5.264	0.657	1.836	6.242	2.167	0.060	0.885	1.236	0.660
1989-91													
TPP/KS:													
coefficient	0.030	0.275	0.632	-1.248	1.271	-0.043	0.561	-4.752	-0.733	-0.056	-1.715	N/A	0.862
std error	0.100	0.606	1.022	1.234	1.245	0.242	0.810	4.015	0.976	0.018	0.371	N/A	0.837
TPC/KS:													
coefficient	-0.018	0.223	0.586	-1.255	1.219	-0.075	0.548	-4.983	-0.703	-0.100	-1.739	N/A	0.937
std error	0.099	0.598	1.007	1.217	1.228	0.239	0.799	3.959	0.962	0.018	0.365	N/A	0.926

SPECIFICATION TESTS:

	F stat Stat.	D of F	Jarque–Bera Stat. (Chi Sq)	D of F	Heteroskedasticity Stat. (F)	D of F	Variable Omission Stat. (F)	D of F
1984-89:								
TPP/KS	9.291	(11,54)	0.507	2	0.490	(1,64)	2.485	(8,54)
TPP/KS	12.466	(11,54)	0.568	2	1.220	(1,64)	1.896	(8,54)
1989-91								
TPP/KS	34.315	(10,55)	31.261	2	0.436	(1,64)	5.217	(8,54)
TPP/KS	82.183	(10,55)	21.416	2	0.432	(1,64)	5.492	(8,54)

contention that total factor productivity is not simply an industry-specific form of disembodied technological progress and embodied technological change is of importance. This, in turn, implies that wages must be affected by prices and disembodied technological change on the one hand and factors specific gains in productivity on the other.

CONCLUSIONS

The starting point of our analysis was to identify the predictions of trade theory concerning changes in employment and wages. Trade theory offers a rich vein of predictions concerning the linkages between world factor and product markets and domestic factor markets.

A careful examination of this theoretical basis yields conclusions which are at variance with much of the previous work concerning trade and labour markets. In particular, there are three key points that arise. Firstly, the volume of tradeables output and employment is, in the context of trade theory, the residual after determination of factor supplies and the factor demands of the non-tradeables sector. This means that the volume of trade cannot in itself influence employment.

Secondly, technology determines trade as much as it determines employment. It is not, therefore, apparent that trade and technology are competing explanations of employment changes. Thirdly, trade theory predicts that domestic technological progress in an open economy will raise wages and employment rather than lower both, as a number of authors have suggested.

We provide measures and estimates of employment, wage and technological change which are consistent with trade theory. Our estimates of employment changes provide evidence to support the contention that, whilst there have been large changes in both tradeables employment and in the techniques of production used in tradeables, these changes are consistent with a response to changes in wages, non-tradeables factor demands and factor supplies.

Next we consider the wage–technology–price linkages and produce econometric estimates of the key theoretical relationships. These at least produce some evidence to suggest that the interaction between world-determined product prices, technology and domestic wages is a key mechanism affecting domestic labour markets. Thus, our main conclusion is that the key linkages which connect changes in domestic technology and wages/employment with world technology and factor prices are product prices.

Notes

* The authors are grateful to Christine Greenhalgh and Mary Gregory for their advice. We are also grateful to Eva Sausavior for research assistance. All views, errors and omissions, of course, are solely those of the authors.

References

Baldwin, R. E. and Cain, G. G. (1995) 'Trade and US Relative Wages: Preliminary Results', manuscript.

Berman, E., Bound, J. and Griliches, Z. (1994) 'Changes in the Demand for Skilled Labour Within US Manufacturing; Evidence from the Annual Survey of Manufacturers', *Quarterly Journal of Economics*, CIX, 367–397.

Bound, J. and Johnson, G. (1992) 'Changes in the Structure of Wages in the 1980s: An Evaluation of Alternative Explanations', *American Economic Review*, 82, pp. 371–392.

Bowen, H. P., Leamer, E. E. and Sveikauskas, L. (1987) 'Multicountry, Multifactor Tests of the Factor Abundance Theory', *American Economic Review*, 77, pp. 791–809.

Courakis, A., Maskus, K. E. and Webster, A. (1995) 'Globalisation, Productivity Growth in Manufacturing and UK Labour Markets', manuscript.

Diewert, W. E. (1976) 'Exact and Superlative Index Numbers', *Journal of Econometrics*, 4, pp. 115–146.

Ethier, W. J. (1984) 'Higher Dimensional Issues in Trade Theory' in R. W. Jones and P. B. Kenen (eds.), *Handbook of International Economics* (Amsterdam: North Holland).

Greenhalgh, C., Gregory, M. and Ray, A. (1989) 'The Changing Structure of UK Production, Trade and Employment: An Analysis Using Input–Output Tables 1974–84', University of Oxford Applied Economics Discussion Paper No. 70.

Jones, R. W. (1965) 'The Structure of Simple General Equilibrium Models', *Journal of Political Economy*, LXXIII, pp. 557–572.

Katz, L. F. and Murphy, K. M. (1992) 'Changes in Relative Wages 1963–1987: The Role of Declining Market Opportunities', *Quarterly Journal of Economics*, CVII, pp. 35–78.

Koenker, R. (1981) 'A Note on Studentizing a Test for Heteroskedasticity', *Journal of Econometrics*, 17, pp. 107–112.

Lawrence, R. Z. and Slaughter, M. J. (1993) 'International Trade and American Wages in the 1980s: Giant Sucking Sound or Small Hiccup?', *Brookings Papers on Economic Activity: Microeconomics*, 2, pp. 161–226.

Leamer, E. E. (1984) *Sources of International Comparative Advantage: Theory and Evidence*, (Cambridge, Mass.: MIT Press).

Leamer, E. E. (1993) 'Wage Effects of a US–Mexican Free Trade Agreement', in P. M. Garber (ed.), *The Mexico–US Free Trade Agreement*, (Cambridge, Mass.: MIT Press).

Leamer, E. E. (1995) 'The Heckscher–Ohlin Model in Theory and Practice', *Princeton Studies in International Finance*, No. 77.

Lebow, D. E. (1993) 'Import Competition and Wages: The Role of the NonTradable Goods Sector, *Review of Economics and Statistics*, LXXV, pp. 552–558.

Maskus, K. E. and Webster, A. (1995) 'British and American Labor Specialization and the Bilateral HOV Theorem', manuscript.

Oulton, N. and O'Mahony, M. (1994) *Productivity and Growth: A Study of British Industry*, (Cambridge: Cambridge University Press).

Revenga, A. L. (1992) 'Exporting Jobs: The Impact of Import Competition on Employment and Wages in US Manufacturing', *Quarterly Journal of Economics*, CVII, pp. 255–284.

Sachs, J. D. and Shatz, H. J. (1994) 'Trade and Jobs in US Manufacturing', *Brookings Papers on Economic Activity*, 1, pp. 1–84.

Trefler, D. (1993) 'International Factor Price Differences: Leontief was Right!', *Journal of Political Economy*, 101, pp. 961–987.

Trefler, D. (1994) 'The Case of Missing Trade and Other HOV Mysteries', manuscript.

Wood, A. (1994) *North-South Trade, Employment and Inequality: Changing Fortunes in a Skill-Driven World*, (Oxford: Clarendon Press).

9 Optimum Inflation, Taxation and Monetary Arrangements in the Open Economy

Peter Sinclair*

INTRODUCTION

Any government's expenditure needs should ideally be met from lump-sum taxes. Taxes on labour earnings distort labour supply. They contravene the Pareto-efficiency principle requiring equally between the marginal product of labour and the marginal rate of substitution between leisure and consumption. Equiproportionate sales taxes on different consumption goods have just the same effect. We know, too, that taxing money balances is distortionary. In a first-best, money should be left untaxed. That requires a monetary policy that engineers a long-run rate of decline in nominal prices equal to the real rate of interest.[1]

In a multi-country world where real interest rates are equalized by capital movements or trade (or in the simplest case by equal rates of time preference), the pursuit of first-best monetary policies in each would lead to equal rates of price deflation. If there were any currency conversion costs, these could and should be saved by the introduction of a global monetary union.

In the world we observe, however, governments resort to distortionary taxes. Probably the major reason for this is that earning abilities vary across the population. Lump-sum taxes that were tailored to meet some distributive objective (such as the equalization of the marginal utilities of consumption) would run into the problem of incentive compatibility. Lump-sum ability taxes, positive on the able and negative on those with very low ability, would give the able an incentive to claim the transfer by pretending to be less able. If the fiscal authority can monitor individual earnings, but not individual ability to earn, and people are apt to lie when it suits them, the first-best will not be achievable.

Truth-telling constraints, and asymmetric information on earnings abilities (visible to the individual, but not to the authorities) combine to make distortionary taxation inevitable, then, when earnings abilities vary.[2] Any exogenous government spending requirement (for public goods, for example) has to be met from distortionary taxation. So, too, will such transfer payments to the poor and needy that the government wishes to furnish.

In these circumstances it is no longer clear that taxing money should be avoided.[3] Seignorage receipts from taxing currency, through the medium of positive long-run nominal interest rates, will allow the authorities to lower the marginal rates of taxation levied on other goods or on factor earnings. An optimal balance of taxation would be achieved where the marginal distortion cost of each tax was the same. Should currency be taxed? Or should it remain tax-exempt, as in the first-best?

The answer to this question is complex. Essentially it 'all depends'. A key element in the story is the economic roles money is asumed to play, and the way it affects the utility and behaviour of those who hold it. A simple and attractive approach is provided by the view that money serves as a time-saver.[4] Higher real money holdings enable the holder to release time for better purposes that would otherwise be devoted to search and transactions.

In this interpretation, money enters utility only indirectly. Money is held up to the point where the value of the marginal saving in time which it provides balances its opportunity cost. The opportunity cost is the nominal rate of interest if, as here, money is taken to be non-interest-bearing fiat currency. The value of the marginal time-saving is proportional to the real wage rate, at least for money-holders who work.

Let c, m and s denote consumption, real money and 'shopping-time'. It makes sense to assume that s is decreasing and convex in m, and non-decreasing in c. So, if s in $s(m, c)$, $s_1 < 0 < s_{11}$ and $s_2 \geq 0$. If R and w represent the nominal rate of interest and the real wage rate, money is held in equilibrium up to the point where

$$-s_1(m,\ c)\ =\ R/w \tag{1}$$

We shall assume that if R is zero, m will be large enough to set s at zero. If all labour income and asset income (net of accumulation) is taxed at a common rate t, equation (1) still holds, provided that R is defined by

$$R = r + \frac{\pi}{1 - t} \qquad (2)$$

where r is the real rate of interest and π the rate of inflation.

Suppose the authorities have just two fiscal instruments, R and t. Their task is to set t and R to satisfy a balanced budget condition, meeting exogenous sending needs through seignorage (taxes on money) and expenditure taxation (original income minus asset accumulation).

If agents are all alike, deriving utility from consumption and leisure, and R and t are set to minimize the utility lost from levying these taxes, the following results hold.[5]

(1) If the demand for money is unit-elastic or elastic in consumption, R should be set to zero, no matter how high the government's revenue need, and whatever the shape of the shopping function s;

(2) when the demand for money is less than unit-elastic in consumption, and finite at a zero value of R, R should be positive if the government has a positive revenue need;

(3) when the demand for money is less than unit-elastic in consumption, and isoelastic in R, R should be zero unless the government's revenue need is sufficiently high *and* the interest-elasticity of money demand is sufficiently low.

In case 2, the issue of whether R should be positive is also sensitive to the shape of the utility function.

In what follows, I propose to extend the analysis to the case of agents who vary in ability to earn. There are three reasons for this: first, it is realistic; second, it allows us to explore the interplay between redistribution and taxation; and third, the significance of the above results is undermined by the reflection that, if all agents really are all alike, nothing is lost by meeting the State's spending needs by an equal poll tax.

ASSUMPTIONS

In order to examine whether countries exhibiting earning ability disparities will seek to tax money, we need to specify assumptions and establish a model. Let us assume as follows:

(a) all residents of the home country share a common utility function, which depends on leisure, $z (= 1 - h - s)$ where h denotes work-time. Consumption of a domestic good is c, and consumption of a foreign good c^*. Utility (u) is Cobb–Douglas:[6]

$$U = \alpha \ell n c^* + (1 - \alpha) \ell n c + \ell n (1 - h - s),$$

$$\text{where } \alpha \text{ is a parameter} \tag{3}$$

(b) shopping-time, s, is isoelastic[7] in real holdings of (domestic) currency, m:

$$s = \frac{\gamma m^{1-\beta}}{\beta - 1}, \text{ where } \gamma \text{ and } \beta \text{ are parameters, } \gamma > 0, \beta > 1 \tag{4}$$

(c) the budget restraint that each agent faces is given by

$$(1 - t)[wh - Rm] + b - c - \frac{p^* c^*}{1 + \theta} \geq 0 \tag{5}$$

Here, b is a lump-sum paid by the government, p^* is the relative price of the foreign good, and θ represents the costs of currency conversion if the home and foreign countries have separate monies. In a monetary union, $\theta = 0$

(d) the ability to earn, w, varies across agents. It is uniform between a ceiling of unity and a floor of zero

(e) labour supply, h, cannot be negative

(f) the government levies tax rates t and R on income and currency respectively, and balances its budget. It has an exogenous revenue requirement, for public goods, of g. Consequently

$$g + b - \int_0^1 [twh(w) + R(1 - t)m(w)]dw \tag{6}$$

(g) the government's welfare objective, ϕ, is to maximize a weighted mean of the utilities of the median and least-advantaged individuals:[8]

$$\phi = \delta \text{ Median } U + (1 - \delta) \text{ Minimum } U, \text{ where } \delta \text{ is}$$

$$\text{a parameter, } 0 \leq \delta \leq 1.$$

DISCUSSION

Some discussion of these assumptions will be helpful. Consumers' preferences give symmetric, rectangular-hyperbolic indifference curves between two kinds of goods enjoyed – leisure (z), and an aggregate for consumption, call it C. C is a weighted geometric mean of home and foreign goods. The share of foreign consumption in consumers' budgets will be α. We may think of α as capturing the size of the economy: in a small country, α will be larger than in a big one.

The shopping time function, equation (3), makes the elasticity of money demand to the ratio R/w equal to a constant, $1/\beta$. If R is zero, m will be infinite, and s will vanish. Higher R will entail lower m and larger s.

The budget constraint shows agents receiving two kinds of income. They earn labour income, wh, which is taxed, plus a transfer, b, which is not taxed. They can be thought of as financing their money-holdings, m, by a loan from the government at a real rate of interest, r; they are given tax credit for that. Their income is devoted to the purchase of domestic and foreign consumption goods (the latter bearing a price of p^* and involving a currency conversion cost of θ in the absence of a monetary union) and also to the inflation-erosion of the value of their money holdings, πm.

The distribution of abilities is the simplest possible. As we shall see, it allows for unemployment: those individuals for whom the non-negativity constraint on work-time h will bind, will not participate in the labour force.

The left hand side of equation (6) gives the government's outgoings – the spending on public goods, g, plus the transfer, b, which is paid to everyone. The right-hand side represents tax receipts. These are of two types: taxes on labour earnings, and taxes on money. The latter equal $[\pi + r(1 - t)]m$, so that they can be written as $(1 - t)Rm$.

The government's objective function allows us to consider differences in political aims and ideologies. At one extreme we may view government as seeking to maximize its reelection chances in a political duopoly: in this case, δ will equal one. It its objective is to maximize the utility of the poorest, however, δ will be zero. The parameter δ may therefore be taken to represent 'right-wingness'; a left-wing government will have lower δ than a right-wing one. We may also view δ as reflecting the intensity of democratic competition; an authoritarian régime with a left-wing bias will have a low δ.

ANALYSIS

The consumer's optimization decision is to maximize equation (3) subject to equation (5) and a non-negativity constraint on h. The resulting supply of labour will be given by

$$h = Max\left[0, 1 - s + \frac{Rm - b/(1 - t)}{w}\right] \tag{8}$$

If b is positive, some low-ability individuals will not participate in the labour force. They will supply no labour. Their proportion in the population will be given by the value of w (call it u) at which $1 - s + \frac{Rm - b/(1 - t)}{w}$ vanishes. We may therefore write

$$\frac{b}{1 - t} = R\bar{m} + u(1 - \bar{s}) \tag{9}$$

where u represents the unemployment rate, and $\bar{m}$ and $\bar{s}$ the money holdings and shopping time of anyone who does not work.

The economy's total output in this model equals the value of total labour earnings. This will be

$$\int_0^1 wh(w)dw = \frac{1}{2}\int_u^1 [w(1 - s) - u(1 - \bar{s}) + R(m - \bar{m})]dw \tag{10}$$

from equation (8) and (9). Equation (10) provides the base for the income tax, which is critical for the government's budget equation.

The other element in government revenue is seignorage, at least if R is set above zero. This is found from the money demand equation, $-s' = R/w$. Given (b), we find

$$m = (\gamma w/R)^{1/\beta} \tag{11}$$

so that $Rm = R^{1 - 1/\beta}(\gamma w)^{1/\beta}$ and $s = \dfrac{R^{1 - 1/\beta}\gamma^{1/\beta}w^{(1 - \beta)/\beta}}{\beta - 1}$. Defining $x \equiv R^{1 - 1/\beta}\gamma^{1/\beta}$, we may write these as

$$Rm = xw^{1/\beta}$$
$$s = \frac{xw^{(1-\beta)/\beta}}{\beta - 1} \quad (12)$$

We may now substitute equations (9), (10) and (12) into equation (6), and derive

$$1 - t = \frac{(1 - u)^2 - 4g + 2xy(\beta - 2)}{(1 + u)^2 - 4x/(\beta - 1) u^{1/\beta} - 2xy\beta} \quad (13)$$

where $y = \dfrac{\beta}{\beta^2 - 1} \left(1 - u^{1+1/\beta}\right) - \dfrac{u^{1/\beta}}{\beta - 1} (1 - u)$. Equation (13)

reveals, unsurprisingly, that the income tax rate increases with the size of the exogenous government spending level, g. If β, the reciprocal of the interest-elasticity of money demand, is large enough ($\beta > 2$ suffices), equation (13) also tells us that the income tax rate is reduced if x (hence R, hence inflation) increases.

The next step is to obtain indirect utility for the consumer. For anyone who works – anyone, that is, whose wage rate exceeds the unemployment rate, u – substitution from equation (8), (9) and (12) into equation (2), and use of the condition $c^* = \dfrac{\alpha c}{p^*(1 + \theta)(1 - \alpha)} \equiv vc$, establishes that

$$U(w \mid w > u) = \ell n(1 + t) + \alpha \ell nv + 2\ell n[w(1 - s) + u(1 - \bar{s})$$
$$- R(m - \bar{m})] - \ell n4w \quad (14)$$

For anyone not working, utility reduces to

$$U(w \mid w \le u) = \ell n(1 - t) + \alpha \ell nv + \ell nu + 2\ell n[1 - \bar{s}] \quad (15)$$

In both equations (14) and (15), $(1 - t)$ is given in terms of u, g and (implicitly) R by equation (13). It is noteworthy that $\ell n(1 - t) + \alpha \ell nv$ is common to both equations (14) and (15).

Armed with equations (14) and (15), we may now find the government's maximand. Given equation (7), social welfare will equal

$$\phi = \ell n(1 - t) + \alpha \ell nv + 2\delta \ell n \left[\frac{1}{2} - \tilde{s} + u(1 - \tilde{s}) - R(\tilde{m} - m) \right]$$

$$- \delta \ell n2 + (1 - \delta)[\ell nu + 2\ell n(1 - \tilde{s})] \qquad (16)$$

Here $\tilde{s}$ and $\tilde{m}$ are defined as shopping-time and money balances of the median individual (who commands a wage rate of $1/2$): $\tilde{s} = x2^{(\beta-1)/\beta} / (\beta - 1)$ and $\tilde{m} = x/2^{1/\beta}R$. Government policy can be inferred directly from maximizing equation (16), subject to equation (13) and a non-negativity constraint on R.

It is easiest to begin by exploring what happens when δ takes either of its extreme values of unity or zero. If $\delta = 1$, the median voter is appointed dictator. In this democratic-rightwing case, b will be set to zero, and u will vanish, too. There exists an equilibrium where the unemployment rate is set at one-half, so that the median voter is unemployed, but this will always deliver lower utility for that voter than the equilibrium with $u = 0$, at least under our assumption of the uniform distribution of the wage.

In our example, g has to be very large before the median voter sees benefit in supplementing income tax by a tax on currency. We reduce equation (13) to

$$1 - t = \frac{1 - 4g + 2xy(\beta - 2)}{1 - 2xy\beta}, \qquad y \rightarrow \beta/(\beta^2 - 1)$$

and set R to maximize (16) with $\delta = 1$, and $u = 0$ subject to these restrictions and the constraint $R \geq 0$. An interior solution obeys

$$\beta - 2 = (1 - 4g)[2(\beta + 1)\left(\frac{1}{2}\right)^\beta - \beta] \qquad (17)$$

Now g must be less than a quarter, otherwise government will usurp so much of social income that consumption is non-positive. Since the expression in square brackets on the right hand side of equation (17) must be positive, equation (17) tells us that money should always be exempt from taxation if the interest-elasticity of money demand is one-half or more. If β exceeds 2, however, so that the interest-elasticity of money demand is less than one-half, money should be taxed if the government's revenue needs (g) are large enough. At $\beta = 3$, for example, the threshold minimum value of g above which money should be taxed is about 0.175. If $\beta = 4$, this threshold falls to 0.137. The lower the interest elasticity of money demand, and the greater the government's revenue requirement for public goods, the likelier it is that the median voter will dictate some tax on money.

At the other extreme lies the authoritarian left-wing policy of maximizing minimum utility. This case arises when $\delta = 0$. It is now (one of) the unemployed who is effectively appointed dictator. The threshold values of β and g at which money starts to be taxed can be obtained thus. First, maximize ϕ subject to $\delta = 0$ and $R = 0$ with respect to the unemployment rate, u. This gives the result

$$4g = 1 - 4u - u^2 \tag{18}$$

or, equivalently,

$$u = \sqrt{5 - 4g} - 2 \tag{19}$$

Now maximize (16) with respect to R subject to equations (13), (18) and $R = 0$. The result is a boundary condition linking β to u:

$$x(\beta - 1)[(\beta - 2)(1 + u) + 2\beta u] = 2(1 + u^2)u^{1/\beta} \tag{20}$$

This Rawlsian conditions gives the same general floor to β for taxing money as the median-voter case. If $u \to 0$, $\beta \to 2$. Consequently if $\beta \leq 2$, it can never be right to tax money, and R should always be zero. With $\beta > 2$, however, taxing money can become worthwhile, but only if g and β are both sufficiently large. The threshold value for g, given β, at which money should start to be taxed, is higher in the Rawlsian case than when $\delta = 1$. With $\beta = 3$, for example, g must exceed 0.229 (and u must be no higher than 0.0204) for money to be subject to positive tax. (With $\beta = 4$, the threshold for g falls slightly to 0.217, when the unemployment rate is about 0.033. We can conclude from this that, at least in this case, the median voter is likelier to benefit from taxing money than the unemployed, but g must be really rather large in either case.

If δ lies between 0 and 1, and not at either of the extremes, the threshold for g at which money should start to be taxed will be less than the Rawlsian but higher than the median-voter cases. There is an important discontinuity to note. There is a jump once δ drops from unity to something only slightly less than unity: optimal unemployment suddenly becomes positive. This is because minimum utility has a value of minus infinity when $u = 0$. Optimal unemployment is very sensitive indeed to δ when δ is large.

In the case where $1 > \delta > 0$, the money-taxation threshold is found by maximizing ϕ with respect to u with R set to zero, to derive the value of g as a function of optimal unemployment. This is then inserted into the income tax rate equation (13). The next step is to maximize ϕ with respect to R subject to the modified version of equation (13), and evaluate the resulting equation linking β and u to δ at the point where optimal R is zero. The final equation, which is highly ungainly and not presented here, reduces to equation (20) as $\delta \to 0$.

One important result that merits emphasis is the point that the long run Phillips curve cannot generally be vertical: higher inflation can raise or reduce unemployment through its fiscal effects. Only by fluke would unemployment not respond.

What other inferences can we draw from our discussion so far? An additional conclusion is that a pair of countries will opt to tax money at similar rates (quite possibly zero) if they are alike in the following three respects:

(a) social welfare is similarly weighted between median and minimum utilities;
(b) the governments' exogenous revenue requirements are similar; and
(c) the interest-elasticities of money demand are similar.

They should both opt for exempting money from taxation if money demand is sufficiently interest-elastic, or government revenue needs sufficiently modest (and in this case we do require similarity in the relevant parameters).

If, however, both β and g are large enough in both economies, both will benefit from taxing money. But it is highly unlikely that they will wish to tax money at similar rates if they exhibit differences in one or more of the parameters β, δ and g. If they both tax money, we should expect there to be a higher nominal interest rate – and hence in all likelihood a higher rate of inflation – in one country, all else being equal, if:

(a) it is more 'right-wing democratic';
(b) its government expenditure is given at a higher level; or
(c) the interest-elasticity of its money demand is lower.

What implications for monetary union does this have? Countries that trade with each other will always stand to gain something by adopting a monetary union. This will enable their residents to save currency conversion costs. In our model, the size of this gain increases with two parameters. These are α (the proportion of consumers' spending devoted to foreign goods) and θ, the currency conversion cost parameter. Both α and θ exert positive effects on v.

If the world consists of two economies of different sizes, we should expect the smaller one to gain more from a monetary union than the larger one. There is a well-attested negative association between an economy's openness (the ratio of its imports to GDP, for example) and the size of its GDP. In big countries, agents should have smaller v than in small ones.

But a monetary union is potentially damaging, too. There will be no difficulty if the two countries both seek to obey the canon of the 'optimum quantity of money' and leave money untaxed. In that case both will gain from a monetary union if their values of α and θ are positive. There is the possibility that one of them might later feel impelled to start taxing money (for example if its government revenue needs suddenly rise sharply, as a result of war perhaps, or political changes leading to a large rise in the 'democracy' parameter, δ). But in that event the monetary union could be dissolved. Monetary union dissolution is not an uncommon phenomenon: the East African union broke up in the 1960s, as did the Anglo-Irish and Southern African unions in the 1970s, and political fragmentation in the former USSR and Yugoslavia was accompanied by monetary union dissolution in the early 1990s.

If the two countries both seek to tax money, but at different rates, at least one of them must lose something by adopting a monetary union. If country A's optimal nominal interest rate, $R*_A$, differs from country B's, $R*_B$, then a monetary union brings disadvantages. Suppose they set their uncommon π to maximize $\phi(A) + \phi(B)$, the sum of their national governments' objective functions. This means they have to compromise, by setting their common inflation rate presumably somewhere between the rates they would have chosen for themselves in isolation. The issue then is whether what at least one, probably both, lose in accepting an imperfect inflation rate is greater or less than what they save in currency conversion costs.

It merits emphasis that a monetary union will require similar long-run inflation rates, but not necessarily similar values of R. This is because their income tax rates may differ. Let us assume that real interest rates are equalized. Since $R_i = r + \dfrac{\pi_i}{1 - t_i}$, setting π_A equal to π_B will entail $R_A = R_B$ if and only if t_A and t_B are equal. A monetary union which is not also a fiscal union may therefore display differences in nominal interest rates between its member countries. It also raises certain problems of coordination. The common monetary authority, if it taxes money, earns seignorage; what will it do with the revenues obtained? If it redistributes them equally to all member countries' residents, that could entail inter-country transfers. A country with a relatively low ceiling to its wage, or a relatively low value of γ, the shopping time parameter, will stand to gain; the other will lose. And because these transfers supplement whatever levels of b the national governments provide for their residents, they are likely to add to unemployment somewhat, particularly in a relatively low-wage country. National governments would have to reset their targets for t and u in the light of these seignorage returns. Furthermore, a country with higher average wages, or relatively high money demand, may gain from leaving the monetary union (or at least threatening to do so) if it perceives an appreciable loss of seignorage revenue to its partner.

SOME FURTHER CONSIDERATIONS

We have seen that countries may seek to set different long-run inflation targets in any one of three cases: if their given government expenditure requirements differ; if their social welfare weights between median and minimum utilities differ; or if their shopping-time transactions technologies differ in the parameter β that governs the interest-elasticity of money demand.

This is not all. There could be other national differences which make countries aim for different rates of tax on money. One is the extent of earning ability disparities. Suppose earnings abilities are more dispersed in country A than country B. We can imagine that mean abilities are the same, but that A displays a greater mean-preserving spread than B. If δ is less than one (but common to the two countries), country A will be keener to redistribute income from rich to poor than B. In the limit, if B's earnings abilities are not dispersed at all, she should eschew distribution and distortionary taxation of all forms entirely, and meet State expenditure needs from poll taxes. A, however, will wish to tax income, and money too, if g and β are large enough; and B will also display unemployment, while A has none. In sum, greater earnings disparity will make it likelier that money should be taxed, and increase the optimal rate of tax money if it is already taxed.

A further influence on optimal money taxation is the shape of the utility function. We have imposed a Cobb–Douglas structure on preferences between consumption and leisure. The elasticity of substitution and leisure between them is therefore constrained at unity. Had consumption and leisure been more complementary than this, optimal income tax rates would have been higher. This is because compensated labour supply becomes less elastic to the income tax rate. So if A and B differ in their residents' preferences, with A's substituting between consumption and leisure with less flexibility than B's, A would be less likely to seek to tax money (all else equal) than B, and A's optimal value of R, if positive, would be lower than B's.

Another possible difference relates to a further feature of our utility function. It is not just Cobb–Douglas: it is also additively separable. We could replace (3) by

$$U = [c^{\alpha}c^{1-\alpha}z]^{1-\varepsilon}/(1 - \varepsilon) \qquad (3')$$

Equation (3') gives equation (3) after minor transformation, by L'Hôpital's rule, when $\varepsilon = 1$. If $\varepsilon < 1$, utility becomes less concave than when $\varepsilon = 1$, and ϕ becomes less sensitive to differences between median and minimum consumption differences for any given value of δ. Two countries alike in all respects, save that ε is larger for B than for A, will, when $1 < \delta < 0$, display different thresholds at which money should start to be taxed. B will be more inflation-averse than A. B will display more unemployment, larger transfers, a higher income tax rate, and a lower probability of crossing the threshold at which money should be taxed.

A final point to emphasize is the fact that we have assumed that optimizing governments take v, and the terms of trade p^* on which it depends, as given. This is perfectly plausible when the countries are small. A large country, however, may observe that its financial policies can affect p^*. Increasing the rate of domestic inflation should increase the authorities' total tax receipts. This should permit a higher level of the transfer payment, b. If provided, that would induce a reduction in the domestic supply of labour and a rise in domestic unemployment. Under these conditions, foreign goods would become more plentiful than before, relative to home output. So p^* should fall, increasing home consumers' indirect utility. The country's terms of trade would improve. In this case, inflation acts rather like an export tax.

If it recognizes this power to affect its terms of trade, this suggests that the government of a large country would be somewhat keener to espouse inflation than a smaller one, all else being equal. Two similarly large countries could be trapped into an inferior Nash equilibrium where each sought to improve its terms of trade by loose monetary policy, but neither succeeded. In such circumstances, a monetary union could be more advantageous than the foregoing analysis suggests. A monetary union could block this route to competitive and ultimately pointless depreciations that could otherwise ensue.

This conclusion must be qualified in one important respect, however. If a group of small countries combines to form a monetary union, leaving some other countries outside, the monetary union would put a stop to competitive depreciations between its members. But they could amplify it *vis-à-vis* the rest of the world; and together, their influence on their external terms of trade would be enhanced rather than weakened.

CONCLUSIONS

This paper has argued that monetary policy is an aspect of tax policy. The question of whether money should be taxed, and if so at what rate, forms part of the broader issue of optimal taxation.

Countries will stand to gain something from forming a monetary union because this will enable residents to save on currency conversion costs. They may lose if a monetary union requires them to accept a rate of inflation that diverges from what they would have chosen in isolation. This paper examines the issue of when and why countries' optimal long-run inflation rates may differ. A simple constrained optimal taxation model is studied: agents vary in earning ability and governments set transfers and a single income tax rate, and possibly a tax on currency to minimize the social welfare cost of satisfying a balanced budget. The optimal trend in the nominal exchange rate between a pair of countries is determined by the gap, in any, between their optimal inflation rates.

We have seen that governments setting optimum monetary policies independently could opt to tax currency at different rates for a variety of reasons. All else equal, we should probably expect country A to choose higher inflation than country B if its exogenous government spending requirement is higher, if its residents' transactions technology makes currency demand less interest-elastic, if it places a higher social welfare weight on median as opposed to minimum utility, and if its earnings ability disparities are greater.

Among other results, one conclusion to stress is that the long-run Phillips curve (the trade-off between inflation and unemployment) cannot generally be vertical. Faster inflation may be associated with higher or lower unemployment in the long run, but not in general, even with the unchanged level of unemployment which much economic theory has led us to expect. Another conclusion is that a monetary union could have the unsuspected advantage of preventing excessive inflation that individual countries might otherwise seek to engineer (as a subtle form of export tax). If the monetary union embraces some, but not all countries, however, there is a risk that it will be tempted into a more inflationary stance, because its power to influence rest-of-the-world prices could be enhanced.

Notes

* Most of this piece was written while the author was visiting the European University Institute of Florence. I should like to thank them, and Professor Artis, for their kind hospitality, and also to record my gratitude to Alec Chrystal, my discussant, to other participants at the IESG conference, and to members of seminars at the Universities of Birmingham, Manchester, Oxford, Sheffield and Warwick. The ideas presented in this paper have benefited greatly from numerous valuable comments.

1. This result was first established by Milton Friedman (1969); much of the subsequent literature is well reviewed by Woodford (1990).
2. Mirrlees (1971) provides the seminal analysis of this problem.
3. The first paper to study the robustness of Friedman's 'optimum quantity of money' result, in a representative-agent setting where government meets a fixed revenue target by distortionary income tax, possibly supplemented by a tax on money, is due to Phelps (1973).
4. This is the approach taken, amongst others, by Dowd (1990), Kimborough (1986) and Guidotti and Vegh (1993).
5. These results are obtained in Sinclair (1995).
6. Sinclair (1995) studies a quasi-linear variant of (3), where utility is linear in the level of leisure, but in the logarithms of c and c^*. That form enables one to obtain closed-form solutions for mean utility, and hence a richer set of welfare results than those reached in the present paper.
7. This is only one of several possible forms for s. Others are examined in Sinclair (1995).
8. Because the utility function (3) will not allow integration over abilities when R is positive, it is not possible to include mean utility in (7). See footnote 6.

References

Dowd, K. (1990) 'The Value of Time and the Transactions Demand for Money', *Journal of Money, Credit and Banking*, pp. 51–64.

Friedman, M. (1969) 'The Optimum Quantity of Money', in *The Optimum Quantity of Money and Other Essays*, (Amsterdam: Aldine) pp. 1–50.

Guidotti, P. E. and Vegh, C. A. (1993) 'The Optimal Inflation Tax When Money Reduces Transactions Costs: a Reconsideration', *Journal of Monetary Economics*, pp. 189–205.

Kimborough, K. P. (1986) 'Inflation, Employment and Welfare in the Presence of Transactions Costs', *Journal of Money, Credit and Banking*, pp. 127–40.

Mirrlees, J. A. (1971) 'An Exploration in the Theory of Optimum Income Taxation', *Review of Economic Studies*, pp. 175–208.

Phelps, E. S. (1973) 'Inflation in the Theory of Public Finance', *Swedish Journal of Economics*, pp. 67–82.

Sinclair, P. J. N. (1995) 'On Optimal Exchange Rate Trends', University of Birmingham Discussion Paper in Economics, 95–28.

Woodford, M. (1990) 'The Optimum Quantity of Money', in B. M. Friedman and F. H. Hahn (eds) *The Handbook of Monetary Economics* (Amsterdam: North-Holland) ch. 20.

10 Tied Aid, Unemployment and Welfare

Sajal Lahiri and Pascalis Raimondos-Møller*

INTRODUCTION

The effect of foreign aid on the welfare levels of both the recipient and the donor country has been a much analysed topic for research in both the theory of international trade and development economics. In the development economics literature, concerns have been raised since the 1960s on the possible adverse effect of foreign aid on domestic savings and growth.[1] The trade theory literature in this respect is much older and dates back to the 1920s when Professors Keynes and Ohlin debated on the effect of foreign aid on international terms of trade.[2] Ever since, the terms of trade effect has been the cornerstone in the analysis of the welfare effect of foreign aid in the trade theory literature.[3] After some early confusion, it is now well established that in a Walrasian stable world economy with two countries, a necessary condition for foreign aid to have perverse effects is that there is some distortion in either of the two countries.[4] It is also known that, under normality and substitutability of goods, untied aid cannot be strictly Pareto-improving in a tariff distorted world.[5]

More recently, the focus of attention has shifted towards tied, rather than untied, aid. This is perhaps a reflection of changes that have actually taken place in the nature of foreign aid.[6] Foreign aid can of course be tied in many ways. In the literature, one finds the analysis of aid that is tied to: (i) increased purchases of export goods from the donor (Kemp and Kojima, 1985); Schweinberger, 1990; Lahiri and Raimondos, 1995a); (ii) more agricultural production (Brecher and Bhagwati, 1982); (iii) production of public goods (Hatzipanayotou and Michael, 1995; Lahiri and Raimondos, 1995b), and (iv) trade policy reform (Lahiri and Raimondos, 1995a and 1995c). In the papers that consider tying of aid to more imports from the donor country (as in (i) above), the motive of the donor in tying aid is only to alter the international terms to trade to its advantage, that is, to benefit from the traditional terms of trade effect. However, there must be other more direct motives. Reduction of unemployment in the donor countries must be one of the major reasons for the tying of foreign aid to increased imports from the donor. Recently, the British government got away with giving 'illegal' tied aid to Malaysia (for the infamous Pergau Dam project) perhaps because it was perceived at home that the deal would create more jobs in the United Kingdom.

In this paper we develop a model in which the donor has, *inter alia*, the direct motive of reducing unemployment at home in tying aid to more imports from it. We consider two alternative ways of modelling unemployment and compare the results. In the first model, we assume that unemployment is involuntary and arises from wage rigidity. The model analysed is an adaptation of the model developed by Neary (1985) to the present context. This model is developed and analysed in the following section.[7]

The second model which is analysed in the penultimate section assumes that labour supply is endogenously determined and, in this sense, treats unemployment as voluntary. The model is an adaptation of the models analysed by Mayer (1991) and Michael (1994). In both sections we derive conditions under which tied aid decreases unemployment in the donor country. We also examine the possibility of transfer paradox and of transfer to be strictly Pareto-improving. The final section of the paper summarizes the main results of the paper.

A MODEL WITH INVOLUNTARY UNEMPLOYMENT

We consider a two-country, two-good model of international trade with perfect competition prevailing in all markets. One country – called the donor – gives aid (denoted by T) to the other – called the recipient – in terms of the non-numeraire good which the donor exports. Aid is assumed to be financed and distributed in a lump-sum fashion. International trade is distorted by quotas imposed by the recipient on the imports of the non-numeraire good. There is no trade restriction for the numeraire good. The domestic relative price of the non-numeraire good is denoted by p.[8] The expenditure and revenue functions in the recipient country are given respectively by $e(p, u)$ and $r(p)$ where u is the utility level. For notational simplicity, the price of the numeraire good and the endowments which do not change in our analysis have been omitted from the arguments of the functions. The only exception is labour in the donor country which we now turn to. We assume the existence of classical involuntary unemployment in the donor country. That is, the wage rate in terms of the numeraire good is rigid in the donor country and this is denoted by $\bar{w}$.[9] The constrained revenue fiction – which gives the income of all factors except labour – is denoted by $R(P, \bar{w})$.[10] For simplicity, we also assume that there is no unemployment in the recipient country.

The equilibrium in the world economy is described by the following equations:

$$e(p, u) = r(p) + PT + (p - P)(\bar{m} + bT) \tag{1}$$

$$e_p(p, u) - r_p(p) = \bar{m} + bT \tag{2}$$

$$E(P, U) = R(P, \bar{w}) + \bar{w}L - PT \tag{3}$$

$$L = -R_w(P, \bar{w}) \tag{4}$$

$$E_P(P, U) + e_p(p, u) = R_P(P, \bar{w}) + r_p(p). \tag{5}$$

Equation (2) represents the trade restriction in the recipient country: compensated excess demand for the non-numeraire good in the recipient country is equal to a quota which is the sum of an exogenous import quota $\bar{m}(> 0)$ plus the part of the transfer that is tied to imports, bT, b being the tying parameter. Equation (5) gives the world equilibrium for the non-numeraire good. In our model, employment level in the donor country can be obtained by partially differentiating the constrained revenue function with respect to $\bar{w}$ and multiplying it by (-1), and this is given in (4). Finally, equations (1) and (3) are the budget constraints for the recipient and the donor country respectively. For the recipient country, the expenditure required to achieve utility level u is equal to the sum of factor incomes $(r(p))$, aid revenue (PT) and quota rent $((p - P)(\bar{m} + bT))$.[11] For the donor country, the expenditure is the sum of non-labour factor income $(R(P, \bar{w}))$ and labour income $(\bar{w}L)$ minus the direct cost of the transfer (PT).

Having described the model, we now turn to its analysis. From equation (4) we obtain:

$$- R_{wP} \, dP = dL \tag{6}$$

Clearly, for our analysis to make sense we need to assume that a higher price (hence production) of the good the donor exports leads to more employment in the donor country. In other words, in view of equation (6) we assume that $- R_{wP} > 0.$[12]

Totally differentiating equations (1) to (3) and making use of equation (6), we get:

$$e_u \mathrm{d}u = [P + b(p - P)] \, \mathrm{d}T - [\bar{m} + (b - 1)T] \, \mathrm{d}P \qquad (7)$$

$$E_U \mathrm{d}U = - P \, \mathrm{d}T + [\bar{m} + (b - 1)T - \bar{w}R_{wP}] \, \mathrm{d}P \qquad (8)$$

Increasing aid ($\mathrm{d}T > 0$) has three effects on the welfare of the recipient country. The first term on the right hand side of equation (7) gives the direct effect of increased income plus the positive effect due to the relaxation of the quota. The second term is the usual term of trade effect. Similarly, for the donor country, the first term is the direct negative effect of aid due to reduced income and the second term is the sum of the terms of trade effect and the employment effect.

From equations (7) and (8) we can say something on the possibility of potential Pareto-improving transfer. Adding the two equations, and the use of equation (6), gives:

$$e_u \mathrm{d}u + E_U \mathrm{d}U = b(p - P)\mathrm{d}T + \bar{w}\mathrm{d}L \qquad (9)$$

Thus, aggregate welfare will definitely improve with aid if it has a positive effect on the employment in the donor country. The first term is the positive effect due to the relaxation of the quota level due to increased aid. The second term represents the effect due to changes in the labour market distortion. It is to be noted that the presence of unemployment in the donor country can make the increase in global welfare due to tied aid larger. Increase in global welfare has the implication that strict Pareto-improving transfer is not impossible. We shall return to this issue later on.

Differentiating the market clearing condition for the non-numeraire good, equation (5), and substituting equations (7) to (8) in it we obtain:

$$Z \, \mathrm{d}P = (C_Y - b)\mathrm{d}T \qquad (10)$$

where $Z = E_{PP} - R_{PP} + [\bar{m} + (b - 1)T - \bar{w}R_{wP}]C_Y$, and $C_Y \, (= PE_{PU}/E_U)$ is the marginal propensity of consumption for the non-numeraire good in the donor country. For the system to be Walrasian stable, Z must be negative.

From equation (10) it immediately follows that an untied aid ($b = 0$) unambiguously worsens the donor terms of trade, and a tied aid improves it if, and only if, $b > C_Y$. The intuition is straightforward. Aid directly reduces the income in the donor country and thus the demand for the non-numeraire good. The extend of this shift in the demand schedule depends on the magnitude of C_Y. The demand for the non-numeraire good in the recipient goes up only if the aid is tied and the extent of this effect depends on the size of the parameter b. Thus, the net effect on the world demand schedule for the non-numeraire good is positive if, and only if, $b > C_Y$. From equations (6) and (10) it follows that aid will increase employment in the donor country if, and only if, $b > C_Y$. Formally:

Proposition 1: *Aid tied to increased imports from the donor reduces involuntary unemployment in the donor country if, and only if, $b > C_Y$.*

It should be noted that when aid is fully tied ($b = 1$), aid unambiguously reduces unemployment in the donor country. Finally, substituting dP from equation (10) into equations (7) and (8) we obtain the welfare equations:

$$ZE_U \frac{dU}{dT} = -P\left(Z - (C_Y - b)\frac{\overline{m} + (b - 1)T - \overline{w}R_{wP}}{P}\right) \quad (11)$$

$$Ze_u \frac{du}{dT} = [P + b(p - P)]\left(Z - (C_Y - b)\frac{\overline{m} + (b - 1)T}{P + b(p - P)}\right) \quad (12)$$

For simplicity, the rest of this section assumes that the initial level of aid is zero, that is, $T = 0$. From the above two equations it follows that: (i) a necessary condition for the donor country to benefit from the transfer is that $b < C_Y$, and (ii) a sufficient condition for the recipient country to benefit from the transfer is $C_Y < b$. Thus, if $C_Y < b$ one gets the normal donor immiserising and recipient enriching effect of tied aid. It also follows that $b < C_Y$ is a necessary condition for tied aid to be strictly Pareto-improving. The reason for the above results is that the relative magnitude of the parameters C_Y and b determine the terms of trade effect and the employment effect. The above results can be summarized as follows.

Proposition 2: *Aid tied to increased imports from the donor country has the following properties:*

(i) *it benefits the donor country only if $b > C_Y$,*
(ii) *it benefits the recipient country if $b < C_Y$, and*
(iii) *it benefits both the countries only if $b > C_Y$.*

A MODEL WITH VOLUNTARY UNEMPLOYMENT

The model developed here is similar to the one in the preceding section except for the treatment of unemployment. Unlike the last section, here we assume that unemployment in the donor country is voluntary. Since the consumers decide on their labour supply, we need to redefine the expenditure function for the donor country which is now represented as $\bar{E}(P, L, U)$ where $\bar{E}_L$ gives us the reservation wage rate for the representative consumer.[13] The revenue function also needs to be redefined. In fact, we no longer need a constrained revenue function. $\bar{R}(P, L)$ here is the normal revenue function representing all factor incomes, R_L being the competitive wage rate. To simplify the notation of the model, we define the trade expenditure functions in both countries as the difference of the expenditure and revenue functions, in other words $s(p, u) = e(p, u) - r(p)$ for the recipient country and $\bar{S}(P, L, U) = \bar{E}(P, L, U) - \bar{R}(P, L)$ for the donor country.

The equilibrium conditions here are:

$$s(p, u) = PT + (p - P)(\bar{m} + bT) \tag{13}$$

$$s_p = \bar{m} + bT \tag{14}$$

$$\bar{S}(P, L, U) = -PT \tag{15}$$

$$\bar{S}_L = 0 \tag{16}$$

$$\bar{S}_P + s_p = 0 \tag{17}$$

The equilibrium conditions (13), (14) and (17) are the same as in the previous section. The budget constraint of the consumer in the donor country is given in equation (15). Equation (16) represents the equilibrium in the labour market in the donor country. It states that the reservation wage of the consumer is equal to the market wage.

We now turn to the analysis of the effect of aid on welfare levels. Totally differentiating the above five equations we obtain:

$$S_u \, du = [P + b(p - P)]dT - [\bar{m} + (b - 1)T]dP \qquad (18)$$

$$\bar{S}_U \, dU = -PdT + [\bar{m} + (b - 1)T]dP \qquad (19)$$

$$-\bar{S}_{LU} \, dU = \bar{S}_{LL}dL + \bar{S}_{LP}dP \qquad (20)$$

$$-\bar{S}_{PU} \, dU = \bar{S}_{PP}dP + \bar{S}_{PL}dL + bdT \qquad (21)$$

Equations (18) and (19) are similar to the welfare equations (7) and (8) except that here there is no direct effect of changes in employment level in the donor country on its welfare. The reason is that, unlike the previous model, unemployment is voluntary and thus is not a distortion. Summing over equations (18) and (19) we obtain:

$$s_u du + \bar{S}_U dU = b(p - P)dT \qquad (22)$$

Comparing equation (22) with equation (9) we can conclude that tied aid is potentially more beneficial to the world when unemployment is involuntary than when it is voluntary. The reason is that whereas in the former case tied aid mitigates the distortion imposed by wage rigidity as well as the trade distortion, in the latter (present) case, it only relaxes the trade distortion.

Substituting dU from equation (19) into equations (20) and (21) we get the following system of equations which can be solved to obtain changes in P and L:

$$\begin{bmatrix} a_{11} & a_{12} \\ a_{21} & a_{22} \end{bmatrix} \begin{bmatrix} dL \\ dP \end{bmatrix} = \begin{bmatrix} w_Y \\ C_Y - b \end{bmatrix} dT, \qquad (23)$$

where

$$a_{11} = \bar{S}_{LL}$$

$$a_{12} = \bar{S}_{LP} + w_Y \frac{\bar{m} + (b - 1)T}{P}$$

$$a_{21} = \bar{S}_{LP}$$

$$a_{22} = \overline{S}_{PP} + C_Y \frac{\overline{m} + (b - 1)T}{P}$$

$$w_Y = \frac{P\overline{S}_{LU}}{\overline{S}_U}.$$

w_Y can be interpreted as the income effect on the reservation wage. Equation (23) is solved to yield:

$$\Delta \frac{dL}{dT} = -(C_Y - b)\overline{S}_{LP} + w_Y \left[\overline{S}_{PP} + \frac{b(\overline{m} + (b - 1)T)}{P} \right] \quad (24)$$

$$\Delta \frac{dP}{dT} = (C_Y - b)\overline{S}_{LL} - w_Y \overline{S}_{LP} \quad (25)$$

where because of the stability of the system we have:

$$\Delta = \overline{S}_{LL} \left(\overline{S}_{PP} + C_Y \frac{\overline{m} + (b - 1)T}{P} \right) - \overline{S}_{PL} \left(\overline{S}_{LP} + w_Y \frac{\overline{m} + (b - 1)T}{P} \right) < 0$$

For simplicity we assume from now on that the initial level of aid is zero, that is, $T = 0$. As is clear from the above two equations, the effect of aid on employment (and terms of trade) is not as clear-cut as in the previous section. The reason is that because of wage rigidity the interaction between the labour market and the commodity market was rather limited in the preceding section, and here the excess demands for labour and the non-numeraire commodity are very much dependent on each other. It is normal to assume that $\overline{S}_{LL} > 0$, and $\overline{S}_{LU} > 0$ (and thus $w_Y > 0$) (see Michael, 1994). Thus, for a given level of P, the excess supply of labour ($\overline{S}_{LL}$) is upward sloping. An increase in aid will decrease the income of the representative consumer in the donor country and thus its reservation wage (since $\overline{S}_{LU} > 0$) for given P. This would increase the supply of labour. However, a change in P may shift the excess supply of labour either way depending on the sign of a_{12} which in turn depends, *inter alia*, on whether leisure and consumption are complements ($\overline{S}_{LP} < 0$) or substitutes ($\overline{S}_{LP} > 0$) in a net sense. For a given level of L, an increase in aid, for reasons explained in the previous section, will shift the world excess demand schedule for the non-numeraire good outward if and only if $C_Y > b$. An increase in L will shift the excess demand for the non-numeraire good inward if and only if leisure and consumption are net substitutes

$(\overline{S}_{LP} > 0)$. These complexities explain why the employment effect is not clear-cut. For example, it is possible that a higher value of the tiedness parameter b may, under certain plausible conditions, make it more likely for aid to reduce employment. From (24) it can be worked out that when $\overline{S}_{LP} > 0$, aid will increase employment if and only if

$$b < \frac{C_Y P \overline{S}_{LP} + w_Y \overline{m}\varepsilon}{P\overline{S}_{LP} + w_Y \overline{m}}$$

where $\varepsilon = -\dfrac{\overline{S}_{PP}P}{\overline{S}_P} (> 0)$ is the price elasticity of the donor's export function. Moreover, from the above it should also be clear that untied aid ($b = 0$) increases employment if leisure and the consumption of the non-numeraire good are net substitutes ($\overline{S}_{LP} > 0$). Formally:

Proposition 3: *When leisure and the consumption are net substitutes, we have:*

(i) *untied aid always decreases voluntary unemployment in the donor country, and*

(ii) *tied aid decreases voluntary unemployment if*

$$b < \frac{C_Y P \overline{S}_{LP} + w_Y \overline{m}\varepsilon}{P\overline{S}_{LP} + w_Y \overline{m}}$$

Turning now to welfare, substituting equation (25) into equations (18) and (19), and setting $T = 0$, we obtain:

$$\Delta s_u \frac{du}{dT} = b(p - P)\Delta - P\overline{S}^2_{PL} + \overline{m}\,\overline{S}_{LL}(b - \varepsilon) \tag{26}$$

$$\Delta s_u \frac{du}{dT} = P\overline{S}^2_{PL} + \overline{m}\,\overline{S}_{LL}(b - \varepsilon) \tag{27}$$

It follows directly that if aid is untied ($b = 0$), aid unambiguously benefits the recipient and harms the donor, as was the case in the previous section. The same results will follow if ($b - \varepsilon$) is negative, that is, tying is limited and the import function is very elastic. However, in the case where ($b - \varepsilon$) is positive, that is, the tying is significant and the import demand function is not very elastic, tied aid can give us transfer paradox as well as strict Pareto improvement.

Proposition 4: *Untied aid always harms the donor and benefits the recipient. With tied aid, however, (i) both countries can benefit, (ii) the donor can lose and the recipient benefit, and (iii) the recipient can lose and the donor benefit.*

CONCLUSIONS

Over the years the nature of bilateral foreign aid has changed. More and more aid packages now include implicit and explicit conditionalities. The conditionalities themselves are diverse. In the development economics literature, it is often argued that the conditionalities are imposed purely for the donor's self-interest, implying that they are not necessarily beneficial for the recipient countries.[14]

In this paper we have analysed welfare effects of aid that is tied to increased imports from the donor. The justification of tying in this way is given in terms of two objectives on the part of the donor: (i) to mitigate trade restriction in the form of quota imposed by the recipient, and (ii) to increase employment in the donor country.

In order to incorporate the above objectives, we developed a model in which the recipient country has a quota on its imports and aid is tied to a relaxation of this quota. We also consider the presence of unemployment in the donor country, and the cases of voluntary and involuntary unemployment are considered in turn.

One of our results is that, while untied aid cannot be strictly Pareto-improving, tied aid can be. We also find conditions under which employment in the donor country increases with tied aid and conditions under which strict Pareto-improving transfer and transfer paradox can take place. We also find that the two types of unemployment can yield very different qualitative result. For example, unlike in the case for involuntary unemployment, we find that a lower level of tiedness of aid may make it more likely for aid to reduce voluntary unemployment.

To summarize, the inclusion of unemployment in the welfare analysis of tied aid not only makes the framework of analysis more realistic, it also throws up a number of interesting results.

Notes

* The authors are grateful to the participants of the conference and, in particular, the discussant John Black for constructive criticism. Raimondos-Møller's research was funded by a grant from the Danish National Research Foundation.

1. See Cassen (1988) for a survey of the literature.
2. See Keynes (1929) and Ohlin (1929).
3. See Kemp (1992) for a survey of the literature.
4. See Bhagwati *et al.* (1985).
5. See Turunen-Red and Woodland (1988).
6. See Bhagwati (1985).
7. Beladi (1990) has also analysed the welfare and employment effects of transfer in the case of binding minimum wages. However, in his model transfer is untied.
8. Unless otherwise stated, the variables and functions of the recipient (donor) country are denoted by lower (upper) case letters.
9. It should be noted that we are not requiring the *real* wage rate to be rigid. Rather, in this context, this assumption is closer to the one of *nominal* wage rigidity. In macroeconomics literature both assumptions are found. Whereas real wage rigidity is easier to justify, the assumption of nominal wage rigidity presumes some degree of money illusion on the part of the workers.
10. See Neary (1985) for the properties of the constrained revenue function.
11. Here we assume that import quota is binding, that is, $\bar{m} + bT < m^*$, where m^* is the free trade level of imports. As a result of this, $p - P > 0$.
12. It should be pointed out that we are not necessarily assuming the donor's export good to be labour intensive. In the presence of unemployment (and possibly specific factors of production), an increase in the employment of labour in one sector does not necessarily imply a reduction of the same in the other sector.
13. See Mayer (1991) and Michael (1994).
14. See, for example, Maizels and Nissanke (1984).

References

Beladi, H. (1990) 'Unemployment and immiserizing transfer', *Journal of Economics/Zeitschrift für Nationalökonomie*, 3, pp. 253–265.

Bhagwati, J. N. (1985) 'The tying of aid', in: G. Grossman (ed.) *Dependence and interdependence* (Oxford: Basil Blackwell) pp. 204–251.

Bhagwati, J. N., Brecher, R. and Hatta, T. (1985) 'The generalized theory of transfers and welfare: exogenous (policy-imposed) and endogenous (transfer-induced) distortions', *Quarterly Journal of Economics*, 3, pp. 697–714.

Brecher, R. and Bhagwati, J. N. (1982) 'Immiserising transfers from abroad', *Journal of International Economics*, 13, pp. 353–364.

Cassen, R. (1988) *Does aid work?* (Oxford: Clarendon Press).

Hatzipanayotou, P. and Michael, M. S. (1995) 'Foreign aid and public goods', *Journal of Development Economics*.

Kemp, M. C. (1992) 'The static welfare economics of foreign aid: A consolidation', in D. Savoie and I. Brecher, (eds), *Equity and efficiency in economic development: essays in honor of Benjamin Higgins* (Montreal: McGill–Queens University Press) pp. 289–314.

Kemp, M. C., and Kojima, S. (1985) 'Tied aid and the paradoxes of donor-enrichment and recipient-impoverishment', *International Economic Review* 26, pp. 721–729.

Keynes, J. M., 1929, 'The German transfer problem', *Economic Journal* 39, pp. 1–17.

Lahiri, S. and Raimondos, P. (1995a) 'Welfare effects of aid under quantitative trade restriction', *Journal of International Economics*, 39, pp. 297–315.

Lahiri, S. and Raimondos, P. (1995b) 'Food aid and food production: a theoretical analysis', forthcoming in a festschrift in honour of Professor J. N. Bhagwati (ed. V. N. Balasubramanyan).

Lahiri, S. and Raimondos, P. (1995c) 'On the tying of aid to tariff reform', *Working paper No. 4*, University of Essex.

Maizels, A. and Nissanke, M. K. (1984) 'Motivations for aid to developing countries', *World Development* 12, pp. 879–900.

Mayer, W. (1991) 'Endogenous labour supply in international trade theory', *Journal of International Economics*, 30, pp. 105–120.

Michael, M. S. (1994) 'The welfare and employment effects of trade and factor taxes with variable supply', *Journal of International Trade and Economic Development* 3, pp. 177–192.

Neary, P. J. (1985) 'International factor mobility, minimum wage rates, and factor-price equalization: a synthesis', *Quarterly Journal of Economics* 100, pp. 551–570.

Ohlin, B. (1929) 'The reparation problem: a discussion', *Economic Journal* 39, pp. 172–183.

Schweinberger, A. G. (1990) 'On the welfare effects of tied aid', *International Economic Review* 31, pp. 457–462.

Turunen-Red, A. H., and Woodland, A. D. (1988) 'On the multilateral transfer problem: existence of Pareto improving international transfers', *Journal of International Economics* 22, pp. 57–64.

Index

accounting evidence 5, 103, 122, 125
adjustment costs 9, 119
    see also labour market adjustment
Andean Pact 24

barrier reduction theory 145

capital 56, 110
capital-intensive techniques 149
Census of Production 124
change in gross output 64, 77
changes in business organization 81
changing economic structure 68
Chilean liberalization 21, 23, 28, 29, 40
comparative advantage 63, 91, 92, 133, 141
    see also revealed comparative advantage
competitive markets 180
consumption of tradeables 189
co-ordination 214
creative destruction 90
current account 56

debt crisis 44
decompositions of employment changes 181
defensive innovation 151, 152
deindustrialization 62, 81, 90, 93, 96, 110, 112, 146
demand for financial services 74, 155
demand for labour 134, 136, 176
demand for skilled labour 150
demand for unskilled labour 140, 149, 150, 160
devaluation 26
developing countries 141
disciplinary effect 137
domestic demand 128
domestic labour markets 180

econometric evidence 6, 105, 132
effective rates of protection 26
effects of trade on wages 143
elasticities of substitution 154
employment in manufacturing 103, 140
    see also sectoral employment
employment income 80

employment-intensity of production 66
exchange rate 49, 69
exchange rate overvaluation 26, 67
exchange rate policy 46
expenditure 220
export intensity 136

factor content 148, 151, 156
    see also labour content of imports
factor demands 176
factor price equalization 171
factor price insensitivity 171, 192
factor requirements 188
factor substitution 79
factors shares 195
final demands 74
financial services 68, 78
foreign aid 219
foreign competition 131

globalization 1, 81, 170
government budget deficits 48
growth-accounting framework 120, 123
growth-theoretic proposition 110

Harris–Todaro mechanism 17
Heckscher–Ohlin (H–O) model 120, 141, 142, 145, 171, 177
Hicks-neutral technological progress 104
high technology manufactures 68, 76
hysteresis 122

impact of trade on labour demand 120, 152
import penetration 63, 66, 69, 79, 96, 101, 146, 147
import substitution 23
inflation 48, 215
inflationary expectations 51
input–output tables 4, 63, 65, 67, 85, 87, 123
inter-industry trade 76
intermediate goods 74, 152
international competitiveness 63
international reserves 53
intra-industry trade 76, 122, 131
intra-sectoral effects of trade 160

Index

intra-sectoral skill intensity 159
investment (see also capital) 57
involuntary unemployment 220, 223

job-shedding 79

labour content of imports 148, 154
  see also factor content
labour demand equations 134
labour legislation 29
labour market adjustment 4, 21
  see also adjustment costs
labour market conditions 11, 20, 141,
  222
labour market equilibrium 11
labour market participation 29
labour productivity 104, 128
  see also productivity growth
labour requirements 64, 67
labour saving 79, 81, 189
labour share 198
labour skills 6
labour unions 49
labour-intensive sectors 144, 159
labour-theoretic approach 106
Latin America: employment reform 2
Leontief assumptions 64, 67, 91
liberalization process 24
low-wage competition 151
lump-sum taxes 203

macroeconomic fluctuations 197
manufactured imports from developing
  countries 158
median-voter 211
Mexican experience 21, 44, 47, 54
minimum wage 13, 40, 49
monetary union 212, 213
money 204
Morocco's experience 22

Nash equilibrium 216
New Earnings Survey 67
'new' theories of international trade 122
nominal anchor policies 47, 49, 50, 51,
  52, 54, 56
non-competing imports 148
non-OECD trade 137
non-traded services 160
North American Free Trade
  agreement 45

occupational employment 188
openness 96

panel data 134
Pareto-efficiency 203, 228
Phillips curve 212, 216
portfolio investment 53
prices 192
probability of being unemployed 34,
  35, 39
probability of remaining
  unemployed 36, 37, 38, 39
probit equations 36
product price movements 157
production processes 75
production-possibility 92
productivity growth 123, 126, 129
  see also labour requirements
protectionists 163
public goods 174

R & D expenditure 151, 161
Rawlsian conditions 211
real exchange rate 25, 48, 50
real interest rate 56
real wage rigidity 11
  see also wage rigidities
reservation wage 224
return on investment 54
revealed comparative advantage 96
  see also comparative advantage
revenue functions 220
Ricardo–Viner model 3, 11, 12
Rybczynski theorem 171, 174, 175

savings 57
sectoral employment 101, 118
sectoral skill intensities 153
sectoral versus factoral biases 159
sector-specific wage rigidity 15
  see also wage rigidities
seignorage 204, 205, 214
shopping time function 207
skill differentials 155, 157, 161
skill-intensive sectors 144, 159
Southern Cone of Latin America 21
specialization 120, 144
stabilization program 26, 51
Standard Industrial Classification 160
Stolper–Samuelson theorem 142
structural change 90
structure of employment 78
subsidies to the unskilled 164
supply chains 75

technical change 64
technical progress 64, 141, 155, 193, 200

technological change 200
technological progress 155, 193
technology 6, 192
technology and employment 66
technology and the demand for
    labour 78
technology indicators 161
the Wood hypothesis 74
Third World competitors 78
tied aid 225, 227
total factor productivity 193, 195, 196,
    197, 198
total factor productivity change 182
trade and technology 176
    see also technology
trade balance 93, 112
trade competitiveness 91, 111
trade expenditure functions 224
trade liberalization 8, 20, 24, 28, 40
trade reform 20, 27, 28, 131

trade theory 111, 170, 176
transmission mechanism 180

unemployment 11, 27, 28, 147, 220,
    224, 250
unemployment and trade performance
    107
unemployment duration 32, 36, 40
unemployment surveys 29
unskilled labour 140, 151
utility function 206, 215

wage differentials 162
wage flexibility 12
wage indexation 27
wage inequality 140
wage rigidities 3, 13, 40, 220,
    226
wages 192
World Bank study 20